OPERATIONAL RESEARCH APPLIED TO HEALTH SERVICES

Edited by Duncan Boldy

CROOM HELM LONDON

©1981 Duncan Boldy ©1980 Crown copyright Chapter 4
Croom Helm Ltd, 2-10 St John's Road, London SW11

British Library Cataloguing in Publication Data

Operation research applied to health services.
    1. Hospitals – Administration
    2. Operations research
    I. Boldy, Duncan
    658.4'034   RA971

    ISBN 0-7099-0380-4

Typesetting by Elephant Productions, London SE22
Printed and bound in Great Britain by
Redwood Burn Limited Trowbridge & Esher

OPERATIONAL RESEARCH APPLIED TO
HEALTH SERVICES

CONTENTS

PREFACE

The development of health operational research (OR) has been slowly gathering momentum, particularly over the last ten to fifteen years. However, although research effort has increased considerably, the potential of OR as applied to the health field is still far from being realised. In the US this state of affairs has been recognised to the extent that a major symposium was organised by the Health Applications Section of the Operations Research Society of America in 1972 in order to debate whether such unease is justified, and if so, to determine an appropriate response. The proceedings were published in 1975 by the Johns Hopkins University Press as the book *Operations Research in Health Care: A Critical Analysis*, edited by Larry J. Shuman, R. Dixon Speas Jr and John P. Young.

Nor has sufficient attention been paid in the UK and the rest of Europe to the implementation aspects of health OR. This accounts for the choice of title of the EURO (Association of European Operational Research Societies) working group, 'Operational Research Applied to Health Services', which is also the title of this book.

Because of its applied emphasis, the book is structured in terms of application areas and not techniques (in contrast to the US book referred to above) and there is a whole chapter devoted to aspects of implementation. Authors have been requested to indicate, where possible, the extent to which particular studies have had an impact. The book is aimed at an OR audience, but it should also be reasonably understood by health services administrators and planners.

Duncan Boldy
Chairman of EURO Working Group
'Operational Research Applied to
Health Services'
University of Exeter

PART ONE

INTRODUCTION

1 HEALTH OPERATIONAL RESEARCH

Duncan Boldy

The title of this book, *Operational Research Applied to Health Services*, is the same as that adopted by a EURO (Association of European Operational Research Societies) working group of which I am currently chairman. The broad aim of this working group, established in 1975, is to promote co-operation between European OR scientists engaged in work in the health services. The choice of such a title, with its implied emphasis on application and hence implementation, is no accident in connection either with the working group or with the book. It recognises that the major challenge for OR scientists working in the health field lies not in developing new and/or more sophisticated techniques, but in using what expertise they currently possess to make much more of an *impact* on the delivery of health care. This gap between theory and impact has been identified both in the UK[1] and in the US[2] and the aim of this book is to help bridge it by reviewing the contribution of OR to various aspects of health services and by presenting accounts of successful case studies.

The structure of the book is in three parts. It may at first sight seem rather strange that this first short chapter of Part One (Introduction) is followed immediately by a somewhat longer chapter on implementation. This is deliberate. Not only does it further emphasise the book's focus on application, but it represents an analogy with an OR study, in that implementation is something that should be borne in mind right from the beginning and is *not* something that only needs to be thought about at the end. In this chapter, Mårten Lagergren stresses the fact that 'implementation must be seen as a *process* which takes place throughout a project'. He structures this process in terms of eight discrete steps, ranging from the conception of the project to the general application of the results at the local level. The problems at each step are discussed and examples of both successes and failures, mainly from his experience of health OR in Sweden, are given. Chapter 2 is one of several that were originally presented, in a less developed and more cursory form, at one of the annual EURO working group meetings.

The other two parts of the book cover, respectively, aspects of strategic and tactical planning. As Ackoff has pointed out, this distinction is in general somewhat relative, in that decisions that appear to be strategic to one person may appear to be tactical to another.[3]

For the purposes of this book I have adopted a split similar to that used in my review of mathematical programming applications to health and social services problems,[4] i.e. I have taken the term 'strategic' to apply to those studies that have concerned themselves with wider aspects of health planning, such as the broad allocation of resources and the optimisation of hospitals.

In a paper recently co-authored with David Clayden, we showed that, based on a comparison of two registers of current health and welfare OR projects in the UK and Ireland, compiled in 1972 and 1977, the major focus of such work has apparently moved away from hospital-based tactical studies, towards more broadly based strategic studies.[5] This can be seen from Table 1.1, by noting the threefold increase in the number of studies labelled 'health and welfare services general'. Such a change of emphasis is not to my knowledge, however, apparent in other European countries with a less centralised health service and a less well-established OR tradition. It is also probably less apparent in the US, leading Young in his introduction to *Operations Research in Health Care: A Critical Analysis* to call for 'much more effort . . . to deal with major systems problems involving regional care strategies, manpower allocations, and distribution of resources'.[6]

Further evidence for this 'switch' in the UK and Ireland is provided by Table 1.2, which presents a comparison by problem area. Although the keyword 'planning' (often linked with the keyword 'forecasting') is a somewhat general term, which could be applied to most projects, given a sufficiently wide interpretation, nevertheless twice as many projects in the UK and Ireland in 1977 compared with 1972 were given such a label.

Part Two of this book contains four chapters which cover various aspects of strategic planning. In Chapter 3, Richard Gibbs presents an overview of health care resource allocation models. Three types of such models are defined: macro-economic, behaviour simulation and system optimisation. The advantages and disadvantages of each type are assessed in turn, paying particular attention to their suitability for incorporation within the Health Care System (HCS) Modeling Task of the International Institute for Applied Systems Analysis. It is concluded that the HCS Modeling Task should concentrate on the behaviour simulation approach, particularly where it is concerned with possible situations of major structural, rather than incremental, change.

In the following chapter I describe, together with colleagues, the development and local application of a resource allocation model (based on the behaviour simulation approach) in the UK. Although based on the techniques of mathematical programming, the 'balance-of-care'

Table 1.1: Comparison of Health and Welfare OR Projects by Main
Focus (UK and Ireland)

	Grouped keywords	No. of projects	
		1972	1977
Health and welfare services	Health & welfare services general	6	18
	Community care	14	18
	Ambulance studies	10	7
	GP and health centre services	10	5
	Ophthalmic, pharmaceutical and dental services	2	4
	Sub-total	40[a](33%)	50[a] (50%)
Hospital services	Hospitals general	23	13
	In-patient specialties	26	19
	Out-patients	12	6
	Hospital staff	15	15
	Hospital support services	26	9
	Discharge/admission policies, appointment systems, etc.	11	9
	Sub-total	95[b] (77%)	68[c] (67%)
	Total projects	123[d] (100%)	101[e] (100%)

Notes:
a. Excluding double counting 2 projects covering both 'Health services general' and 'Community care'.
b. Excluding double counting of 18 projects.
c. Excluding double counting of 3 projects.
d. Excluding double counting of 12 projects.
e. Excluding double counting of 17 projects.

Source: reproduced, with permission, from the *Journal of the Operational Research Society,* vol. 30, no. 6 (1979), p. 508.

Table 1.2: Comparison of Health and Welfare OR Projects by Problem
Area (UK and Ireland)

Main	No. of projects	
keywords	1972	1977
Planning (planning & forecasting)	24	47
Equipment and/or facilities	32	3
Measurement and/or monitoring and/or performance	28	13
Demand and/or supply	20	10
Personnel	18	11
Financial	18	7
Organisation	15	11
Scheduling	12	13
Total projects	123[a]	101[a]

Note:
a. Most projects were described by more than one keyword, hence the column
totals add up to a figure greater than the total number of projects.

Source: reproduced, with permission, from the *Journal of the Operational
Research Society*, vol. 30, no. 6 (1979), p. 509.

model does not purport to indicate a single optimum allocation of health
and social services resources; rather, it calculates the resource
consequences of possible alternative courses of action. As such, its use
is seen as iterative, in that health and social services decision makers can
review and update their assumptions in the light of the results from
successive runs of the model.

The question of how big a hospital should be is of obvious importance
and is an aspect which has been tacked by a number of OR scientists. In
Chapter 5, Dietrich Fischer explores this question within the wider
framework of how to determine the appropriate structure of a total
hospital system. In the context of the German hospital system, three
interrelated models are presented and discussed.

1. a parametric cost model, which allows for a relative assessment of
cost resulting from hospital size and function;
2. an LP model for determining the optimum resource allocation *within*

a hospital of a certain size and function;
3. an LP model for determining the optimum size of a hospital forming part of a hierarchical system.

One of his conclusions is that the varying results of many earlier investigations into the optimum size of an *individual* hospital are probably due, at least in part, to the lack of consideration of such a hospital as part of a wider hospital system.

Chapter 6 concludes the strategic planning section of the book with an account of an approach to the planning of services for the elderly developed at Duke University in the United States. The OR contribution was to devise a formal structure within which to consider the problem of what alternative programmes of care to develop. Based on the concept of a 'service package', a mathematical model was defined, having two main components: a service generation component, linking services with their cost, and an effectiveness component, linking the services assigned to a target population to their expected impact. Despite difficulties in operationalising the second of these two components, the effectiveness component, there are now around 80 documented applications of the Duke OARS (Older Americans Resources and Services) methodology throughout the US, ranging from the initial clinical assessment of individual elderly persons to programme evaluation.

Although I have already drawn attention to the apparent recent change of emphasis in health OR towards studies of a more strategic nature (at least in the UK), nevertheless tactical studies probably still predominate. Indeed, as pointed out by Ciaran O'Kane in Chapter 7 (the first chapter in Part Three of the book, which is devoted to aspects of tactical planning), about two-thirds of the studies current in 1977 in the UK and Ireland were focused mainly on hospital services (see Table 1.1). In his chapter, O'Kane outlines the development of OR in the hospital field and indicates the particular features of hospitals which make them an attractive area for study, yet one which presents a number of particular difficulties. A brief description of a number of hospital studies is then given, with an assessment of their impacts, where known, and the chapter concludes with a detailed account of a case study involving the modelling of the operation of a diagnostic X-ray department.

Health Services are labour intensive; for example, in the UK something like 75 per cent of the National Health Service revenue budget is spent on staff. The majority of this goes on nurses. In Chapter 8, John Hershey and his colleagues draw attention to the extent of nursing activities and the apparent availability of appropriate OR techniques, as reasons why a great deal of attention has been given by OR scientists and industrial engineers to the management of nurses. This attention is likely to continue and even intensify as hospital costs become subject to increasingly tight control. In their chapter, Hershey *et al.* discuss the strengths and weaknesses of the various quantitative procedures that have been developed to support nurse staffing activities, viewed in the context of an over-all conceptual framework of nurse staffing management. They conclude that nurse staffing research has concentrated on activity analysis, workload prediction, corrective allocations and shift scheduling, with too little attention being paid to manpower planning, improved performance monitoring or co-ordination with other hospital activities such as admission and treatment scheduling. The chapter also contains a detailed discussion of a particular approach to nurse scheduling, which has been successfully applied.

Chapter 9 considers primary health care, a field which has not as yet attracted a great deal of attention from OR scientists, but which Tony Hindle believes is 'one of the most fruitful areas of potential innovation'. In his chapter, Hindle indicates the range of questions which should be amenable to an operational research approach and discusses various illustrative applications with which he has been involved, both in the UK and in the USA.

Ambulance service planning has, like nurse staffing management discussed above, attracted a lot of attention from OR scientists. It appears, at least at first sight, to represent an appropriate area for the application of existing OR techniques for the handling of logistic problems. However, Robert Raitt argues, in his introduction to Chapter 10, that 'questions of ambulance deployment have exhibited many distinctive structural characteristics that have posed new modelling problems'. In his chapter, Raitt focuses on the particular deployment problems that are unique to ambulance services and reviews the various approaches that have been adopted. Following a section on implementation, the final part of the chapter is devoted to an account of the ambulance planning work carried out in the UK by the National Health Service OR Group. The group have developed an analytical approach (based on queuing theory) to emergency ambulance planning which is, as Raitt points out, 'now an established tool for ambulance service planning within the UK having been applied to approximately thirty different services'.

Having now completed my task of introducing the book, its purpose, emphasis and structure, it only remains for me, as editor, to wish you, the reader, 'bon voyage'.

Notes

1. Duncan Boldy and David Clayden, 'Operational Research Projects in Health and Welfare Services in the United Kingdom and Ireland', *Journal of the Operational Research Society*, vol. 30, no. 6 (1979).

2. Larry J. Shuman, R. Dixon Speas Jr and John P. Young (eds), *Operations Research in Health Care: A Critical Analysis* (The Johns Hopkins University Press, Baltimore and London, 1975).

3. R.L. Ackoff, *A Concept of Corporate Planning* (Wiley, New York, 1970).

4. Duncan Boldy, 'A Review of the Application of Mathematical Programming to Tactical and Strategic Health and Social Services Problems', *Journal of the Operational Research Society*, vol. 27, no. 2, ii (1976).

5. Boldy and Clayden, 'Operational Research Projects in Health and Welfare Services in the United Kingdom and Ireland'.

6. Shuman *et al.*, *Operations Research in Health Care.*

2 IMPLEMENTATION OF OR PROJECTS IN HEALTH CARE

Mårten Lagergren

What is Implementation?

Implementation might loosely be described as the impact of the OR project on the subject of study. This concept of implementation has attracted a lot of attention in the OR literature in the last decade, because it has been recognised more and more that this is often the weak point of OR. If this is not true as a general statement, it certainly seems to be true as regards OR in health care. Shuman, Wolfe and Speas note that 'very few if any OR projects have had a profound effect on the delivery of health care'.[1]

Stimson and Stimson, in their very complete and critical review of OR studies in hospitals,[2] quote Young as saying that 'upon reflection I am hard pressed to name a single instance where the application of OR has initiated or led to a major decision in the health services'.[3] These statements from well-informed authors represent a very grave criticism of the practice of OR.

It is also obvious that implementation should be seen as the goal of OR. As Bennis puts it: 'Implementation is the problem and the relationship between researcher and user is the pivotal element.'[4] If the OR project has not had any impact on reality, the money and effort spent on the project are obviously wasted. Implementation can, however, imply many different things. I propose to discuss in a more penetrating way what we should mean by implementation in order to understand better what *kind* of implementation we can hope for and the reasons for non-implementation.

Implementation can be defined in several ways implying more or less strong demands on the results. Huysmans states: 'We will say that an OR recommendation is implemented if the manager or managers affected by the recommendation adopt the research results in essence and continue to use them as long as the conditions underlying the research apply.'[5] Tobin and Outfield, in relation to the airline industry, give an even stronger definition: 'It is our belief that a planning model has not been implemented in a real sense unless it is an integral part of the planning system seen by the planners themselves as an important part of their equipment.'[6]

18

Obviously, there is a difference here between the implementation of recommendations and of models. The former is more difficult to assess; the latter perhaps more difficult to achieve. Quade, considering the problem of politically infeasible alternatives, contends that:

> It is vitally important that these currently impractical alternatives be examined. Otherwise the policymakers, the politicians and the public will not know the real cost implications, that is to say the opportunities foregone, by their present politically dominated policy . . . for this purpose, consideration of how to win acceptance and secure implementation may not be very relevant.[7]

The meaning of this seems to be that there is more to implementation than just getting the decision maker to accept the recommendation or adopt the model. This line of thought will be pursued in the following attempt to clarify the issue of implementation.

Implementation as a Contribution to Problem Solving

The task of OR is to treat problems. Problems can be described as situations that are considered unsatisfactory by the concerned observer, in this context the decision maker. A solution to a problem is arrived at when the problem ceases to be a problem, i.e. when the situation is no longer considered unsatisfactory. This might result from a conscious effort to solve the problem or the problem might in some cases somehow solve itself.

From the total problem, as perceived by the decision maker, an OR problem might be derived and defined. In some cases this OR problem is a redefinition of the total, original problem. Mostly, however, the OR problem will constitute a sub-problem of the total problem, that is supposed to be amenable to an OR approach.

The definition of the OR problem is an indirect statement of the demand we put on the solution. The OR problem is not 'solved' until the problem, as it was defined, ceases to be a problem. This we can call a completely successful implementation. We might thus state that full implementation is achieved when the situation that the OR project was supposed to treat has been changed — as a consequence of the results of the OR project — into a satisfactory state as judged by the decision maker. Implementation thus depends on the stated purpose, including the desired level of ambition of the OR project. This level of ambition might be to treat the total problem or to treat certain parts of it or even just to illuminate certain aspects.

An example might be helpful to illustrate this point. Suppose the total problem is that the out-patient care unit is operating inefficiently, with long waiting times for patients, low capacity, etc. as consequences. In this situation, the OR problem might be defined as inefficient admission procedures. The desired solution to this OR problem will be the development and introduction of a well-functioning admission procedure. (This is not meant to be an ideal OR formulation of the problem, just an example of how an OR problem might be defined.)

Note that the out-patient care unit might still be operating very inefficiently and the decision maker might be very unhappy about the situation. No blame can, however, be put on the OR project, as this has fulfilled its required purpose and thus achieved a successful implementation. (The original definition of the OR problem is, of course, another question.) Note also that implementation in this sense can be achieved to a higher or lower degree depending on whether the result contributed more or less to the solution of the stated problem. Later we shall introduce the concepts of 'strong' and 'weak' implementation in the context of a multi-level organisation, in order to describe the level of impact.

It follows from the definition of implementation given above, that the implementation of an OR project does not necessarily require changed practices or even that a proposed alternative is adopted. If the purpose of the OR project is to illuminate certain aspects of the problem, then the OR problem might be defined as 'insufficient knowledge about certain properties of the system concerned' and implementation mean that the decision maker acquires a new body of knowledge concerning his total problem. The crucial point is that the project has made an impact on reality at the required level.

Whether the decision maker will be happier or not depends to a great extent on whether the formulation of the OR problem was meaningful. In many cases this seems to be the deeper problem. Often the OR problem is defined too narrowly, making implementation easier to achieve but less helpful as regards the total problem.

Implementation in a Multi-level Organisation

A common feature of health care organisations is that they are multi-level with the lower levels having more or less autonomy. Hence, even if the central level perceives a problem, it might lack the direct power to implement solutions.

The central level might, for example, be very well aware of, and disturbed by, the inefficient operation of out-patient care units. The only way to change the situation, however, is to go through the lower levels — in the Swedish case the county councils and the primary care districts. Due to the limited development resources at the local level and the fact that problems are much the same in all local units, it is convenient to give a central development agency the task of working on common local problems. In such a case it is possible to define different degrees of implementation:

1. implementation of the first degree ('weak' implementation) — OR project results are accepted at the central level as a basis for recommendations to the local level;
2. implementation of the second degree ('strong' implementation) — recommendations resulting from the OR project are generally adopted at the local level.

The desired degree is, of course, part of the purpose of the OR project and the resulting degree of implementation must be judged against this stated purpose. As described earlier, the level of ambition can be varied. If the purpose is confined to the illumination of an aspect of a common problem, then 'weak' implementation consists of arriving at this clarification and translating it to the decision makers at the central level. 'Strong' implementation will also include the lower levels.

Acceptance of OR project results as a basis for recommendations from the central level usually requires that a local test application has proved successful. Thus, 'weak' implementation in this case must be preceded by at least one successful local implementation. This might sometimes be difficult, since the conditions for a central agency to work on local problems are usually less favourable than for the local level itself. It is also noteworthy that in this case the local test implementation *per se* is of only marginal value. A central OR project that only accomplishes change in one local unit seldom covers its costs.

Problems with 'strong' as opposed to 'weak' implementation are by no means a special feature of health care organisations. They are encountered in all big organisations — especially perhaps in the governmental sector. Pressman and Wildavsky have given a vivid description of the problems associated with a federal programme in the USA when one tries to implement it in a local setting.[8] To get the central decision makers to accept a recommended policy ('weak' implementation) is thus quite a different thing from getting it to work in practice ('strong' implementation).

The Process towards Implementation

It is a common mistake to believe that implementation is something one tries to achieve when the OR project is completed. Nothing could be more wrong! Many authors on the subject of implementation emphasise that the achievement of implementation must be seen as a *process* which takes place throughout a project.
Huysmans, in the preface of his book on implementation, stresses

> the need to consider the interdependence between social, psychological and technical aspects of the system under study during all phases of an OR project – from the moment of identifying management's problem and formulating it in OR terms to the point of implementing the recommendations made on the basis of the analysis.[9]

As regards health care, Pondy, in a paper on 'behavioural perspectives', points out that 'successful implementation requires that those affected by system changes must be involved from the very first planning stages of any study'.[10] He argues further that it is not possible to distinguish between 'design strategies' and 'implementation strategies'. These two processes must be seen as intimately related: 'The evaluation of a model must include the likelihood of its successful implementation and continued use.'[11] Similarly, Stimson and Stimson contend that 'one reason for failure to implement OR studies in the hospital field is that the recommendations of these studies do not seem to consider the complicated process that characterises implementation'.[12]

My experience confirms completely these observations. As a reflection of this I have chosen to structure the rest of this chapter in terms of a process – the process towards implementation. This process, illustrated in Figure 2.1, is shown – somewhat arbitrarily – as composed of eight discrete steps, of which the first is the conception of the project idea and the last is the 'strong' implementation, i.e. the general application of the results at the local level.

The context I have in mind is that of a health care organisation consisting of at least two levels with OR resources employed at the central level. This could apply to a national system like the Swedish (which has at least three levels) or to a regional system, like a Swedish county council or a group of hospitals.

Figure 2.1: The Process Towards Implementation

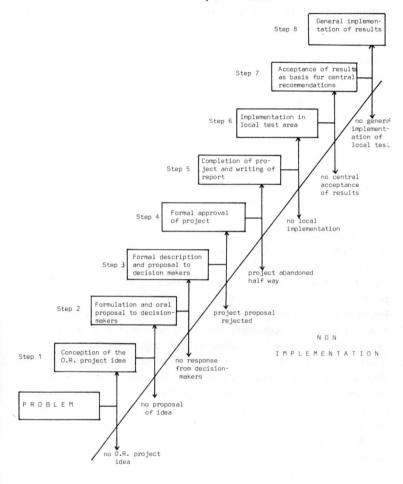

As already pointed out, 'strong' implementation is generally very difficult to attain, there being many chances for abortion along the way. I now propose to discuss the problems at each step, the risk of abortion and possible ways to surmount the difficulties. Examples of success and failure — mainly from the experience of health care OR in Sweden — are given.

Step 1: Conception of the OR Project Idea

It is safe to say that most potential health services OR projects do not even reach the first step towards implementation. The OR project idea is simply never conceived. Several reasons may account for this. Two important ones are the lack of OR tradition and the lack of trained OR personnel. These two in combination have the effect that problems in the majority of cases are never identified as OR problems — neither the total problem nor parts of it. The situation is demonstrated by two observations. The international literature reveals that many problems that are treated with OR methods in countries with a well-developed OR tradition and a good supply of OR personnel are not treated that way in other countries with a less fortunate situation from the OR point of view. One good example in the case of Sweden consists of resource allocation problems, e.g. the relative requirement for hospital beds and other resources, where modelling in Sweden is almost non-existent. It is also possible to observe, in retrospect, that studies have failed to use OR methods in cases where their value would have been obvious if somebody present had been aware of the possibilities. One example of this is the central planning, in Sweden, for the training and distribution of doctors in different specialities. This is a problem that seems to be extremely well suited to a simulation approach.

Stimson and Stimson point out that operational researchers, by concentrating on problems of certain types (e.g. queuing, scheduling, inventory control, etc.), have failed to recognise many problems that are deemed important by hospital administrators.[13] They mention in this context, *inter alia,* problems concerning:

1. cost allocation;
2. quality of care;
3. continuity of care;
4. manpower and personnel administration;
5. planning for the future.

One reason for this might be poor communication between operational researchers and administrators — a subject I will return to later on. Connors has pointed out that:

There is a tremendous opportunity for the improvement of our health services system. Selective interjection of OR at crucial points and on key issues can be an influential force in predicting probable outcomes of alternate changes and courses of action, as well as testing and evaluating changes in our delivery system that are already taking place.[14]

Among the problems he deems likely to be most beneficial are:

1. development of organisations for comprehensive care to a defined population;
2. planning for health services;
3. financing health services;
4. developing a rational information system by reassessment of information requirements;
5. health manpower data and planning.[15]

The conclusion to be drawn seems to be that there is a need for conceiving *relevant* OR project ideas. The only way this can be achieved is through a more continuous exchange of problems and ideas between OR people and administrators. This requires, in turn, changes in the education of both categories and also the more continuous effort of joint professional meetings and other similar arrangements. Quoting Stimson and Stimson once again:

changes in education should mean that the operations researcher will have more knowledge about how to deal with problems in the health field, and the hospital administrator will have greater knowledge of quantitative methods of management and in general will be better able to participate in OR studies. As a result the two should be able to work together more closely and productively than before.[16]

Step 2: Formulation and Oral Proposal of the Project Idea to the Decision Makers and Other Concerned Groups

The idea that a certain problem might be identified and treated as an OR problem must be communicated to the people concerned. Commonly, this is first done orally. You meet with the person(s) and express your ideas. Traditionally, the counterpart of the analyst has been called 'the decision maker'. As pointed out by Lockett and Polding, this is a very simplified notion.[17] In reality the situation is much more complex. They propose instead the interaction model shown in Figure 2.2

Figure 2.2: A Model of Possible Interactions

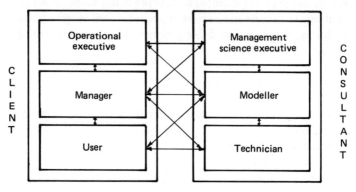

Source: A.G. Lockett and E. Polding, 'OR/MS Implementation — a variety of processes', *Interfaces,* vol. 9, no. 1 (November 1978).

Assuming that the project idea has been conceived by the modeller — perhaps together with the manager — the idea must then be communicated on the one hand to the operational executive and on the other hand to the management science executive. It might also be wise to contact the users, perhaps through their union representatives. The technicians, if such people are employed, might also have valuable opinions concerning, for example, technical feasibility of data collection or processing.

As a rule the two executives are the most important people at this stage, since they control the budget. Many times, however, an OR idea is conceived but never even reaches the ears of the concerned superiors. The reason for this is that the person or group that conceived the idea realises immediately the impossibility of getting the decision makers to appreciate the value of the approach. Alternatively, they recognise that there is nobody available with the required training to work on the conceived OR problem.

The following is an example from Swedish experience: within the context of a personnel planning project the idea of developing a simulation model to illustrate the flow of personnel to, from and within a local health care organisation was suggested. It was clear to everybody working on the project that such a model would greatly enhance the understanding of the complex movements of personnel and put the vast amount of unorganised data into a meaningful context. However, scarce OR resources and the lack of understanding on the part of the decision-making group made it meaningless even to bring the idea forward.

Scarce OR resources provide, of course, a very tangible reason for not pushing an idea forward. On the other hand, the fact that OR resources are scarce is a reflection of a set of established priorities which have ruled out a more substantial recruitment of OR capability. We are therefore posed with the question: why do some people not consider OR worth while?

Huysmans introduces the concept 'cognitive style' or 'ways of reasoning' to explain why certain people easily adapt to the OR approach while others simply will not accept the OR way of thinking.[18] He identifies two ideal types of 'ways of reasoning':

1. analytic reasoning – reducing problem situations to a set of underlying causal relationships and seeking to detect these relationships and manipulate decision variables so as to reach the 'optimum' solution;
2. heuristic reasoning – emphasises workable solutions to total problem situations and the searching for analogies with familiar problems rather than causal relationships.

From an experiment he concludes that the manager's way of reasoning has a major influence on the implementation of OR solutions. We might be safe to add that it is likely to have a major influence upon the decision to engage in an OR project at all.

Heuristic ways of reasoning are not, of course, an exclusive feature of the health care sector – executives that adhere to this approach can be found in all areas, industrial as well as governmental. However, it is reasonable to believe that this way of reasoning is more common in the health care sector than, for example, in defence. As pointed out by Pondy, the health care sector has a number of special traits:

> The health system is more nearly a loose coalition of personnel than a well-defined hierarchy. Decision-making tends to be dispersed rather than centralised. The form of social control tends to be based on collegial and professional values rather than hierarchical and bureaucratic values and goals tend to be multiple rather than unitary.[19]

Such an environment is more likely to foster a heuristic way of reasoning than an analytic one.

What then can be done in order to make the decision makers in health care more ready to adopt ideas of OR projects? Huysmans sees the solution in terms of education but points out immediately that 'it is uncertain to what extent education can affect a person's approach to problems'.[20] Education is also proposed by Connors as a means for achieving more OR impact on hospital operations.[21] The author also stresses the need for a continuous educational effort: 'But formal education is but a start and progress will not be made unless basic education is reinforced in practice and experience.'

Other authors point to the necessity of changes in the practice of OR in order to adapt to conditions pertinent to the public sector in general and health care in particular. Stringer ascribes the tardy development of OR in the public sector *vis-à-vis* industry not to the slow adoption of new ideas by political bodies, but to the slowness of OR itself in adapting to the special nature of public problems.[22] A common criticism in this context is the reluctance of OR practitioners to apply results from the behavioural sciences. I will return to this problem later on in this chapter.

Step 3: Formal Description and Presentation of the Project Idea to the Decision Makers

If the project idea is presented to the decision makers they might react in several ways. They might be favourable and recommend the production of a formal paper about it, they might say that this sounds very interesting but . . . , or they might simply reject it. In the last two cases this is the end of it (if you are not persistent or do not try other channels).

To undertake an OR project requires more than OR resources. It will also require time from the manager and the user (cf. Figure 2.2) and perhaps also money for computer time, etc. The OR personnel might also be usable on other projects. Lack of resources on the part of the consultant or the client is thus a common reason for non-implementation at this step. However, this might not be the whole truth. If the OR tradition is weak, most of the competing projects will be non-OR and they will perhaps seem more practical to the decision makers and easier to grasp. Lack of resources might be used as an excuse for rejecting an idea if one has difficulty in understanding what is being proposed.

Another reason might, of course, be that the problem area lacks priority or does not fit into the organisational context. An example where low priority could hardly have been the problem is as follows.

A project idea concerning the study of the long-term supply of health care personnel, which also involved a simulation of their flow, was rejected because the supply problem was considered so big that it required much more resources than were available. As a consequence, nothing has been done about the long-term supply problem, which is generally judged to be of paramount importance.

The two reasons for non-implementation that we encounter here might be labelled low priority and low understanding. The problem with low priority has already been touched upon. Stimson and Stimson, among others, have pointed out that operational researchers have not addressed themselves to the problems that the decision makers perceive as most urgent[23] and Connors has commented that 'operations researchers have accurately been criticised as viewing the hospital as a laboratory to their research trade and to conduct self-conceived projects'.[24] This latter situation is, of course, only possible in an environment where the researchers have the money and power to start projects of their own — i.e. in a university setting. The implementation problems will then face them — probably to a greater degree — at a later stage.

The problem of low understanding is, to some extent, a problem of confidence. Quade points out that:

personal acceptance usually comes before acceptance of ideas. [The retained] . . . information depends on the way the analysis is presented and on the decision maker's confidence in the man and the organisation from which he comes . . .[25]

. . . the analyst [should] keep his client relations good. If they are not he may never win acceptance for his analysis and may not even be listened to attentively.[26]

Radnor, Rubinstein and Tansik argue that results and understanding tend to reinforce each other so that:

As the client begins using OR/MS recommendations, he forms opinions of the OR/MS activity based upon the project's result. Good results may lead the manager to associate positive rewards with the OR/MS activity and poor results may tend to evoke a negative reward relation. Given that a favourable relation evolves, the client acquires a propensity to engage in similar activities in the future.[27]

Of course, there could be reasons other than low priority or low understanding that bring an OR project idea to a halt at this stage. Often OR projects are perceived as threats to one or more of the 'actors' involved. This might especially be the case for the users – doctors and other categories of health care personnel. The OR approach – especially if it seems to be too much inspired from industrial engineering and/or implies computerisation – might, true or not, be perceived as intruding on professional autonomy or as devaluating professional skills. To the extent that the users' opinions are held in high esteem, this can be a ready cause for abandoning a project before it is born.

The OR approach to a problem can also be perceived as a more subtle threat, namely if it is too much out of line with the usual thinking of the organisation. Huysmans cites a number of examples where this seems to have been the cause of non-implementation.[28]

The problem of threat can only be handled by the development of 'mutual understanding' in the sense of Churchman and Schainblatt.[29] This means, amongst other things, participation in the project by all parties concerned working together in a multidisciplinary team. The ideal form of project organisation in order to achieve implementation will be dealt with later on in this chapter.

Step 4: Formal Approval of the Project

When a formal description and presentation of the project idea has been made the project enters the formal decision-making process. This usually means that more people are involved in the process of reviewing the project which thus will be subject to a more thorough examination concerning its potential value and the resources required.

In this step, awareness of need and judgement of potential value will perhaps play a greater role than mere OR tradition and general attitudes. It might be assumed that, if the project idea has reached so far, at least some influential people understand what it is all about and are able to explain this to others. The project will thus be judged in a more professional way. Typically, questions will be raised concerning the correct definition of the OR problem, the availability of data, the possibility of modelling particular parts of the system, the relative importance of qualitative factors and so on. Assuming a test application is intended, there will be questions concerning the conditions required for undertaking it. The resources required and the likely difficulties and limitations will then be judged against the perceived general value of the project.

For example, a formal proposal for developing a general model of

the flow of services in a health care area was rejected because it was
felt that:

1. There was no direct connection to a specific problem. There was a
   risk that the model would try to treat all problems and solve or
   illuminate none.
2. Knowledge was insufficient concerning the connection between
   different parameters such as demand for care, distribution of patients,
   length of stay and existing resources. In general the structure was
   considered too 'weak' to be amenable to a formal OR model.
3. The project was not sufficiently connected with the local health care
   authorities (the proposal came from a university).

The perceived need for the project is, of course, an essential factor at
this stage. Stimson and Stimson argue that academics tend to choose
problems according to their intellectual interest: 'This practice leads to
studies in which a technique seeks a problem rather than to studies in
which the analysis of a problem suggests the technique.'[30] The choosing
of problems according to their academic interest will not necessarily, of
course, lead a researcher to propose those projects that are felt to be
most needed by the decision makers.

Another 'professional deformation' on the part of the operational
researchers, relevant in this context, is the tendancy to enlarge a problem
in order to involve all relevant aspects. Peter Szanton, writing from his
experience as head of the New York City Rand Institute, says:

> the problems attacked analytically should be within the power of
> the client to deal with. The better and the more conscientious the
> analyst, the more likely he is to be concerned with larger and more
> fundamental problems − and the more likely he is then to identify
> difficulties or to propose conclusions which the client, at least over
> the short run, has no substantial power to effect.[31]

It is obvious that there is no 'need' for the decision maker to engage in
a grand project when he does not have the power to implement the
promised findings.

Stimson and Stimson argue the same way when they say: 'operations
researchers seem to assume that the hospital administrator has unlimited
power to make changes and has many more resources available to carry out
changes than is usually the case.'[32] This brings us to the second criterion
for project approval: the estimate of the potential value of the project.

Analysts are often required to state in quantitative terms the potential benefits and costs of their projects. Though costs could (and should) be readily calculated, benefits tend to be much more difficult to assess. Stimson and Stimson comment on this problem thus: 'the lack of specific data on the costs and benefits of implementing and maintaining the new procedures suggested in the OR studies is a barrier to their acceptance.'[33] They report several instances where proposed savings have been calculated in a misleading way, for example in terms of nursing time 'saved' without any assurance that this 'saving' could be transferred into money savings or into more time for the patients.

Wagner points out the essential value of a deeper insight into a problem achieved by sensitivity testing:

> Careful managerial scrutiny of comparative case studies provides the principal means by which an executive can confirm his understanding of the underlying model, its assumptions and its data . . . The benefits a manager receives from a planning oriented model stem largely from such insightful sensitivity testing.[34]

It is clear that these types of benefits are much harder to put into money terms. On the other hand, they seem at least as important. After all, the purpose of OR is to support decision making and, since insight must be the crucial basis for good decision making, it comes rather natural to put a high value on it.

A fair assessment of the value of insight, hopefully achieved through an OR study, cannot be reached without an environment of mutual understanding in the sense of Churchman and Schainblatt. It is also apparent that an evaluation of the type of insight that Wagner describes is closely dependent on what has earlier been called 'the cognitive style'. Either one likes analytic reasoning and values the kind of insight reductionistic modelling gives one or one does not. The value of the study will thus be dependent on the frame of mind of the decision makers.

One important feature of the formal approval of a project is that it should involve the conscious and explicit support of top management. The importance of obtaining top-management support has been pointed out by many authors. Here it will suffice to cite Radnor, Rubinstein and Tansik: 'the level of top-management support . . . [is] . . . a key variable in determining whether an OR/MS activity would be successful in an organisation.'[35]

It might be possible in the short term to engage in an 'underground' project without real support from top management but sooner or later one will find oneself in difficulty. On the other hand, top-management support is a necessary rather than a sufficient condition for success. For example, Lockett and Polding report a number of cases where the high initial involvement of top management was not sufficient to achieve successful implementation. They contend that the effective support of concerned middle management might be more crucial.[36]

Step 5: Completion of the Project and the Writing of a Report

The first prerequisite for getting results accepted is, of course, that one has results in the first place. Many obstacles lie in the way of the successful completion of OR projects in health care. I will only mention a few. Some of these have — reasonably enough — already been mentioned in connection with the reviewing process:

1. lack of relevant data;
2. weak structure of the system;
3. qualitative parts tend to dominate;
4. difficulty in reaching the right level of abstraction.

To this list might be added the problems that emanate from working with the people in a local test application. As soon as the OR project has a potential impact on the working conditions or balance of power in the test area — and it usually has — people will react in different ways to the project. If this problem is handled badly — or if one is just plain unlucky — then there will be a high chance of rejection. I will return later on to this highly important problem area — essentially the problem of how to work as a change agent. First I would like to give two examples of non-completion, each one due to different reasons.

The first example relates to another health care area simulation model project. This one was conceived and funded by local health authorities. It was a rather grandiose project, the construction of a general model with only tenuous links with any specific problem. No experienced OR people were involved. The technical side was handled by computer experts, who were fascinated by data-base techniques. As a natural consequence, the project failed to reach the right level of abstraction and got stuck in detail. It was thus rather easy to see from the outside that the project would fail. Decision makers lost interest when problems started to mount and the project was abandoned half-way.

The other example concerns an attempt to improve patient planning and assignment routines within the surgical department of a big hospital. The department consisted of several wards, but admission planning and the assignment of patients to wards were not connected, leading to poor resource utilisation. Nobody appeared to be responsible for choosing which patients were picked from the waiting lists, and when.

The problem is not difficult in theory. Patients need to be combined into one waiting list and selected for particular wards according to the extent of empty beds and nursing dependency. In practice, however, due to the internal problems of the department it was impossible to introduce a strict routine. Doctors would not subordinate themselves to the head of the department and insisted on picking their own patients. The project had to be abandoned.

This case is instructive since it illustrates very well the problems run into when there is a failure to recognise people as people rather than as 'components'. The literature on implementation is replete with lost causes where this fundamental condition has not been observed and authors unanimously stress the importance of involving concerned users and of paying attention to the psychological and social aspects of the OR project. For example, Peter Szanton, New York City Rand Institute, writes:

> First there must be support for the analytic effort from the potential decision makers within the government. The support need not be wholehearted or entirely free from scepticism but it must exist. Where it is absent the analyst will find his access to data restricted and the participation of city staffs in the study foreclosed.[37]

Wagner, who generally takes a rather technical standpoint in these matters, finds it important, however, to point out that:

> it is both difficult and foolish to impose an operations research system on an operating management that has not been a party to the system's design. Anyone with only a modicum of experience knows that the best of plans can be so cleverly sabotaged by a group of unwilling personnel that the promulgator looks like a fool.[38]

It is, however, not only a question of psychology. Participation is also a crucial factor as regards the quality of the analysis. Wagner continues: 'When operating management has not been actively engaged in the study, there is substantial likelihood that the proposed methods of the system will not be sufficiently comprehensive and flexible to handle the inevitable exigencies.'[39]

Returning to the special conditions of health care (cf. Step 2), it is even more obvious that the successful completion of an OR project requires full participation and a sympathetic attitude on the part of the doctors, nurses and other categories of health care personnel. Stimson and Stimson make the critical remark 'Physicians on the medical staff have been largely ignored in OR studies in hospitals'.[40] They also point out that many of the problems worrying hospital administrators stem from the fact that physicians often have different goals from their own. To quote Stimson and Stimson again, 'until OR studies deal with the very real administrative problems caused by physicians and others pursuing their own goals administrators may think operations researchers just don't understand the situation'.[41]

How then is one to face these difficult psychological and social problems? Huysmans points out in the preface to his book that: 'The OR practitioner . . . must not only command the tools of OR analysis, but must also be able to make effective use of results from other disciplines, particularly those of the behavioural sciences.'[42] The essential meaning of this is that the gap between the behavioural approach of the social scientist and the technical approach of the operational researcher as regards the accomplishment of organisational change must be bridged. The operational researcher must perceive himself as a 'change agent', who is equipped with certain tools and a certain problem-analysing ability, but who essentially is in the business of stimulating and helping others to think and do something about their own organisation problems.

This clearly implies a team approach to problem solving. A multidisciplinary team in health care could, for example, be composed of administrators, doctors and nurses, computer and other specialties, an operational researcher and a social scientist. Alternatively, the operational researcher would – if his/her education and training permits – combine the two latter roles.

The combined role of change agent and operational researcher might be described as follows:

1. to act as a promoter of change;
2. to contribute to analysis and problem solving by using OR thinking and methods;
3. to formulate suggestions that are more far-reaching than otherwise would have been advanced;
4. to act as a neutral bystander capable of seeing problems with fresh eyes.

A quotation from Ackoff might suitably conclude this discussion:

An objective of OR is not simply to understand the performance of
the organisation studied, but to improve it and to enhance the
organisation's ability to diagnose and prescribe for its ills. Hence,
one result of intervening in an organisation should be a strengthening
of its capability to solve its own current and future problems.[43]

With this approach to a project, what purpose then does the writing
of a report serve? Should completing a project successfully be looked
upon as a sufficient end in itself and the writing of a report as just
unnecessary paper-work? Or do other reasons exist for engaging in the
rather tedious task of report writing? In ideal circumstances, report
writing should make a small contribution to implementation. If co-
operation with the decision makers has been intimate and continuous,
then there should be little need, from an implementation point of view,
to present the results in an exhaustive report. It might seem more
appropriate to show the usefulness of the OR team by tackling the next
urgent project. Indeed, it can be argued that if report writing seems
necessary in order to get the results implemented, then they will
probably not get implemented anyway!

Two reasons stand out, however, for writing a report, even in the
best of circumstances. First, as pointed out in the description of Step 2,
the situation is generally more complex than that of a single analyst (or
a group) and decision maker. Decision makers exist at different levels
within both the client and consultant organisations and numerous other
people might be involved in a project or have a right to be informed
about its outcome. Hence, the formal report is an essential part of the
communication process.

Second, the writing of a report has an intrinsic value for the OR
team as a full consistent documentation of assumptions, methods,
reasoning and conclusions. It is astonishing how fast one forgets about
the details of a study and how difficult it is after a year or two to
reconstruct assumptions and thinking that seemed perfectly clear the
moment they were made. Another aspect, of course, is that people
sometimes leave the organisation. Written documentation is then
necessary for reasons of continuity.

My advice, therefore, is that one should resist the temptation to
skimp the report-writing stage, even if it seems pointless at the time as
regards implementation. In the long run any skimping will be self-
defeating for the OR team and this the customer must be made to
understand and accept.

Step 6: Implementation of Project Results in a Local Test Area

As mentioned before, central OR projects in a multi-level organisation often involve a local test application. Lack of success in that application makes it, of course, unlikely that the recommendations will be accepted elsewhere.

The failure of a local implementation rests on the same premisses as abortion during the course of a project. The involvement of local people is extremely important; indeed, it is vital if the solution is to work after the special project people have left the area. It is not uncommon for the presence and persuasive power of the project people to keep the project alive during the test period. However, as soon as they have left, local powers, possibly suppressed, often regain control and old habits can be resumed.

Huysmans distinguishes between sustained and autonomous implementation.[44] In the former case, implementation requires the continuous involvement of the researcher; in the latter no such continued support is necessary. It is clear that sustained implementation at the local level will soon absorb all available central OR resources and in that way effectively block further progress. The possibility that other local units will be encouraged to adopt the proposed solutions will also diminish considerably, if it is clear that continuous analytical efforts are required to make the solution work.

As a consequence, it is important to accomplish autonomous implementation in the test area. This is very much dependent on how change has been achieved: if it has responded to a locally perceived essential problem, if the local staff have been sufficiently involved and so on. Are they sufficiently prepared to handle the changed system; have they accepted the essential ideas?

Again an example — this one successful for a change. As part of a project concerned with developing a system of five-year planning for health care areas, an interactive budget simulation model was developed for use in the test area. The model made it possible to calculate financial consequences of different planning alternatives under different economic assumptions, e.g. economic growth, growth of operations, inflation rate, level of taxation, etc. The purpose was to improve the quality of planning by making it possible to consider alternatives.

The model was in many aspects a long step forward. The personnel involved were not even familiar with using computers in batch mode, let alone interactive modelling. They had never been used to calculating alternatives, undertaking sensitivity analyses, etc. Perhaps due to the fact that planning was essential and that the model relieved them from tedious manual work, they overcame the difficulties and gained — after a time — complete control over the system. The model has been altered and improved several times. As a consequence, other models have been developed using the same interactive system.

In this case the problem to surmount was the unfamiliarity of the personnel to the technical solution. This was somewhat aggravated by the fact that they had never asked for the essential capability of the new system — to do 'what-if' analyses. Nevertheless, local implementation proved successful. Success, however, has been limited to that. No other county council has followed.

An important factor when it comes to implementation is the power structure. OR projects often imply efforts — conscious or not — to change this structure. Many times, however, project people have recognised that the structure seems to be made of rubber. It regains its form as soon as pressure is relieved.

Change as a consequence of the implementation of an OR project does not, of course, differ from any other form of organisational change. The same rules apply. Commenting on the well-known Harwood experiments, Lawrence emphasised that it is not the technical change *per se,* but the social change by which it is accompanied, that is resisted.[45] Thus the technical and social change can never be viewed separately. The organisation must be seen as a socio-technical system and the introduction of each technical change must be paralleled by an adaptive social change such that the motivation for efficient performance will remain.[46] Generally speaking, power structures are too 'solid' to permit OR projects to break them. It is therefore wise to try to minimise the social change inherent in implementation and — unless very strong support is at hand — avoid solutions with too revolutionary repercussions.

For central operational researchers working in a local test area, there are also other problems of importance for implementation. In particular, it is essential for them to get sufficiently involved in the operations of the local unit so as not to be regarded too much as outsiders. Radnor, Rubinstein and Tansik relate a successful case where the OR analyst located himself in the department where the project was to take place in order to create a 'sense of belonging' in the clients.[47] On the other hand, they report on a not so successful project where clients spoke of the 'know-it-all attitude' of the OR manager.[48] No doubt personal feelings of this kind are of great importance in the subtle area of organisational behaviour.

Local implementation should not, of course, be seen as an isolated event taking place when the local OR project is finished. This much should be clear from what I have already said. Local implementation must be seen as the product of a conscious continuous effort from the conception of the OR idea through to the writing of the report. But for a central OR unit local implementation is not the end; the worst is still to come!

Step 7: Acceptance of Results as a Basis for Recommendations from the Central Level

A successful local test application is only a step on the way to general implementation. There are many reasons why the results of a local application, however successful, can fail to be accepted as a basis of a central recommendation.

One reason might be that the local conditions are judged to be so special that the results are not felt to be applicable on a wider scale. Successful test applications are often achieved by enthusiasts, whose sheer enthusiasm can be a reason for others to be sceptical. Hence, enthusiasm must not be a necessary condition for the success of a proposed system.

Quade points out that results from OR (policy) studies tend to be less incremental in nature than policies arrived at by the usual processes. Because of this they tend to meet more resistance from people who have not thought deeply enough about the problems. Quade recommends providing ongoing information about the study to the decision makers:

> When, and if, an analyst presents his findings, they should not come as a surprise to the client and the staff. For if he has been sensible, he will have consulted with them during the course of the study and given them a good idea of what to expect.[49]

Translated to the context of a local test application, this means that the important central decision makers should be kept continuously informed about the test project and the thinking that is evolving.

In other cases, results might be so controversial that they must be suppressed. The central level wishes to develop uniform solutions. Local solutions that do not fit into this structure cannot be promulgated for general application. In such cases the usual reason seems to be that central decision makers are unaware of what kind of results an OR project might produce. Different decision makers might also start different projects in the same problem area, but with different objectives. In the course of time co-ordination becomes necessary and, depending on the relative power of the decision makers, some solutions are likely to be dropped.

Huysmans, discussing the importance of organisational and individual managerial values and their interrelationships, concludes: 'It is not enough to find the "right" solution; the researcher who aims at implementation of his findings has to come up with the *right* solution to the *relevant* problems.'[50] Stimson and Stimson also point out that 'the extent to which the results of research are implemented is related directly to the extent to which existing relationships within the organisation are disturbed'.[51] And later, 'studies in other organisations [than health care] show that changes that threaten existing social relationships are strongly resisted'.[52]

This applies not only to a local setting but even more so to the central level. The reason for this is that conditions at the central level are much more institutionalised. Whereas at the local level much can be left to the discretion of local individuals, e.g. doctors and shop stewards, decisions at the central level will certainly follow the policy lines of different central decision bodies: central government agencies, unions, etc. Thus, only small movements are allowed and local OR projects that do not fit into this picture have a very small chance of achieving the status of a central policy recommendation.

A third cause for failure to achieve central recommendation is that the OR solutions are felt to be too complicated. This seems to be a usual fate for more advanced OR projects. For example, one OR project that was very successful at the local level consisted in developing different simulation models of a large clinic-chemical laboratory. The purpose of the project was to study different problems concerning the efficient operation and equipment of the laboratory, for example the effect of different workloads on request-to-report time, the effect of having small emergency laboratories handling priority samples *v.* having one laboratory carrying out all required analyses, and the benefit of using multi-channel analysers. The project gave many interesting special results and generated a much improved understanding of the complicated operations of the laboratory.

Further implementation of such a project might go along three different lines:

1. project results and insights can be communicated to other similar laboratories;
2. the computer models can be used to study other laboratories;
3. the conceptual system model can be used when modelling other laboratories.

In reality, only the first of these lines has been pursued — and only to a rather limited extent, interestingly enough more along international than along national channels. It took more than two years for the central agency that financed the project to publish a report. The other lines of further development have not even been officially proposed — far less attempted.

The reason for this remarkable non-implementation seems to be lack of understanding and interest on the part of the central decision makers. There is nothing controversial about the results. The knowledge arrived at seems to pose no threat to the laboratory personnel or to the county council managers. One explanation lies in the fact that health care managers generally are non-technical. Thus there is a general lack of interest on their part in technically oriented problems. Laboratory operations and equipment problems do not arouse any great emotions despite the fact that substantial amounts of money are involved.

One further reason for the difficulty in achieving more general acceptance of an OR project lies in the limited possibilities of making a valid assessment of the benefits. This problem has already been touched upon in the context of project approval. Wagner points out two reasons why it is so hard to compare 'before and after':

1. sufficient data about past operations may not be available;
2. it is only in exceptional circumstances possible to make a completely parallel comparison between two systems operating under different sets of procedures.[53]

To make matters worse still, health care is an activity that is guided by many different values — many of which are not readily quantifiable. In such an environment, where it is not possible to use such yardsticks as profits, costs, etc., evaluations tend to be based on the opinions of superiors.[54]

Thus, we are back to square one: the crucial element in implementation, even at this level, is the mutual understanding resulting from a continuous, intimate working relationship between researcher and client (here to be taken in a general sense).

Step 8: General Implementation of Project Results at the Local Level

This could be seen as the ultimate goal of all OR projects that are concerned with change at the local level. Anything less might be regarded in some respects as a failure. At the same time, it is obvious that this is a rare event. For instance it has never — to my knowledge — been achieved by a Swedish health services OR project!

Total implementation is, of course, in most cases unrealistically ambitious. The process of implementation is so slow and the pace of change so fast that it is doubtful if it is meaningful to try to implement the same solutions in the last area as in the first. As Ackoff points out, 'The effectiveness of a solution claimed to be optimal at the time of its implementation tends to deteriorate over time.'[55] General implementation at the local level will thus always be a diffuse, slow process where it is not always possible to discern clearly what is implemented and what not.

The problems in this context have already been touched upon. One problem is the tendency to absorb scarce OR resources in sustained implementation. Another is the lack of persuasive power on the part of the central level. Some examples will illustrate this.

In the context of a central study, a simple model was developed for estimating the demand for delivery care units. The model would state the number of beds needed in an area, with a certain specified risk of running a deficit under particular circumstances. Actual delivery care planning is performed by the county councils, none of whom was found to have used the recommended model in its planning. Two reasons were found for this:

1. the model was considered too complicated (although in fact it was relatively simple);
2. delivery care planning is not a question of calculations but of politics. The number of beds is determined by existing resources and the power to close units. Everybody knew that there were far too many units and that the power to close them was inadequate. So there was no need to know the exact required number, since it would be unattainable anyway.

Another, more successful, example concerns the planning system of a medical care centre. In this case a highly successful test application had been demonstrated. The purpose of the project was to increase the accessibility, to shorten waiting times – both in the waiting list and in the waiting room – and to ensure a good patient-doctor continuity. Different computer models were used to develop an efficient patient planning and assignment procedure, manual routines were developed for the planning of personnel working time, medical care programmes were agreed upon among the doctors, etc.

The result of this project has been a much improved service at the centre. The project has also given a good general insight into the problem of how to operate an out-patient care unit efficiently and it has proposed general solutions and recommendations. The problem is that there are several hundred out-patient units. The procedures at these units are not changed by someone reading an article in the county council journal. The proposed solution includes many practical aspects that involve all personnel. It also requires a different way of thinking – an acceptance of the fact that the care centre has limited resources and is supposed to serve all inhabitants in the area, not only those who are patients. This thinking is not readily accepted among doctors since it stands in conflict with their fundamental professional attitude – 'nothing but the best for my patient'.

So, in spite of enthusiastic central recommendations from the highest level, implementation at the local level is slow and time consuming. The plan is to implement in at least one care centre in each of the 26 county councils and hope that the rest of the centres will follow. This alone is obviously a heavy task.

One essential point in general implementation must obviously be to avoid 'sustained' implementation, i.e. an implementation that is dependent on the continued support of the operational researcher. On the one hand, this calls for explicit and complete understanding on the part of the manager and users – not mere acceptance.[56] But this is not enough. OR resources are obviously too scarce to make it possible to implement solutions in all concerned units at the local level.

Two solutions are suggested to this dilemma. The first is to try to create a problem-solving atmosphere rather than to solve problems. Again quoting Ackoff, 'there is an urgent need for OR and MS to devote their efforts to the design of decision-systems that learn and adapt quickly and effectively – rather than the production of optimal decisions that don't'.[57] Similarly, Pondy states: 'The issue, it seems to me, is not how to build better models, but how to create a problem-solving relationship within which better models are likely to be built.'[58] This clearly implies that the operational researcher takes on more the role of a change agent, encouraging and helping clients to find their solutions rather than trying to sell his own.

The other way is to create an effective diffusion process which allows problem-solving approaches and – in relevant cases – solutions to spread with a force of their own. Education and training, meetings and cross-professional conferences are important tools in this effort. Even writing articles and books could make a modest contribution to this goal! The important thing for the operational researcher in health care to realise is that local change, which is the change that really matters in quantitative terms, must usually be accomplished indirectly. Direct change can generally only be achieved at the central level — which in turn means indirect change at the local level — or in an insignificant number of local units.

Taking into account the different problems that are inherent in local change, it might seem more encouraging for the operational researcher to work on central-level problems. Without devaluing the need for more refined and deliberate health care policy, unless this policy is implemented in the local units actually responsible for the delivery of health care, nothing has really been accomplished. Therefore, working on central problems does not relieve the analyst from the responsibility of implementation. Quade makes this point clear, arguing that:

> the ultimate goal of policy analysis is not just to help a policymaker discover what might best be done in some ideal or abstract environment but to help in a practical sense by taking into account the problems of acceptance and implementation associated with the real context.[59]

The eight steps to implementation represent a long ladder to success. It will come as no surprise that so few projects reach the highest steps. However, the difficulties must not keep us from trying. In the pursuit of experience, knowledge and understanding, each step that is reached has a value of its own. So keep on climbing and falling!

A citation from Pressman and Wildavsky provides an appropriate summary of the message this chapter has been trying to convey:

> People now appear to think implementation should be easy; they are therefore upset when expected events do not occur or turn out badly. We would consider our effort a success if more people began with the understanding that implementation under the best of circumstances is exceedingly difficult. They would, therefore, be pleasantly surprised when a few good things really happened.[60]

Notes

1. L.J. Shuman, H. Wolfe and R.D. Speas Jr, 'The Role of Operations Research in Regional Health Planning', *Operations Research*, 22 (March-April 1974), pp. 234-48.

2. D. Stimson and R. Stimson, *Operations Research in Hospitals, Diagnosis*

and Prognosis (Hospital Research and Educational Trust, Chicago, Ill., 1972), p. 41.

3. J. Young, 'No Easy Solutions', in George K. Checko (ed.) *The Recognition of Systems in Health Services* (Operations Research Society of America, Arlington, Va., 1969), pp. 395-8.

4. W. Bennis, 'Commentary', *Management Science*, 12 (October 1965), p. 13.

5. J. Huysmans, *The Implementation of Operations Research* (John Wiley and Sons, New York, 1970), p. 1.

6. N.R. Tobin and T.E. Outfield, 'The Implementation of O.R. Models on Planning Procedures', paper presented at IFORS Conference (August 1972).

7. E.S. Quade, *Analysis for Public Decisions* (Elsevier, Holland, 1975), p. 253.

8. J. Pressman and A. Wildavsky, *Implementation* (University of California Press, California, 1973).

9. Huysmans, *Implementation of Operations Research*, p. V.

10. L.R. Pondy, 'Behavioral Perspectives', in L.J. Shuman, R.D. Speas Jr and J.P. Young (eds.), *Operations Research in Health Care: A Critical Analysis* (The Johns Hopkins University Press, Maryland, Baltimore, 1975), p. 409.

11. Ibid., p. 406.

12. Stimson and Stimson, *Operations Research in Hospitals*, p. 62.

13. Ibid., pp. 41-2.

14. E.J. Connors, 'Hospital System Aspects', in Shuman, Speas and Young (eds.), *Operations Research in Health Care*, p. 26.

15. Ibid., pp. 26-31.

16. Stimson and Stimson, *Operations Research in Hospitals*, p. 77.

17. A.G. Lockett and E. Polding, 'OR/MS Implementation – A Variety of Processes', *Interfaces*, vol. 9, no. 1 (November 1978), p. 46.

18. Huysmans, *Implementation of Operations Research*, pp. 38-9.

19. Pondy, 'Behavioral Perspectives', p. 405.

20. Huysmans, *Implementation of Operations Research*, p. 37.

21. Connors, 'Hospital System Aspects', p. 23.

22. J. Stringer, 'O.R. for "Multi-organizations" ', *Operational Research Quarterly*, 18, no. 2 (1967), pp. 105-20.

23. Stimson and Stimson, *Operations Research in Hospitals*, p. 42.

24. Connors, 'Hospital System Aspects', p. 23.

25. Quade, *Analysis for Public Decisions*, p. 255.

26. Ibid., p. 256.

27. M. Radnor, A.H. Rubinstein and D.A. Tansik, 'Implementation in O.R. and R&D in Government and Business Organisations', *Operations Research*, vol. 18, no. 6 (November-December 1970), p. 979.

28. Huysmans, *Implementation of Operations Research*, pp. 16-17.

29. W.C. Churchman and A.H. Schainblatt, 'The Researcher and the Manager: A Dialectic of Implementation', *Management Science*, 11 (February 1965), pp. 69-87; W.C. Churchman and A.H. Schainblatt, 'On Mutual Understanding', *Management Science*, 12 (October 1965), pp. 40-2.

30. Stimson and Stimson, *Operations Research in Hospitals*, p. 58.

31. P. Szanton, 'Analysis and Urban Government: Experience of the New York City – Rand Institute', *Policy Sciences*, 3 (1972), p. 158.

32. Stimson and Stimson, *Operations Research in Hospitals*, p. 61.

33. Ibid., p. 60.

34. H.M. Wagner, *Principles of Operations Research* (Prentice Hall, New Jersey, 1969), p. 927.

35. Radnor, Rubinstein and Tansik, 'Implementation in O.R. and R&D', p. 980.

36. Lockett and Polding, 'OR/MS Implementation', p. 49.

37. Szanton, 'Analysis and Urban Government', p. 158.

38. Wagner, *Principles of Operations Research*, p. 931.
39. Ibid.
40. Stimson and Stimson, *Operations Research in Hospitals*, p. 47.
41. Ibid., p. 49.
42. Huysmans, *Implementation of Operations Research*, p. V.
43. R. Ackoff, 'Some Ideas on Education in the Management Sciences', *Management Science*, 17 (October 1970), pp. 2-4.
44. Huysmans, *Implementation of Operations Research*, p. 28.
45. P.R. Lawrence, 'How to Deal with Resistance to Change', *Harvard Business Review* (May-June 1954).
46. E.L. Trist and K.W. Bamforth, 'Some Social and Psychological Consequences of the Long-wall Method of Coal-getting', *Human Relations*, vol. 4-1 (1951), pp. 3-38; A.K. Rice, *Productivity and Social Organizations; The Ahmedabad Experiment* (Tavistock Publications, London 1958).
47. Radnor, Rubinstein and Tansik, 'Implementation in O.R. and R&D', p. 985.
48. Ibid., p. 985.
49. Quade, *Analysis for Public Decisions*, p. 255.
50. Huysmans, *Implementation of Operations Research*, p. 13.
51. Stimson and Stimson, *Operations Research in Hospitals*, p. 63.
52. Ibid., p. 63.
53. Wagner, *Principles of Operations Research*, p. 932.
54. Radnor, Rubinstein and Tansik, 'Implementation in O.R. and R&D', p. 979.
55. R. Ackoff, 'Optimization + Objectivity = opt.out', *European Journal of Operational Research*, vol. 1, no. 1 (1977), p. 2.
56. Huysmans, *Implementation of Operations Research*, p. 28.
57. Ackoff, 'Optimization + Objectivity = opt.out', p. 2.
58. Pondy, 'Behavioral Perspectives', p. 406.
59. Quade, *Analysis for Public Decisions*, p. 253.
60. Pressman and Wildavsky, *Implementation*, pp. xii-xiii.

PART TWO

ASPECTS OF STRATEGIC PLANNING

3 HEALTH CARE RESOURCE ALLOCATION MODELS

Richard Gibbs

Background

This review of health care system (HCS) resource allocation models was written whilst the author was working at the International Institute for Applied Systems Analysis (IIASA). Its purpose was to review the literature on HCS resource allocation models, to classify the models into different types, to consider their advantages and disadvantages, and to assess the type that is most appropriate for the IIASA HCS Modeling Task.

The IIASA HCS Modeling Task

The main task of the IIASA Health Care System Modeling Team is to build a national HCS model and to apply it as an aid to HCS planning in collaboration with national centres. The long-term strategy for this task, as set out in earlier papers by Venedictov[1] and Kiselev,[2] envisages the construction of a mathematical simulation model relating activities both within the HCS and between the HCS and other interacting systems (e.g. the population, environment and socio-economic systems). The purpose of the simulation model is to illuminate the future consequence of alternative policies both for the HCS and for the interacting systems and thus assist planners to examine strategic options.

Shigan, Hughes and Kitsul describe the progress towards achieving the long-term aims of the previous paragraph.[3] Figure 3.1 summarises this progress. The figure represents the processes by which people fall ill and by which health resources are provided and used for their treatment. So far five groups of sub-models have been developed. Population projections are used by morbidity models to predict health needs. These estimated needs can then be used to estimate resource requirements at a certain normative level, or they can be partially satisfied according to a resource allocation model, which has some inputs from a resource supply model. The decision maker can choose his policies, standards and performance indicators. Beyond the health care system are the external systems of environment and economy. At some later date, it is hoped to include models of these systems within the over-all framework. Also not included in the suite of models are the feedbacks between the

49

Figure 3.1: Schema for a National HCS Model

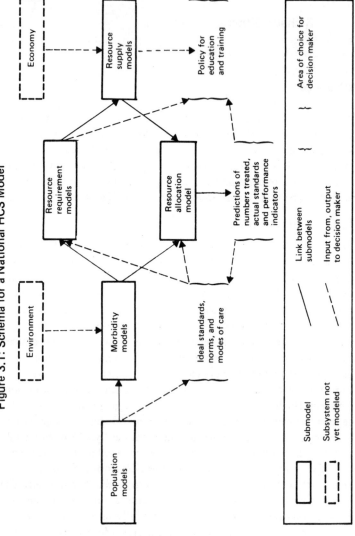

various sub-models (e.g. the allocation of resources to preventive medicine should in the long term alter patterns of morbidity). Again, it is hoped eventually to include these feedbacks within the model framework.

The five sub-models described above have been used to analyse data from several countries. Most of the sub-models are available as computer programmes, which experience has shown are readily transferable from computer to computer. This chapter is concerned with one of the sub-models: the resource allocation sub-model.

The Literature Review

This builds upon the start made by the review-analysis of national HCS models by Fleissner and Klementiev.[4] Their review-analysis was concerned with reviewing all types of national HCS model whereas this chapter is concerned only with models dealing with resource allocation; it considers certain models in more detail and attempts to go beyond reviewing into drawing conclusions about the appropriateness of different types of model for different tasks. The previous review-analysis suggested a classification of national HCS models into three types: econometric, simulation and optimisation.[5] A modified version of this classification is employed in this chapter where the following three types of resource allocation model are defined:

1. macro-econometric – models consisting of linear equations (or transforms of linear equations) relating aggregate variables such as consumption, supply and price of health services, and population attributes, the parameters of which are estimated by multiple regression analysis of current or historic aggregate data;
2. behaviour simulation – models based on hypotheses concerning the behaviour of physicians, patients and other decentralised decision makers in the HCS;
3. system optimisation – models designed to identify the set of resource allocations that optimise a defined objective function of the HCS.

Each type of model is reviewed, in turn, and their advantages and disadvantages are assessed. Following this, the way in which each type of model could fit into the HCS modelling schema of Figure 3.1 is considered and the appropriateness of each type of model for the IIASA HCS Modeling Task is assessed.

Macro-economic Models

Introduction

Many examples of macro-econometric models can be found in the literature on health system resource allocation.[6] The common characteristic of these models is that their hypotheses are expressed in terms of linear relationships (or transformations of linear relationships) between aggregate amounts of quantities such as consumption, supply, price of health care services, and factors describing attributes of the population and the environment. The other distinguishing feature of the approach is that the coefficients of the equations expressing these relationships are estimated by multiple regression analysis using cross-section and/or time series data. This estimation process also allows for testing of the hypotheses in the sense that those equations which fail tests of statistical significance are rejected. This means that a large number of alternative equations (hypotheses) can be tested and the eventual econometric model consists of the sub-set of equations (hypotheses) which have survived the tests.

Three examples of the macro-econometric approach will now be considered in detail: Yett *et al.*[7], Feldstein[8] and D. Harris.[9] These examples illustrate the wide range of relationships which have been examined using this approach. Following this, the advantages and disadvantages of the approach will be assessed.

The Model of Yett et al.

Some authors, particularly those from countries where the HCS has a predominant private sector, offer hypotheses in which the consumption of health care is dependent mainly upon supply and price variables. Consider, for example, the model of Yett *et al.*, which describes the HCS with a set of 47 equations.[10] The model can be illustrated by examining the four equations describing one particular sector of the HCS, the in-patient activity of short-term voluntary and proprietary (STVP) hospitals; these equations are displayed in Table 3.1.

Equation (1) represents consumption (P-DP) as a function of price (P-HP), price reimbursement (HBEN/P-HP), the activity of a 'competing' set of hospitals (PDGA) and an attribute of the population (%OLD). Equation (2) represents price as a function of price in the previous year (P-HP$_{t-1}$), the intensity of bed utilisation (OCCP), weighted wage rates (W-RN, etc.), staffing levels (EMBD) and current capital valuation (KPBD). Equation (3) is a definitional equation showing that occupancy is the ratio of consumption to supply. Equation (4) represents supply

**Table 3.1: Four Illustrative Equations from the Model of Yett *et al.*
Describing the In-patient Activity of STVP Hospitals**

(1) $\quad$ P-DP $\quad=\quad$ -36.2394 P-HP/P-OP + 61.1378 %OLD + 656.3433 HBEN/P-HP
$\quad\quad\quad\quad\quad\quad$ (-2.38) $\quad\quad\quad\quad$ (5.67) $\quad\quad\quad\quad\quad$ (4.91)
$\quad\quad\quad\quad\quad\quad$ -0.9308 $\quad$ PDGA + 317.8782, $\quad \bar{R}^2$ = .81, $\quad$ S.E. = 119.4853.
$\quad\quad\quad\quad\quad\quad$ (-9.32)

(2) $\quad$ P-HP $\quad=\quad$ 0.8971 $\quad$ P-HP$_{t-1}$ − 0.1418 OCCP + 2.1657 (.25 W-RN + .07 W-AH + .13 W-PN + .55 W-NM)
$\quad\quad\quad\quad\quad\quad$ (22.40) $\quad\quad\quad\quad$ (2.04) $\quad\quad\quad\quad$ (3.48)
$\quad\quad\quad\quad\quad\quad$ + 7.0271 EMBD + 0.0525 KPBD − 0.8362, $\quad \bar{R}^2$ = .96, $\quad$ S.E. = 3.4737.
$\quad\quad\quad\quad\quad\quad$ (4.05) $\quad\quad\quad\quad$ (0.56)

(3) $\quad$ OCCP $\quad=\quad \dfrac{\text{P-DP}}{0.00365\ \text{BEDP}}$.

(4) $\quad$ BEDP $\quad=\quad$ 0.7958 DEBP$_{t-1}$ + 0.7645 P-DP + 0.0226 HBFF$_{t-2}$ − 0.0554, $\quad \bar{R}^2$ = .99,
$\quad\quad\quad\quad\quad\quad$ (15.25) $\quad\quad\quad\quad$ (3.74) $\quad\quad\quad\quad$ (1.26)
$\quad\quad\quad\quad\quad\quad\quad\quad\quad\quad\quad\quad\quad\quad\quad\quad\quad\quad\quad\quad\quad\quad\quad\quad\quad\quad\quad$ S.E. = 0.1092.

where
P-DP = annual number of in-patient days provided by STVP hospitals (millions);
P-HP = average daily service charge in STVP hospitals (dollars);
P-OP = average revenue per out-patient visit at STVP hospitals (dollars);
%OLD = percentage of population aged 65 and over;
HBEN = benefits *per capita* for hospital care paid by private and public insurance programmes (dollars);
PDGA = weighted average of in-patient days provided by government-aided hospitals per thousand population;
OCCP = average percentage occupancy rate in STVP hospitals;
W-RN = annual wage paid to general duty hospital RNs (thousands of dollars);
W-AH = annual wage paid to health professionals (thousands of dollars);
W-PN = annual wage paid to practical nurses (thousands of dollars);
W-NM = annual wage paid to non-medical hospital employees (thousands of dollars);
EMBD = number of personnel per bed in STVP hospitals;
KPBD = value of plant assets per bed in STVP hospitals (thousands of dollars);
BEDP = number of available beds in STVP hospitals;
HBFF = Hill Burton funds for hospital construction (millions of dollars).

(BEDP), consumption (P-DP) and the availability of capital building funds in the year before last (HBFF$_{t-2}$). Although some of these variables occur in some other equations in the model, these four equations suffice to illustrate the approach. Essentially, the equations represent how the aggregate quantities of consumption, supply and price of hospital services mutually influence each other; only one quantity, %OLD, describes a feature that is exogenous to the hospital system.

The endogenous variables in the complete model include variables describing in-patient and out-patient care, including not only STVP hospitals but also state and local government ones, and a number of categories of health manpower (e.g. surgical specialists in private practice, registered nurses). The exogenous variables consist mainly of variables describing insurance parameters (e.g. percentages of the population enrolled in different types of scheme) and aspects of federal or other government intervention such as parameters of the Medicare scheme, availability of federal funds for new hospital construction, and the output of medical schools.

The coefficients of the equations in the model were estimated separately by multiple regression analysis of cross-section data. The performance of the model was then tested by initialising the endogenous

variables to the 1975 levels for the State of California, solving the
equations simultaneously year by year, and comparing the results with
historical data for California for the period 1968 to 1977. Yett *et al.*
illustrate how the model can be used as an aid to planning by forecasting
the year-by-year consequences for the endogenous variables of policy-
generated changes in the exogenous variables.

The Models of Feldstein

Although the macro-econometric approach has been most widely used
in countries the HCS of which have strong private sectors, it has also
been used in countries with predominant public sectors. For example,
one of the most well-known studies is that by Feldstein of the UK
National Health Service.[11] In the UK the consumer usually pays no
direct price for health care services. Thus price variables are irrelevant.
Feldstein chose not to include population and environmental variables
(except for population as the denominator in certain consumption and
supply variables). So his equations represent consumption variables as
functions of supply variables alone.

Most of Feldstein's equations treat aggregate consumption as a
function of various groups of supply variables at differing levels of
aggregation. Consider, for example, one of the production functions he
suggests for UK acute hospitals (equation 4.15 of Feldstein):[12]

$$W = AM^{0.387}B^{0.465}N^{0.047}S^{0.069}$$

where W = weighted number of in-patients treated per annum;
        A = constant;
        M = supply of doctors;
        B = supply of beds;
        N = supply of nurses;
        S = other supplies.

Such an equation allows one to predict the aggregate consumption of
hospital care in terms of the supplies of the different inputs of a hospital.
With equations of this type Feldstein analyses the likely consequences for
hospital output (i.e. aggregate consumption) of changes in input ratios
and proceeds to compute input ratios that are optimum under stated
conditions. One of his most interesting findings is that an increase in the
ratio of doctor supply to the other hospital inputs, within the same
total expenditure, would be expected to elicit an increase in production,
i.e. an increase in the number of in-patients treated.

In another part of his analysis (Chapter 7), Feldstein represents disaggregated consumption variables as functions of a single aggregate supply variable. The equations are of the form:

$$\log C_i = a_i \log S + b_i$$

where C_i = consumption by disease type i;
S = aggregate supply of acute hospital beds;
a_i, b_i = coefficients to be estimated.

Thus the coefficient, a_i, is the elasticity of consumption by disease type i with respect to supply. Feldstein used three types of consumption variable for each disease type: beds used, and its two components — cases treated and mean length of stay. An illustrative set of his results, for certain disease types, is shown in Table 3.2. Consider, for example, the results for haemorrhoids. These can be interpreted as implying that a 1 per cent increase in aggregate bed supply is associated with a 1.14 per cent increase in beds used for haemorrhoid patients, which in turn is composed of a 0.70 per cent increase in the number of haemorrhoid cases and a 0.44 per cent increase in their mean length of stay.

In interpreting these results and considering their relevance to this type of analysis, we can start by quoting from Feldstein's text:

The elasticity values for acute appendicitis and acute upper respiratory infections are quite satisfactory. Appendectomies are very inelastic to bed scarcity while the less serious respiratory infections are highly elastic; in addition, the former's elasticity is properly concentrated on the mean stay while the latter's is almost completely in the number of admissions. The values for peptic ulcer also seem appropriate, showing a low overall elasticity which is concentrated on the mean stay.

The results for some other disease groups are not as satisfactory. Cases of abdominal hernia and of haemorrhoids show greater than average overall elasticity. It seems inappropriate that important surgical repair procedures such as these should occupy a smaller proportion of beds in regions of greater relative scarcity and that the number of cases treated should be no less elastic than average.

In contrast, it would seem desirable that admissions for tonsillectomy and adenoidectomy should be highly elastic; in regions where beds are relatively more scarce, tonsillectomy and adenoidectomy cases should occupy a smaller proportion of available

Table 3.2: Elasticities of Consumption, by Selected Diagnoses, to Aggregate Bed Supply[a] for English Acute Hospitals in 1960 (Standard errors in brackets)

Disease (1)	Beds used[b] (2)	Admissions[b] (3)	Mean stay (4)
Acute appendicits	0.15(0.36)	-0.16(0.33)	0.31(0.17)
Acute upper respiratory infections	2.57(1.00)	1.53(0.52)	1.04(0.74)
Peptic ulcer	0.85(0.52)	0.29(0.40)	0.56(0.51)
Abdominal hernia (female)	1.39(0.44)	0.52 (0.22)	0.87(0.44)
Haemorrhoids	1.14(0.62)	0.70(0.48)	0.44(0.24)
Tonsils and adenoids	0.55(0.46)	0.23(0.38)	0.33(0.38)
Arteriosclerotic heart disease	2.22(0.70)	1.14(0.51)	1.08(0.99)
Malignant neoplasms	0.58(0.30)	0.68(0.29)	-0.10(0.20)
Varicose veins (female)	1.40(0.70)	0.78(0.41)	0.62(0.67)
Males	1.03(0.14)	0.66(0.13)	0.37(0.15)
Females	0.97(0.11)	0.63(0.17)	0.34(0.21)
All persons	—	0.65(0.15)	0.35(0.15)

a. Elasticities calculated with respect to total number of beds per 1,000 population.
b. Per 1,000 population, 1960.

Source: M.S. Feldstein, *Economic Analysis for Health Service Efficiency* (North-Holland, Amsterdam, 1967), Table 7.10.

beds. The decision to operate for tonsillitis has often been cited as an example of medical fashion that is not founded on medical knowledge. Nevertheless, one in twenty hospitalisations in Britain are for tonsillectomy and adenoidectomy. And, more important for our current discussion, the number of these procedures and the length of stay show very low elasticity to bed scarcity.

Arteriosclerotic heart disease, including coronary, usually presents very serious medical cases; nearly a third of hospital admissions in this category die in hospital. Despite this, the number of cases admitted is extremely elastic to bed scarcity. Patients with malignant neoplasms (cancer) also have a high hospital fatality rate; more than a fifth of all admissions die in hospital. This is about 50 per cent higher than in the United States, reflecting in part the greater tendency in Britain to keep terminal cancer cases in hospital after there is no longer any hope of helping them. As the table shows, this length of stay is unaffected by relative bed scarcity.

Women with varicose veins enter hospital for a surgical operation. The high elasticity of bed use for varicose veins, with the greater proportion of this due to the number of cases, probably reflects a greater reliance on alternative methods of out-patient treatment, as well as a generally lower rate of care, in those regions in which beds are relatively more scarce.

It is difficult to understand why such striking examples of inappropriate elasticities should have been found. It may be possible that some of the results can be explained by differences among the regions in the actual incidence of the diseases. Since the hospital statistics on which this study has been based provide the only sound measure of morbidity for these conditions, the influence of area-specific incidence rates could only be studied for those diseases in which mortality is a good indicator of morbidity. Doing so for heart disease and cancer does not suggest that the geographical pattern of mortality would explain our findings.

We shall not try to offer any behavioral explanations of the individual elasticity values. To do so properly, we should have to develop a complex theory of medical admission and treatment decisions based on the factors that motivate patients to seek care and the way in which doctors diagnose and treat each type of disease. But again it is likely that any explanation should begin by recognizing that the doctors themselves are not aware of the allocation patterns that they have established.[13]

Although Feldstein considers that some of his elasticity estimates are inappropriate, there is good reason to believe that they correctly represent hospital practice, or at least hospital practice as it was in 1960. At that time tonsillectomy and adenoidectomy were common treatments for cases of infections of the tonsils and adenoids — although this practice is much less common today — and the low elasticity values are therefore plausible. Similarly, the high elasticity values for hernia and haemorrhoids are consistent with the fact that there were (and often still are) long waiting lists for these conditions in areas of relative bed scarcity. Thus, given the prevailing medical practice and within the ranges of his data, Feldstein could reasonably claim that his elasticity values represent how the pattern of admissions and length of stay would be likely to respond to changes in the levels of total bed availability.

The Model of D. Harris

Most econometric studies in this field, like those of Yett and Feldstein, have placed relatively little importance on factors exogenous to the HCS. There are, however, some notable exceptions, e.g. D. Harris,[14]

Fleissner[15] and Newhouse.[16] In the study by Harris, variables describing
consumption are represented as functions of both supply variables and
variables describing certain population characteristics. The variables
describing population chatacteristics were derived from a factor analysis
of 21 population characteristics in the 56 New York State counties (see
Table 3.3). Four factors were identified and Table 3.3 shows the loadings
of each of the original 21 characteristics on each factor and the
commonality estimates (h^2) which state the proportion of variance in
each characteristic explained by the four factors. From inspection of
the loadings Harris interprets the factors as follows:

Factor 1:   'metropolitan/middle class' — predominant in counties with
             a metropolitan character and high socio-economic status.
Factor 2:   'age/illness' — predominant in counties with large elderly
             populations and chronic morbidity.
Factor 3:   'fertility/family' — predominant in counties with high
             fertility, large young population and low educational level.
Factor 4:   'city/inner suburb' — predominant in counties containing a
             central city and a high proportion of unmarried women.

Harris then fitted a number of equations relating these factors and
supply and consumption variables by multiple regression analysis of
cross-section data from 56 New York State counties for 1970. Harris's
equations were based on a three-stage causal model. The stages of
causation are studied by path analysis, an elaboration of multiple
regression analysis, which reveals the causal effect of one variable on
variables at later stages in the model both directly and via variables at
intermediate stages. The model structure and results are shown in
Figure 3.2. The numbers on the linking arrows are the standardised
partial regression coefficients; they measure the effect of each causally
prior variable on each subsequent one. The numbers on the arrows
without origins are the square roots of the unexplained variance.

The results in Figure 3.2, coupled with the zero order matrix (not
shown here), allow one to trace causation. For example the population
factor 1, 'metro/middle class', has a weak net negative effect on the
hospital admissions variable, as revealed by a zero order correlation
coefficient of -0.13, but the path analysis reveals that this is the net
sum of two strong countervailing indirect effects. The first, positive,
indirect effect is via the positive causal effects (a) from factor 1 to
physician supply and (b) from physician supply to hospital admissions.
The second, stronger, negative, indirect effect is via (a) the negative effect

Table 3.3: Factor Analysis of Population Characteristics for 56 New York State Counties (Definitions from 1970 Census)

Variable	Factor 1	2	3	4	h^2
1. Median family income	*0.927*	-0.243	0.034	0.071	0.924
2. Personal income *per capita*	*0.876*	0.096	-0.210	0.099	0.830
3. Population per sq. mile	*0.867*	0.014	-0.179	-0.077	0.789
4. Size of population	*0.827*	-0.050	-0.089	0.160	0.720
5. % of families below poverty level	*-0.774*	0.205	-0.059	-0.129	0.661
6. % of workforce in white-collar jobs	*0.771*	-0.308	-0.258	0.158	0.780
7. % of population living in urban areas	*0.738*	-0.135	-0.107	*0.483*	0.807
8. % non-white	*-0.674*	-0.018	-0.092	0.149	0.486
9. County located in SMSA	*0.560*	-0.230	0.241	*0.514*	0.689
10. % of population over 25 who have completed 13 or more years of school	*0.551*	*-0.548*	*-0.391*	-0.127	0.773
11. Crude death rate	*-0.497*	*0.782*	-0.194	0.083	0.903
12. % of population age 65 and over	*-0.428*	*0.811*	-0.287	0.083	0.930
13. Median age	0.252	*0.894*	-0.174	0.094	0.902
14. % reproductive age females (15-19)	0.251	*-0.797*	*0.438*	0.121	0.904
15. % of population under age 5	-0.121	*-0.441*	*0.846*	0.044	0.926
16. Crude birth rate	*-0.477*	*-0.407*	*0.576*	0.165	0.752
17. Fertility ratio[b]	-0.314	0.018	*0.905*	-0.099	0.927
18. % females (14 and older) married	0.213	0.256	*0.795*	-0.346	0.862
19. County has central city	0.249	-0.109	-0.056	*-0.681*	0.540
20. Sex ratio	-0.176	-0.170	0.302	*-0.056*	0.531
21. Infant mortality rate	-0.059	*0.335*	0.038	*0.494*	0.361

a. Variables in each factor are indicated in italics.
b. Number of children age 5 and under per female between 15 and 54 years of age.
Source: D.H. Harris, 'Effect of Population and Health Care Environment on Hospital Utilisation', *Health Services Research*, 10 (1975).

of factor 1 on hospital bed supply and (b) the positive effect of hospital bed supply on admissions.

From his results Harris concludes that, for the most part, hospital consumption variables depend causally on supply variables and that the effects of population characteristics on consumption are mainly transmitted indirectly via supply variables and only to a small extent directly. This, according to Harris, leads to the following implications.

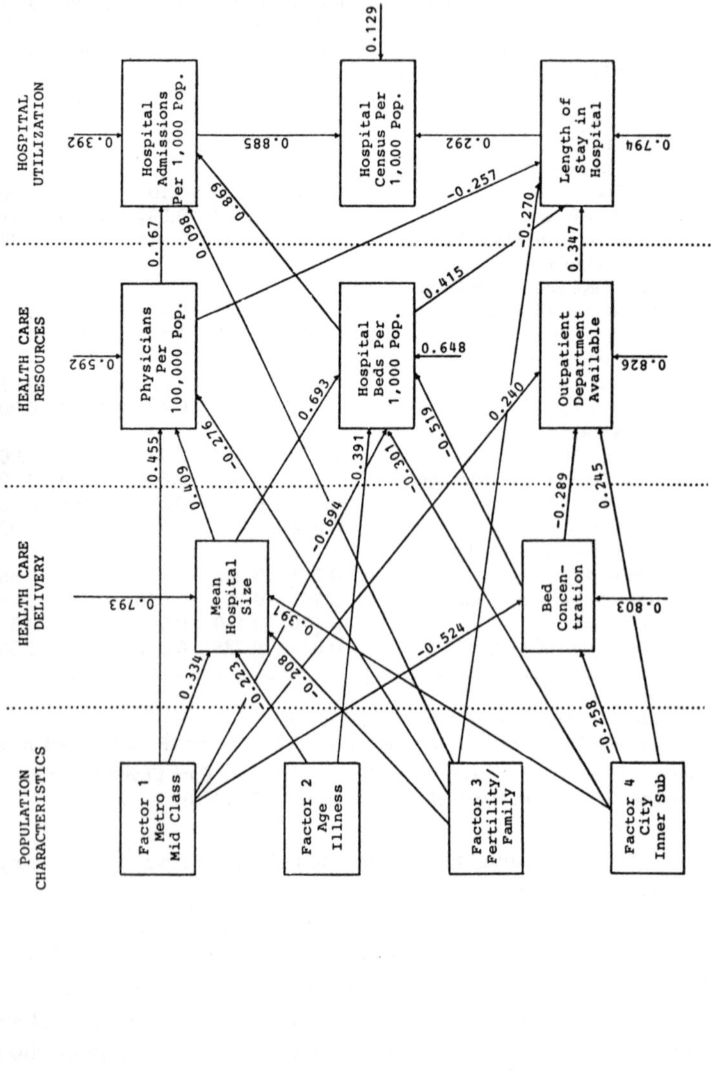

Figure 3.2: The Results of Harris's Study, Expressed in Terms of Path Analysis

The results of the present study, coupled with those of a companion study, using longitudinal data, should help end the controversy surrounding Roemer's thesis,[17] at least in urbanized areas. It should now be clear that supply can create its own demand rather than that demand leads to congruent levels of supply. To supply additional beds to areas with current high demand (utilization) in an attempt to 'satisfy' the 'unmet need' in these areas is thus seen as a futile exercise. Additional beds will always lead to additional use, and health care expenditures will continue to rise. To base hospital construction priorities primarily on past use and current demand is hopeless since areas will never have 'enough' beds.

Excessive hospitalization and its high costs can be reduced by controlling the number of beds available to a local population and its physicians, as well as by controlling the supply of physicians. Money that would have been spent on hospital stays can then be used to help finance and develop more rational health care delivery systems that make more extensive use of ambulatory care and other substitutes for inpatient care.

Harris suggests a sequence of causation, as shown in Figure 3.2, of the following type: population characteristics → health care delivery → health care resources → hospital utilisation. If one accepts this sequence, which is based purely on *a priori* considerations, then one can also accept the important result that hospital utilisation depends mainly on supply factors. This result can then be used in planning, as Harris suggests, by adjusting planned levels of supply so as to achieve some desired levels of utilisation.

Review

Having looked at three examples of the macro-econometric approach to modelling HCS resource allocation, let us assess its advantages and disadvantages.

First the advantages. The approach has been widely used. The three examples described above illustrate both the wide range of relationships that have been studied and the importance of the relationships which show how the pattern of consumption of health services is influenced mainly by the pattern of supply. The approach is relatively easy to apply since standard methods and computer programmes exist and results are relatively easy to compare using a standard terminology.

The data requirements are not usually excessive. The approach has been successfully used in both private and public HCS and there are grounds for believing that certain types of macro-econometric model might be universally applicable, at least among the IIASA member countries.

There are, however, some important disadvantages and limitations. Macro-econometric models relate aggregate amounts of quantities in linear (or transformation of linear) equations and the coefficients are estimated from regression analysis of cross-section or time series data describing current or historic values of these quantities. It follows that the application of such models in a predictive or planning mode is only valid, strictly speaking, for situations in which:

1. the value of each variable is within the range observed in the data;
2. there is no structural change in the HCS or related systems, e.g. a large-scale introduction of screening or a massive pollution of the water supply;
3. there is no major change in the way in which key resources are used, e.g. telephonic medical consultation, the use of hospitals more for nursing care and concentrating medical care more on ambulatory and domiciliary settings.

Thus the approach is only strictly valid for describing incremental changes around the *status quo*. The hypotheses underlying the equations describe how total quantities of the variables relate to each other in the present and/or recent past.

The approach is essentially descriptive — it allows one efficiently to summarise the current or recent historic relations between variations in the variables. This is a serious limitation if the main reason for building a model of the HCS is to assist decision makers to consider non-incremental changes.

We now turn to the second type of resource allocation model — behaviour simulation models.

Behaviour Simulation Models

Introduction

In this type of model there are hypotheses concerning the behaviour of the consumers and the suppliers of health care, i.e. patients and HCS personnel. These models can directly represent how scarce resources are rationed between competing demands. Three examples will be described: Rousseau,[18] McDonald *et al.*[19] and Klementiev.[20]

The Model of Rousseau

Rousseau starts by dismissing the approach in which resource requirements are calculated directly from population characteristics. He supplies evidence showing

> that on the contrary the demanded resources or consumption of resources is directly related to the available resources and that in practice and in the global perspective one has to accept the hypothesis that the demand could never be saturated, or if we can envisage a saturation, it is not at a level society can afford.

Here he echoes the conclusion of D. Harris and many others.[21] Indeed, no author of an HCS resource allocation model has argued against this conclusion.

Rousseau tackles the problem of allocating known quantities, A_i, of medical services (treatments) by category to different categories of physicians (specialists), each with a given capacity, M_s, of work. The variables in the model are the allocations X_{is} of services to physicians. The behavioural hypothesis is based on two assumptions:

1. there exists an ideal scheme of practice that would be attained if enough resources were available;
2. the observed practice is as close as possible to the ideal scheme, given the resource constraints.

Clearly, Rousseau faced a serious difficulty in quantifying the parameters of ideal practice. In the lack of other information he chose (1) to set these parameters equal to the observed mean values of X_{is} over the nine districts of Quebec and (2) to assume that the objective function of the HCS in the different districts was to minimise the sum of squared deviations from the 'ideal' practice. Rousseau found that, under these conditions, his model produced a set of values of X_{is} that not only corresponded closely with observed practice but also corresponded significantly closer than a second set of values derived (without the model) by assuming that a district allocates its resources in the same proportions as the Quebec average. Thus there is some evidence that the model can satisfactorily represent how the HCS allocates its resources. Having tested the model in the descriptive setting, Rousseau plans to apply the model to predicting how resource allocation would change in the future if additional resources are made available. In this way the model could be used by planners to examine the consequences of alternative strategies for resource investment.

Rousseau concludes in his paper that, since 'the control variables for the planning agency are very limited', resource allocation models should, like his,

> be of the type 'user optimization' rather than 'system optimization' in the sense that the models should predict how the different actors in the system *would* react given certain constraints rather than try to model how they *should* react for the well-being of the whole system.

This can be viewed as a positive response to the problem posed by Feldstein (see earlier) of developing 'a complex theory of medical admission and treatment decisions'. It might be argued that, in countries with predominant public sectors in the HCS, 'the control variables for the planning agency' are not so limited as in Canada and system optimisation may be more feasible. However, even in these countries one suspects that many of the decisions on resource allocation are taken by individual clinicians and other staff in the HCS at the point of delivery of care rather than by the central planning agencies and so we may reasonably assume that Rousseau's conclusion holds for these countries too.

The Model of McDonald et al.

Another behaviour simulation model is the inferred worth model of the UK National Health Service, by McDonald *et al.*[22] This model, and its application in a local area, is described in detail in Chapter 4. Briefly, there are three groups of variables which describe the allocation of scarce resources:

1. Cover — the number of patients, categorised by disease type and other factors, who receive treatment (d_i);
2. Modes — the usages of alternative forms of treatment that are permitted for each patient category (x_{il});
3. Standards — the average amounts of resources consumed per patient in a given category in a given mode (u_{ilk});

where i denotes patient category, l denotes mode, and k denotes resource. Thus the model represents the response of the HCS to the scarcity of a resource in terms of:

1. treating fewer patients, in one or more categories (less cover); or
2. treating them in different ways (shift in the balance of mode use); or
3. treating them less intensively (lower standards); or

4. some combination of these.

The central hypothesis of the model is that the HCS attempts to maximise a function of the cover, modes and standards variables. This function is a *de facto* utility function or, in Rousseau's terms, a 'user optimisation' function. It is termed the inferred worth function because its parameters are estimated from observations of the effects of the prevailing value system in the HCS. In other words, the model is fitted to historical data on resource allocation. In running the model the inferred worth function is maximised subject to constraints on resource availability. In applications the model is used to estimate the consequences, in terms of cover, modes and standards, of setting the vector of resource availability to different values. It is therefore used with planners as a device for examining options in long-term strategic planning of resource investment in the HCS.

The underlying theories of this model and that of Rousseau are somewhat similar (although there are considerable differences in the types of variables in the two models). Both models envisage local decision makers in the HCS attempting to optimise their own objective function subject to over-all resource constraints. A further similarity is that both models postulate an ideal scheme of practice. In McDonald's model this is expressed in terms of:

1. total numbers, D_i, of sick individuals by category (i.e. the maximum numbers that ought to be treated);
2. the ideal standards, U_{ilk}, for patients of a given category in a given mode.

For several instances the current performance of the HCS in England is below these ideals (in other words, demands for health care are not saturated). Experience with using the model suggests that budgetary and resource constraints prevent the HCS from attaining these ideals and are likely to continue to so prevent it for the foreseeable future; i.e. the demands for health care will never be fully saturated. In effect, the inferred worth model represents the HCS striving to achieve these ideals, within resource constraints. It also represents the different degrees of priority which the HCS places on the attainment of the different ideals; these differing priorities are incorporated as parameters in the inferred worth function. Thus the model represents resource allocation as the outcome of a rationing process in which these differing priorities of demand are balanced against constraints on resource supply.

The main features of the McDonald model that are not present in the current version of the Rousseau model are:

1. the complete range of HCS resources is represented, not merely physician time;
2. the model represents the consumption of combinations, or packages, of resources by patients rather than a single resource per patient;
3. the estimation of ideal performance is based not on an average of current performance but on information from surveys, medical literature and professional opinion;
4. the model is more concerned with alternative locations (modes) of care, e.g. hospitalisation *v.* domiciliary care, rather than care by one medical specialist *v.* another.

The Model of Klementiev

A third, and rather different, type of behaviour simulation model is contained within the HCS model design suggested by Klementiev.[23] The over-all model describes certain aspects of morbidity, resource supply and resource allocation. The morbidity aspect of the model, which has been further developed since, considers the processes by which individuals transfer between the states healthy, latent sick, revealed sick, treated sick, dead, and between different stages of sickness. Three stages of sickness are defined for degenerative disease, corresponding to out-patient treatment, acute in-patient treatment and terminal care. Latent sick individuals can become revealed sick either by self-referral to a physician or via the screening process. The resource allocation aspect of the model is based on a queue discipline hypothesis which can be roughly expressed as follows:

1. In a given time period the patients in each stage of the disease who are in the state of being treated have prior claims on physician resource for that stage. The remaining availability of physician resource is then calculated.
2. The number of revealed sick (but not being treated) in each disease stage who can transfer in the given time period to the state of receiving treatment will be determined by either the remaining availability of the physician resource (supply), or the number of revealed sick not yet receiving treatment (demand), whichever is smaller.

Although this model is still at an early stage of development, it has already been run for one class of disease, degenerative disease, but on hypothetical data (see Olshansky[24]). Thus there has not yet been an opportunity to test the ability of the model to fit data on the real performance of the HCS.

The model is designed to enable the user to examine the consequences of policy options for (a) the proportion of physician resource devoted to screening rather than to treatment and (b) the proportions of the physician treatment resources devoted to each of the three stages of the disease. 'Inefficient' decisions on these proportions result either in patients accumulating and waiting at one or more stages in the treatment process or in under-utilisation of one or more of the treatment resources.

A somewhat similar approach, though with more dimensions, has been used to simulate the care of elderly handicapped individuals in the UK; see, for example, R. Harris.[25] In this simulation model a number of categories of elderly handicapped are defined, in terms of severity of handicap, home situation, etc., and a priority ordering of categories is stated. For each category a number of alternative forms of care are defined, e.g. hospital, residential, domiciliary care, with a preference ranking. The model simulates how the HCS allocates clients to the alternative forms of care by a queue discipline mechanism. That is to say that, if the first preference form of care is not available for clients in a given category, the model allocates them to the next highest-ranked form of care that is available. In the model, higher-priority client categories are allocated to a package of care before the lower-priority categories so that, in general, the high-priority categories are more likely to be allocated to a high-preference form of care. The model can be used to simulate the consequences of providing different mixes of resources (services) for the care of the elderly. The approach has similarities with that described in Chapter 6.

The queue discipline mechanism has been suggested in other models — for example in the model of the effects of establishing a health screening programme described by Atsumi and Kaihara.[26]

Review

In considering the relatively sparse literature on behaviour simulation models it is interesting to note the variety of hypotheses. Rousseau describes specialist physicians striving to attain an ideal distribution of activities between themselves. Klementiev and R. Harris suggest a system of patient selection based on a queuing discipline. McDonald suggests that the participants in the HCS are striving after ideals in the numbers and types of treatment and that the degrees to which the ideals are approached in practice is a result of striking a balance in priorities. The adequacy of the hypothesis is crucial in a behaviour simulation model since, by contrast with a macro-econometric model, it is not possible to test rapidly a large number of alternative hypotheses. If this approach is to be pursued, it is evident that much thought will need to be given to hypothesis construction.

There are some important advantages in the behaviour simulation approach to resource allocation. It can operate at a disaggregated level, if necessary, since the basic hypotheses describe the behaviour of physicians and other personnel at the local level. More importantly, and in contrast to the econometric approach, it can in principle be validly applied to exploring situations in which there is a structural, rather than a merely incremental, change in HCS, since, through its hypotheses, it contains a type of information about the behaviour mechanisms of the actors in the HCS that is not usually contained in macro-econometric models. An analogy from physical science may serve to illustrate this point. Boyle's Law and Charles's Law describe the relationships between the pressure, volume and temperature of a fixed mass of gas and were established by observing the behaviour of samples of different gases within certain ranges of the three variables; in some respects the equations of these Laws are analogous to the equations of macro-econometric models of the HCS. By contrast, the kinetic theory of gases is based on hypotheses concerning the behaviour of gas molecules and was found not only correctly to predict the macro-relationships of Boyle's and Charles's Laws, within the ranges where they apply, but also correctly to predict the deviations from the Laws outside these ranges, for example near the liquefaction points of gases. Provided that their hypotheses are sound behaviour simulation models of the HCS have analogous properties. Thus they can, in principle, be used to examine the consequences of:

1. major changes in the balance of resources in the HCS, outside the range of current or recent historic variation;
2. changes in the ways in which resources are used;
3. changes in medical technology (provided that the changed technology coefficients can be forecast);
4. changes in the pattern of morbidity.

Another advantage is that, by attempting to represent the real-life process of resource allocation, the model may be more transparent to the HCS planner than the more abstract representation of most econometric models; thus the planner may be more willing to use a behaviour simulation model since its mechanism is more likely to correspond to the mental model which he already possesses and which has been built up through his personal experience of the HCS.

Thus the behaviour simulation approach is strong in areas where the econometric approach is weak. However, the reverse is also true. Firstly, there has been comparatively little experience in the application of behaviour simulation models to the HCS as a whole and the few models that have been used are somewhat different, one from the other. Thus there are no standard methods, programmes and terminology for this approach and the results of different models are not so readily comparable. More importantly, behaviour simulation models are relatively difficult to build since they require an intimate understanding of the workings of the HCS and relatively difficult to apply since they usually require data (for parameter estimation) on the preferences and priorities within the HCS that may not readily be available. Lastly, it may be that a universal behaviour simulation model does not exist, even among the IIASA member countries. That is to say, there may be such differences in the factors governing the behaviour of patients and HCS personnel in different countries that no one behavioural model would be valid for all.

Let us now turn to the third type of resource allocation models – system optimisation models.

System Optimisation Models

Introduction

We come now to the group of models concerned with optimising some assumed objective function for the HCS. We term this approach 'system optimisation' after Rousseau, who distinguishes it from 'user optimisation'.[27] There are many examples in the literature of optimising models applied to health care problems, but only a few are concerned with the HCS as a whole. The most commonly used technique for this type of model is mathematical programming. A useful review of this field of work has been made by Boldy.[28] He concludes that, in the field of strategic planning of the HCS, classical system optimisation models are unlikely to be as useful as models of a more exploratory nature:

> In the strategic planning area, there have been a number of mathematical programming models developed for planning the prevention and control of disease or population growth and a start has been made towards their implementation. However, perhaps the

most potentially valuable mathematical programming models are those such as are being developed by OR Service of the DHSS, which are concerned with exploring the wider aspects of allocating resources both between the different health and social services care sectors and between the various patient/client groups. Because of the general lack of detailed knowledge concerning the relative effectiveness of given forms of care provided to given types of patient/client, a situation which is likely to continue for the foreseeable future, such mathematical programming models are likely to be used in a 'what-if' rather than an optimizing manner. In other words, their use is likely to lie in the exploration of the resource consequence and other effects of different policy options so that a more well-informed decision can be made.[29]

Boldy regards 'the general lack of detailed knowledge concerning the relative effectiveness of different forms of care' as the main objection to the application of classical system optimising models, whereas Rousseau's main objection is that system optimisation is inconsistent with the behaviour of physicians at the point of delivery of health care. To assess these two objections and to consider also the advantages of the system optimisation approach, we will consider two examples of the approach being applied in a real planning situation.

The Model of Feldstein et al.

The first example is the model of Feldstein, Piot and Sundaresan which was applied to the planning of the control of tuberculosis in the Republic of Korea.[30] The authors propose an objective function of the form:

$$\sum_j V_k B_{kj} x_j$$

where V_k = social benefit of type k;
$\quad\quad x_j$ = amount of activity j;
$\quad\quad B_{kj}$ = amount of benefit per unit of activity.

The function is to be maximised subject to resource constraints of the form:

$$\sum_j A_{ij} x_j \leqslant m_i \quad \forall\, i$$

where m_i = availability of resource i;

A_{ij} = amount of resource consumed per unit of activity.

The technology coefficients A_{ij} were estimated from experience with TB programmes elsewhere; the benefit coefficients B_{kj} were calculated on the basis of an economic analysis of research findings and physicians' judgements concerning the clinical outcomes of each activity. The output from the model showed the optimum set of counter-tuberculosis activities for different categories of population defined in terms of age and urban/rural split. The model was run for four different forms of the objective function in which social benefit was expressed respectively in terms of temporary disability, permanent impairment, excess mortality, economic loss. Sensitivity analyses involving changes in parameters in the objective function were performed. The results enabled the authors to propose some robust conclusions for the design of a tuberculosis control programme in Korea.

The sensitivity analysis is particularly interesting since it is argued in this chapter that uncertainty in quantifying the objective function is one of the major disadvantages in using optimising models. The robustness of the results of Feldstein *et al.* is in contrast to the sensitivity found by Ashford *et al.* in an application of linear programming to maternity services.[31] Ashford *et al.* found that there was 'a fundamental disagreement about the relative merits of different procedures' between the various experts consulted. This led Ashford *et al.* to run their model with three different objective functions to reflect these differing views. They found that the use of one of these three led to 'a radically different solution' to that obtained with the other two.

On the basis of these contrasting experiences we can only conclude that the scientist who decides to build a system optimising model for the HCS can have no confidence in advance that his model will not founder on uncertainty in the objective function. Indeed, we must fear that the more comprehensive the scope of the model, i.e. the wider the range of HCS activities covered in the model, the greater is the risk of encountering areas where no single valued objective function can be satisfactorily applied.

The Cost Minimisation Version of the Model of McDonald et al.

Another optimisation model is the early version of the McDonald model.[32] For this version of the model the authors chose as the objective function the minimisation of the total resource cost. Thus they avoided the problems, described above, of quantifying a maximisation of benefits function. This version of the model was designed to identify the set of resource allocations and associated resource availabilities that minimises total resource costs subject to upper bounds on the availability of individual resources, lower bounds on the number of patients to be treated and specifications of the alternative types of treatment permitted for each category of patient:

$$\text{Minimise} \sum_k \sum_i \sum_l C_k x_{il} U_{ilk}$$

subject to

$$\sum_l x_{il} \geqslant D_i \quad \forall i$$

$$\sum_i \sum_l x_{il} U_{ilk} \leqslant b_k \quad \forall k$$

$$x_{il} \geqslant 0 \quad \forall i, l$$

where i = patient category;
  k = resource type;
  l = mode type;
  C_k = unit resource cost;
  x_{il} = number of patients i treated by mode l;
  U_{ilk} = amount of resource k consumed per patient i in mode l;
  b_k = maximum availability of resource k;
  D_i = minimum number of patients of type i to be treated.

(An alternative version of this model, and its limitations, is discussed in Chapter 4.)

The only variables in this formulation are the x_{il}. The D_i and the U_{ilk} are constants representing the ideal numbers of treated patients and standards of treatment. The problem as formulated above was quickly shown to be infeasible. In other words, if realistic constraints on resource availability were assumed, there was no allocation that could treat all D_i patients at the required standards, U_{ilk}. Feasible solutions could only be obtained by relaxing some of the resource constraints to an extent that would permit very large growths of these resources from their current levels, e.g. a trebling of the number of home nurses. Such solutions were unrealistic. Thus, although the solutions had a theoretical validity, they were of little practical value to planners.

In order to produce solutions that were both feasible and realistic, the data input was modified. The values of first the patient demands, D_i, and then later the standards of treatment, U_{ilk}, were lowered to levels that corresponded more nearly with the prevailing levels in the HCS. Feasible solutions were indeed obtained in this exercise and the results were of some limited practical value. However, the behaviour of the model was unsatisfactory in one important respect. The model tended to select modes of care where the prevailing standards were low rather than those where the prevailing standards were close to the ideals, U_{ilk}. An example will clarify this phenomenon.

Consider a typical patient category in the model from the group of categories of elderly chronically disabled patients. One of the permitted modes of care for this category is long-term care in a geriatric hospital. An alternative mode is a package of community-based care services, such as home nurses, home helps and day centres. The ideal standards for this mode of care (showing the main services only) are displayed in Table 3.4. This mode is typical of the domiciliary and community-based modes of care defined for other categories of elderly disabled patient in the model but the precise mix of services and the ideal standards vary from one category to another (for example, the categories with greater physical disability have, in general, higher ideal standards). Estimates of the prevailing standards for this mode of care are also shown in Table 3.4; in general they are significantly lower than the ideals.

Table 3.4: Example of a Community-based Mode of Care for an Elderly Disabled Patient with Ideal and Prevailing Standards

Service	Ideal standard	Estimate of prevailing standard
Home nurse (visits p.a.)	35	7
Home help (visits p.a.)	135	82
Day centre (attendances p.a.)	150	13

Now the behaviour of the model in this situation is to tend to select the domiciliary mode of care, for all patient categories for which it is permitted, in preference to the geriatric hospital mode, for two reasons:

1. the objective function of the model is cost minimisation and, at prevailing standards, the community-based mode is cheaper for all

categories (whereas at ideal standards for the more disabled categories it would be more expensive);
2. the community-based mode, at prevailing standards, makes relatively low demands on scarce resources (whereas, at ideal standards, the constraints on resource availabilities would more tightly limit the use of these modes).

Thus the main result from running their version of the model consisted of a decrease in hospital-based modes of care and an increase in community-based care relative to the prevailing actual situation in England. Such a shift in the balance of care would, in theory, elicit large financial savings in the provision of hospital services and relatively small increases in expenditure on additional community-based services.

This aspect of the model's behaviour is at variance with the behaviour of the HCS in the real world. It is well known in England that many elderly disabled patients are hospitalised precisely because the alternative domiciliary care could only be offered at unsatisfactorily low standards. In other words, decision makers at the point of care delivery reject one form of care at low standards, despite its cheapness, in favour of another one at high standards. This type of difference between the behaviour of the model and the real HCS also occurs for most other categories of patient defined in the model, e.g. the mentally ill and the acute ill. It arises because the objective function of the model, cost minimisation, is different to that of the HCS. This difference is important and the results obtained from running this formulation of the model are of limited practical value. This is an example of the danger foreseen by Rousseau of developing models for 'system optimisation' rather than 'user optimisation'. Even if the central authority of the HCS, in this case the Department of Health and Social Security, had subscribed to the 'system objective' of cost minimisation, the model's results would still have been of little practical value since this objective is inconsistent with the 'user objective' being pursued by the actors in the HCS. Following this experience, McDonald's team proceeded to modify their model into a 'user optimisation' version, the inferred worth model, which has been described earlier as an example of behaviour simulation.

Review

Two examples of system optimising models have been given here and, by considering the different ways in which they were applied, we may draw some conclusions about the appropriateness of this type of model. The model of Feldstein, Piot and Sundaresan was applied to a very specific sector of the HCS, the counter-tuberculosis programme. In this particular sector it appears to be possible to estimate the benefits of alternative activities on a number of different scales and it seems that the main conclusions from the model are not crucially affected by the choice of scale. Furthermore, the paper gives the impression that decision makers in Korea were both willing and capable of designing and implementing this programme at the level of detail specified in the model (e.g. by specifying the population groups at whom mass screening is to be directed). To the extent that this was true, the optimising model was appropriate. By contrast, the cost minimisation version of the McDonald model was concerned with the resource allocation in the HCS as a whole and it became evident that, even if the central decision makers for whom the model was developed wished to allocate resources so as to minimise costs, they were not in a position to do so. They had, and still have, the main say in deciding the aggregate availability of many of the key resources in the HCS but the decisions to allocate these resources between competing patient groups rest mainly with individual personnel at the point of care delivery.

Let us assume, as mentioned earlier, that there is a significant degree of decentralised decision making in the HCS of all countries. Then we may conclude that 'system optimising' models are likely to be appropriate only for certain individual sectors of the HCS where there is a strong influence from the centre and where the clinical outcomes of the alternative procedures are reasonably well known, but that system optimisation is unlikely to be appropriate for planning the HCS as a whole.

There are many advantages in using optimising models of resource allocation. There are a number of well known techniques, such as linear programming, which can readily be applied and for which computer programmes are available. The models are relatively easy to build and most of the data are relatively easy to obtain (with the exception of parameters for the objective function in benefit maximisation models – see below). Optimising models are capable of exploring situations in which major structural changes are envisaged rather than mere incremental changes, provided the technology coefficients can be safely assumed to remain unchanged. By their very nature, they are capable of incorporating a planner's goals into the objective function and so they hold out the promise, in principle, of leading the planner to the desired solution in one step rather than by a series of model manipulations and runs which is required with macro-econometric and behaviour simulation models.

On the other hand, there are the two serious disadvantages mentioned earlier. Firstly, there is the difficulty of defining an objective function which corresponds to some formal quantitative statement of the objectives of the HCS. Objectives like 'maximise the health of the population' are easy to state qualitatively but notoriously difficult to express in an acceptable quantitative form. HCS planners themselves are particularly aware of this difficulty and, in the experience of this author, are not aware of employing any single readily quantifiable conceptual objective function when they are planning services for the HCS as a whole.

A second disadvantage is that the solutions produced by the model are likely to be of theoretical rather than practical interest since there is no guarantee that the real behaviour of the HCS will ever follow the 'system optimising' behaviour of the model. As Boldy has observed for system optimising models of hospital location, 'these models tend to ignore aspects of patient behavior and as such are unlikely to be implemented, consequently more complex models have been developed involving the simulation of such aspects'.[33]

Assessment of the Appropriate Type of Resource Allocation Sub-model for the IIASA HCS Model

Introduction

In this section the ways in which the three types of resource allocation sub-model reviewed in the previous sections would fit into the over-all HCS model are considered and the appropriateness of each type is assessed.

The Role of Each Type of Resource Allocation Sub-model in the Over-all HCS Model

If there were no constraints on the supply of HCS resources, then planning the HCS would be a relatively simple matter. The appropriate model schema would be a simple variant of the schema illustrated in Figure 3.1 which included four sub-models concerned with population, disease prevalence estimation, resource allocation and resource supply. In this variant, shown in Figure 3.3, the resource allocation sub-model is really no more than a list of standard, ideal, resource requirements per unit of prevalence or, for screening resources, per unit of population; the required supply of each resource can then be calculated by combining these figures with the outputs of the population and disease prevalence sub-models.

It is assumed here, following D. Harris,[34] Rousseau[35] and many

Figure 3.3: Model Schema for the Case of Unconstrained Resource Production

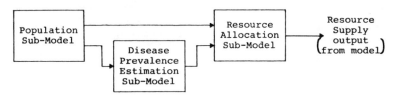

others, that this case, of unconstrained HCS resource supply, does not exist in real life and that in all countries the total potential demand for health care exceeds the capacity of the HCS to provide it, i.e. the demands for health care cannot be fully saturated by the delivery system. Thus the simple schema in Figure 3.3 does not apply and the process of resource allocation in the HCS is one of allocating scarce resources between competing demands. Let us now consider how the three types of model considered in this chapter represent this resource allocation process and how the HCS model schema of Figure 3.1 would apply for each type.

With the macro-econometric type of model information is usually supplied to the model on one or more of the following variables: supply and price of resources and population attributes. (In some cases, such as the model of Feldstein, population features only as a denominator in the supply variables.) The output usually includes the consumption of health care services, e.g. numbers of patients treated in various categories. In no instance is information on demand or disease prevalence supplied as an input. The fraction of disease prevalence that receives treatment (i.e. consumption divided by prevalence) would have to be calculated outside the model. Thus the model schema has to be adapted as in Figure 3.4.

With this type of model the planner can submit options on policies for resource supply and discover the model's estimates of the consequent pattern of consumption.

With the behaviour simulation type of model both the demands for health care and the supply of resources can be supplied as input data and the model can estimate the outcome in terms of variables such as the fraction of demand or prevalence that is met by the service, i.e. the fraction of patients who receive treatment and the fraction who do not, and the types of treatment they receive. The model schema for this case is shown in Figure 3.5. Planners' options for resource supply can be

Figure 3.4: Model Schema for Using the Macro-econometric Resource
      Allocation Sub-model

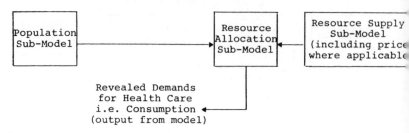

tested out with the model as with the macro-econometric case of Figure
3.4, but in this case the structure of demand and disease prevalence is
part of the input of the resource allocation sub-model; this would be an
important advantage in a situation where the structure of disease
prevalence is expected to change within the planning horizon.

Figure 3.5: Model Schema for Using the Behaviour Simulation type
      of Resource Allocation Sub-model

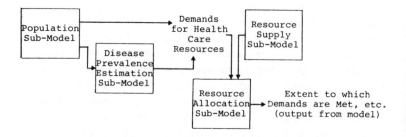

With the system optimising type of model information can be
supplied on the demands for health care but for resource supply all that
is required is a set of upper bounds on the maximum supply of the main
resources. The model then calculates an optimum allocation of resources
to demands, within the constraints, and thus produces the optimum
pattern of resource supply. The model schema for this case is shown
in Figure 3.6.

Assessment

Having considered the different ways in which the three types of

Figure 3.6: Model Schema for Using the System Optimising Type of Resource Allocation Sub-model

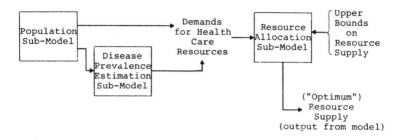

resource allocation sub-model would fit into the over-all HCS model schema, let us assess the appropriateness of each type for the IIASA HCS Modeling Task. The advantages and disadvantages of each type of model have been described in the previous three sections and are summarised in Table 3.5.

The only disadvantages or limitations of the econometric approach are its high level of aggregation, its use of linear equations and the limitation of its validity to situations of only incremental change. Apart from these, the advantages of the approach, as compared with the other two approaches, are very strong. Thus, if the IIASA HCS Modeling Task is to be concerned with the study of incremental changes in the HCS, there is a clear case for concentrating on the econometric approach.

If, however, as seems more likely, the HCS Modeling Task is to be concerned with situations of major structural changes in the HCS, then the behaviour simulation approach is the most strongly indicated *ab initio*. The main doubts about using this approach concern, firstly, the reliability of the behavioural hypotheses under conditions of structural change and, secondly, their universality. It appears that the only way to resolve these doubts is by the classical scientific procedure of building a model and testing it under a range of different situations.

It is therefore recommended that the IIASA HCS Modeling Team should embark on the construction of an HCS resource allocation sub-model of the behaviour simulation type. The point of departure would be the existing behaviour simulation model of Klementiev, which is based on a queue discipline hypothesis.[36] However, the work would need to enlarge considerably upon this model and draw upon the experience of Rousseau[37] and McDonald,[38] who have shown that the

Table 3.5: Summary of Advantages and Disadvantages of Three Types of Resource Allocation Model

	Macro-econometric models	Behaviour simulation models	System optimisation models
Advantages			
1.	Well tried and successful.	1. Easy to use at disaggregated levels.	1. Standard techniques and terminology.
2.	Standard techniques and terminology.	2. In principle can be applied to situations of structural or major change from the *status quo*.	2. Easy to compare results.
3.	Easy to compare results.		3. Most of the data are relatively easy to obtain (apart from coefficients of objective function).
4.	Data requirements reasonable.	3. Relatively acceptable to HCS planner since hypotheses likely to correspond with planner's experience.	
5.	Large number of tried hypotheses can be tested, therefore easy to build model.		4. In principle can be applied to situations of structural or major change from the *status quo*.
6.	Probably applicable universally.		5. In principle supplies the HCS planner with the 'correct' solution in one step.
Disadvantages			
1.	Hypothesis limited to linear relations (or transformations of linear relations) between aggregate quantities.	1. Relatively little experience at strategic level.	1. Impossible to define satisfactory objective function for HCS system as a whole.
2.	Results not valid outside the range of variables in the data used for estimation of coefficients and therefore model is not appropriate to situations of structural or major change from the *status quo*.	2. Standard techniques and terminology not available.	2. Unrealistic since real behaviour of HCS participants will not correspond to 'system optimum' allocations.
		3. Results difficult to compare.	
		4. Relatively difficult to build since deep understanding of HCS behaviour is required.	
		5. Some of the data may be difficult to obtain.	
		6. May not be applicable universally.	

behaviour of the HCS, particularly the way it adapts to resource scarcity, cannot be adequately represented solely in terms of queuing mechanisms and that some account has to be taken of the value system of the actors in the HCS.

Although it is recommended that the HCS Modeling Task should concentrate on the behaviour simulation approach, this is not meant to imply that nothing can usefully be learnt from experience with macro-econometric and system optimising models. In any case, the three types of approach, as applied in practice, are not entirely mutually exclusive (for example, Feldstein used his *econometric* hospital production function as part of a procedure to suggest the *optimum* mix of hospital inputs). Thus, it is to be expected that, in building a behaviour simulation model of resource allocation in the HCS, there will be some recourse both to econometric methods (e.g. for those aspects of the HCS which are not likely to be subject to structural change) and to optimisation methods (e.g. for representing 'user optimisation' behaviour).

Notes

1. D.D. Venedictov, 'Modeling of Health Care Systems', in *IIASA Conference '76*, vol. 2 (International Institute for Applied Systems Analysis, Laxenburg, Austria, 1976).

2. A. Kiselev, *A Systems Approach to Health Care*, RM-75-31 (International Institute for Applied Systems Analysis, Laxenburg, Austria, 1975).

3. E.N. Shigan, D.J. Hughes and P.I. Kitsul, *Health Care Systems Modeling at IIASA; A Status Report*, SR-79-4 (International Institute for Applied Systems

Analysis, Laxenburg, Austria, 1979).

4. P. Fleissner and A. Klementiev, *Health Care System Models: A Review,* Research Memorandum, RM-77-49 (International Institute for Applied Systems Analysis, Laxenburg, Austria, 1977).

5. Ibid.

6. See, for example, the bibliography assembled in US Department of Health, Education, and Welfare, *An Analysis of Health Manpower Models,* Monographs and Data for Health Resources Planning Series, DHEW Publication no. (HRA) 75-19 (Washington, DC, 1974).

7. D.E. Yett *et al.*, 'A Macroeconometric Model of the Production and Distribution of Physician, Hospital, and Other Health Care Services', in D.D. Venedictov (ed.), *Health System Modeling and the Information System for the Co-ordination of Research in Oncology,* CP-77-4 (International Institute for Applied Systems Analysis, Laxenburg, Austria, 1977).

8. M.S. Feldstein, *Economic Analysis for Health Service Efficiency* (North-Holland, Amsterdam, 1967).

9. D.H. Harris, 'Effect of Population and Health Care Environment on Hospital Utilisation', *Health Services Research,* 10, 229 (1975).

10. Yett *et al.,* 'A Macroeconometric Model'.

11. Feldstein, *Health Service Efficiency.*

12. Ibid., p. 98.

13. Ibid., pp. 220-1.

14. Harris, 'Effect of Population and Health Care Environment on Hospital Utilisation'.

15. P. Fleissner, 'An Integrated Model of the Austrian Health Care System', in N.T.J. Bailey and M. Thompson (eds.), *Systems Aspects of Health Planning* (North-Holland, Amsterdam, 1975).

16. J.P. Newhouse, 'Forecasting Demand and Planning of Health Services', in Bailey and Thompson (eds.), *Systems Aspects of Health Planning.*

17. Roemer's thesis is that hospital utilisation is primarily dependent upon supply factors: M.I. Roemer and M. Shain, *Hospital Utilisation Under Insurance,* Hospital Monograph Series, no. 6 (American Hospital Association, Chicago, 1959).

18. J.-M. Rousseau, 'The Need for an Equilibrium Model for Health Care System Planning', in E.N. Shigan and R. Gibbs (eds.), *Modeling Health Care Systems – Proceedings of an IIASA Workshop,* Conference Proceedings (International Institute for Applied Systems Analysis, Laxenburg, Austria, forthcoming).

19. A.G. McDonald, G.C. Cuddeford and E.M.L. Beale, 'Mathematical Models of the Balance of Care', *British Medical Bulletin,* 30, 3 (1974), pp. 262-70; A.G. McDonald and R.J. Gibbs, 'Some Requirements for Strategic Models of Health Services Illustrated by Examples from the United Kingdom', in Venedictov (ed.), *Health System Modeling and the Information System for the Co-ordination of Research in Oncology;* R.J. Gibbs and I.L. Coverdale, 'Some Compatible Inter-related Sub-models of the National Health Service', paper presented at the International Cybernetics Conference, Vienna, Austria (April 1976).

20. A. Klementiev, *Mathematical Approach to Developing a Simulation Model of a Health Care System,* RM-76-65 (International Institute for Applied Systems Analysis, Laxenburg, Austria, 1976).

21. Harris, 'Effect of Population and Health Care Environment on Hospital Utilisation'.

22. See note 19.

23. Klementiev, *Mathematical Approach to Developing a Simulation Model of a Health Care System.*

24. W. Olshansky, *Basic Model of Health Care Systems,* internal paper

(International Institute for Applied Systems Analysis, Laxenburg, Austria, 1976).

25. R. Harris, *The Development of Resources and Services for the Long Term Care of the Elderly, the Use of Operational Research in European Health Services – Report of a Working Group* (WHO, Copenhagen, 1975).

26. K. Atsumi and S. Kaihara, 'Planning a National Medical Information System: A Systems Approach', in Bailey and Thompson (eds.), *Systems Aspects of Health Planning*.

27. Rousseau, 'The Need for an Equilibrium Model'.

28. D. Boldy, 'A Review of the Application of Mathematical Programming to Tactical and Strategic Health and Social Services Problems', *Operational Research Quarterly*, 27, 2, ii (1976), pp. 439-48.

29. Ibid., pp. 446-7.

30. M.S. Feldstein, M.A. Piot and T.K. Sundaresan, *Resource Allocation Model for Public Health Planning – A Case Study of Tuberculosis Control* (WHO, Geneva, 1973).

31. J.R. Ashford, G. Ferster and D. Makuc, 'An Approach to Resource Allocation in the Re-organised National Health Service', in G. McLachlan (ed.), *Problems and Progress in Medical Care: Essays on Current Research* (Ninth Series: *The Future and Present Indicatives* (Oxford University Press for the Nuffield Provincial Hospitals Trust, London, 1973).

32. R.R.P. Jackson, 'Contribution to the Delivery of Health Care', in D. Howland (ed.) *Cybernetic Modelling of Adaptive Organisations: Proceedings of a Conference Held in Oporto, 27-31 August 1973* (NATO Advisory Panel on Operational Research, 1974); see also note 19.

33. Boldy, 'A Review of the Application of Mathematical Programming to Tactical and Strategic Health and Social Services Problems'.

34. Harris, 'Effect of Population and Health Care Environment on Hospital Utilisation'.

35. Rousseau, 'The Need for an Equilibrium Model'.

36. Klementiev, *Mathematical Approach to Developing a Simulation Model of a Health Care System*.

37. Rousseau, 'The Need for an Equilibrium Model'.

38. See note 19.

References

The IIASA Health Care Systems Modeling Task: Recent Publications

A Committee Report to IIASA by the Participants in an Informal Meeting on Health Delivery Systems in Developing Countries, CO-79-10 (1979)

Fleissner, P. *Chronic Illnesses and Socio-Economic Conditions: The Finland Case 1964 and 1968*, WP-79-29 (1979)

Hughes, D.J. *A Model of the Equilibrium Between Different Levels of Treatment in the Health Care System: Pilot Version*, WP-79-15 (1979)

———, E.A. Nurminski and G.D.H. Royston. *Nondifferentiable Optimization Promotes Health Care*, WP-79-90 (1979)

Rousseau, J.M. and R.J. Gibbs. *A Model to Assist Planning the Provision of Hospital Services*, CP-80-3 (1980)

Rutten, F.F.H. *Physician Behaviour: The Key to Modeling Health Care Systems for Government Planning*, WP-79-60 (1979)

Shigan, E.N. (ed.) *Systems Modeling in Health Care. Proceedings of an IIASA Conference, November 22-24, 1977*, CP-78-12 (1978)

———, D.J. Hughes and P.I. Kitsul. *Health Care Systems Modeling at IIASA: A Status Report*, SR-79-4 (1979)

————, P. Aspden and P.I. Kitsul (eds.) *Modeling Health Care Systems: June 1979 Workshop Proceedings,* CP-79-15 (1979)

Richard Gibbs acknowledges with thanks the help he received from colleagues in preparing his contribution; however, he alone is responsible for the views expressed, which should not necessarily be ascribed to the Department of Health and Social Security.

4 PLANNING THE BALANCE OF CARE[1]

Duncan Boldy, Reginald Canvin, John Russell
and Geoffrey Royston

Background and Introduction

The Structure of the UK Health and Social Services

In the UK, health services (doctors, nurses, hospital beds, etc.) are
administered by local health authorities and social services (home helps,
social workers, etc.) by the Social Services Departments of local
government authorities. Central government provides almost all the
health and much of the social service finance and requires that field
authorities produce plans for their service provision, with health and
social services being planned jointly where appropriate. These authorities
have considerable autonomy in planning their services, although central
government expects national priorities to be observed. Service field
workers (doctors, social workers, etc.) have, in turn, considerable
freedom in the allocation of available resources between client groups
(e.g. elderly, physically handicapped, mentally ill) and also in the forms
of care which people receive. For many types of patient or client there
are often several alternative forms of care that are judged to be
professionally acceptable (e.g. domiciliary, community or institutional
care for the elderly). The structure of the health and social services as
outlined above is illustrated, in a simplified form, in Figure 4.1.

The Model

The availability of alternative forms of care with often considerably
different costs provides an opportunity for health and social service
authorities to provide a more cost-effective mix of resources. However,
because of the somewhat complex interrelationships between the whole
range of health and social services required to care for the various groups
of patients or clients, the selection of an agreed balance poses
considerable difficulties, particularly in the absence of a model capable
of exploring the various consequences of possible courses of action. An
added complication is that UK public expenditure is being severely
curtailed, thus presenting health and social services managers with what
appear to be more difficult choices relating to the rationing of scarce
resources.

Figure 4.1: UK Health and Personal Social Services Planning and
Operational Structure

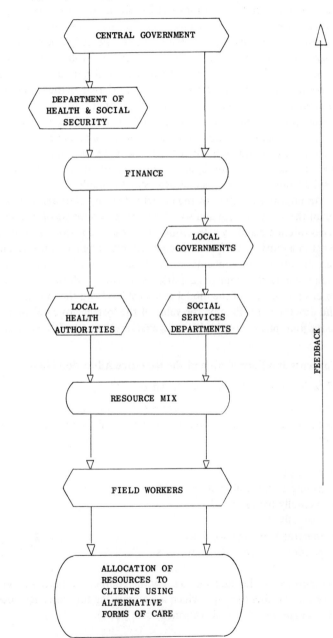

The resource allocation model described in this chapter was originally developed at a national level, to enable policy makers to explore the balance between different forms of health and social services (e.g. in-patient care, day care, domiciliary care) and also between different types of patients or clients (e.g. the elderly and the mentally ill). The model has been designed to estimate how field workers would allocate resources to clients and utilise alternative forms of care and also to suggest resource mixes that would be cost effective. Although based on the techniques of mathematical programming, the model does not purport to indicate a single optimum allocation of health and social services, but rather to suggest or examine possible alternative courses of action and to calculate the service consequences. As such, its use is seen as iterative in that managers can review and update their assumptions in the light of the results from successive calculations using the model.

An important feature of the model is that, by considering in some detail the agreed health and social service requirements of different types of clients and by calculating the resource consequences, it can assist in a move away from 'incremental' planning based principally on past provision. The concepts and form of the model are now described, then the data requirements are discussed. This is followed by a section describing the use of the model at a local level and the model's scope and development. Finally, the value of the 'balance-of-care' approach to the joint planning of health and social services in the UK is considered.

Concepts and Formulation of the Resource Allocation Model

Client Groups, Categories and Packages of Care

In allocating health and social services resources, clients are usually categorised into client groups. Current main client groups in the model are:

1. elderly;
2. younger physically handicapped;
3. mentally handicapped;
4. mentally ill;
5. maternity and gynaecology;
6. children in care of social services.

The purpose of the model is to show the conflicts and interactions between the client groups, which are competing for scarce resources over a planning time-scale (normally five years).

The mechanism for allowing choice in the allocation of resources is based on the concept that there exists a number of alternative modes of care for many types of patients. Each mode is a 'package', consisting of amounts of various resources. The alternative modes are all judged to be professionally acceptable, although requiring different service components. Thus there is the possibility of choosing modes of care in such a way as to make the best use of those resources which are available.

In order to apply the above principles, patients in each client group are divided into categories by a suitable classification. For example, the physically handicapped client group is divided into 18 categories: three factors of age and three levels of handicap, and whether living alone or with others. Over all, there are some 150 categories of patients, for the majority of which a number of alternative modes of care can be considered as professionally acceptable.

An example of the alternative modes of care assumed to be available for a category of the mentally ill client group is shown in Table 4.1. There are three possible types of accommodation (combined together in the table), three types of work situation and two types of support services, giving 18 alternative modes in all (six shown). The amount of each individual resource in a mode is defined to be the desirable or 'ideal' standard of provision of that resource within the particular 'package' of care. In the above example the ideal standards for one mode might consist of five attendances per week at a place of work — i.e. 250 attendances a year — 17 visits per year from a community psychiatrist nurse and 6 attendances per year at an out-patient clinic.

Figure 4.2 gives an overview of the structure used in the model (showing an example from the elderly client group).

The 'Minimum Cost' Model

Based on the above structure a linear programme model was initially formulated as follows, with a minimum cost objective function.

Input variables:
  D_i = number of patients in patient category i to receive care
  R_k and R^*_k = maximum and minimum availability of resource k
  U_{ilk} = 'ideal' standards of allocation of resource k to patient category i in mode of care l
  C_k = unit cost of resource k

Determine:
  d_{il} = number of patients in category i to be treated in mode l

Table 4.1: Example of Possible Modes of Care for a Category of
Person with a Mental Illness (Category: schizophrenic;
in the community; no suitable home; able to work.)

Alternative modes of care	Accommodation		Resources Work		Support	
	Group home, hostel or lodgings	Sheltered workshop	Adult training centre	Day centre	Community psychiatric nurse	Out-patient etc.
1	√	√			√	√
2	√	√				√
3	√		√		√	√
4	√		√			√
5	√			√	√	√
6	√			√		√

Note:
The six alternative modes of care consist of three pairs, one for each of the three
different work situations. For each pair, the second alternative consists of more
frequent out-patient visits, in order to compensate for not receiving the treatment
and support of a community psychiatric nurse.

r_{jk} = amount of resource k allocated to client group j (a client
group j comprises a given set of patient categories i)

Minimise:
$$\Sigma_j \, \Sigma_k \, C_k \, r_{jk}$$

Subject to:
$$r_{jk} = \Sigma_{i \epsilon j} \, U_{ilk} \, d_{il}$$
$$\Sigma_l d_{il} = D_i \text{ for all i and}$$
$$R_k^* \leqslant \Sigma_j r_{jk} \leqslant R_k \text{ for all k.}$$

The model was used to find the set of resources and their allocation
between client groups (within some constraints) that was most cost
effective. However, with the 'packages' of care allocated at the 'ideal'
standard, the minimum cost solutions obtained were often considerably
greater than existing health and social service budgets and, if realistic
budget constraints were imposed, a feasible solution could not always
be obtained. Furthermore, there was no way of representing the priorities
of the field workers for allocating scarce resources between and within
client groups. An extension to the basic model was proposed, termed

Figure 4.2: Structure of the Balance of Care Model

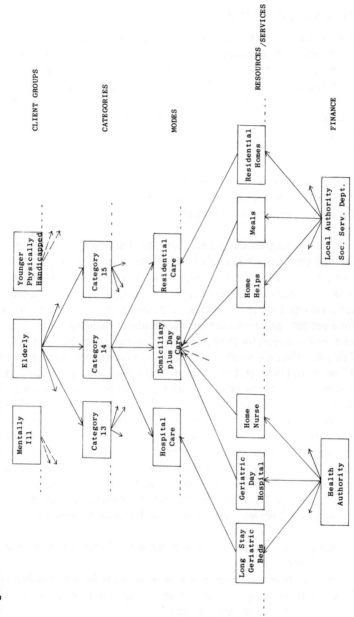

the inferred worth model.

The Inferred Worth Model

The inferred worth model was developed to provide a structure which would reflect the ways in which the resource allocation process responds to resource scarcity through a rationing process, taking account of the field workers' priorities throughout the health and social services. This task has been approached by trying to infer their priorities from the decisions that have been made, as reflected by the current pattern of care. Three possible ways of adapting to the scarcity of resources have been considered:

Option 1:   treating patients by different modes;
Option 2:   treating patients less intensively;
Option 3:   treating fewer patients.

We are mainly concerned here with the first two options. The way the first option is accommodated in the structure of the model has already been described. The concept underlying the second response to resource scarcity is that, when there are insufficient resources available for ideal standards to be achieved, the amount of the resource provided for a patient can be less than the ideal without changing the mode of care. For example, for the category of schizophrenics illustrated in Table 4.1, the ideal number of visits from a community nurse might be 17 per year. However, if nurses were scarce and only, say, 8 visits on average could be provided, then this form of care in the community might still be valid; this rationing would be described by the model as a standard of 47 per cent (8/17) which would, as we shall see, incur a certain penalty cost. This concept of 'elastic' resources cannot be applied to most institutional or residential resources, for example hospital beds and residential homes, but can be widely applied to resources used in community care, such as day centres, social workers, meals, etc.

For the model to respond realistically to resource scarcity, by allowing standards less than 'ideal', a mechanism is needed that:

1. ensures standards are increased as far as possible, but not past the 'ideal' level:
2. reproduces the priorities which are observed to hold in practice, i.e. which standards are low and which are high for different resources between and within client groups.

This is achieved by using a type of utility function h_{jk} (the inferred worth function) as illustrated in Figure 4.3. This is a monotonically increasing function which imposes a penalty cost for failing to achieve 'ideal' standards. It has the same form for each elastic resource in each client group. Requirement (1) is met by making it a function with a gradient greater than the cost of care at standards below the 'ideal' (so the model tries to raise standards) but equal to the cost of care at 'ideal' standards (so the model does not try to raise standards beyond 'ideals'). Requirement (2) is met by having an elasticity parameter (ϕ_{jk}) for the inferred worth curve for each elastic resource k in each client group j which can be set, as described later, so that the observed priorities (hence 'inferred' worth) of the system at some selected time are reproduced by the model. Provided that these requirements can be met, the exact functional form of the inferred worth curve is not critical. The one chosen is of a type commonly used for utility functions:

$$h_{jk}(s_{jk}) = A_{jk} s_{jk}^{-\phi_{jk}} + B_{jk}$$

where:

$h'_{jk}(1.0) = C_k t_{jk}$, since the marginal worth of raising standards already at ideal levels equals the marginal cost (t_{jk} being the allocation of resource k to client group j needed to achieve 'ideal' standards)

and:

$h_{jk}(1.0) = 0$, i.e. no penalty at ideal standards

hence:
$$A_{jk} = -B_{jk} = \frac{-C_k t_{jk}}{\phi_{jk}}$$

and so:
$$h_{jk}(s_{jk}) = \frac{C_k t_{jk}}{\phi_{jk}} [1 - s_{jk}^{-\phi_{jk}}]$$

A similar set of functions can be defined that allows the number of patients treated in each category to be varied. This facility, option 3 above, is not discussed further.

It can be seen that the penalty from the inferred worth functions for each resource standard in each client group depends on the cost of attaining 'ideal' standards, the standard achieved and the calibration parameter, ϕ_{jk}. The inferred worth model then uses the following objective function to maximise the total inferred worth, net of cost.

Figure 4.3: The Form of the Inferred Worth Functions

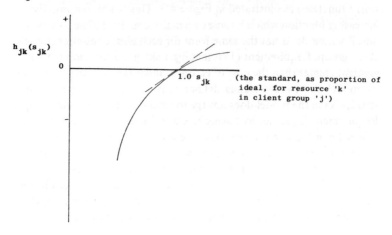

(the standard, as proportion of
ideal, for resource 'k'
in client group 'j')

Maximise:

$$\Sigma \ \Sigma \ [h_{jk}(s_{jk}) - C_k r_{jk}]$$
$$j \quad k$$

subject to:

$$\Sigma \ d_{il} = D_i \text{ for all } i$$
$$l$$

$$R^*_k \leqslant \Sigma \ r_{jk} \leqslant R_k \text{ for all } i$$
$$\qquad j$$

$$\Sigma \ \Sigma \ C_k \ r_{jk} \leqslant Q(Q \text{ is total expenditure available})$$
$$j \quad k$$

where:

$$r_{jk} = s_{jk} \ t_{jk} \text{ and}$$
$$t_{jk} = \Sigma \ \Sigma \ U_{ilk} d_{il}$$
$$\quad i\epsilon j \ l$$

The inferred worth model will thus utilise resources so as to produce the highest attainable standards according to field workers' inferred priorities. Hence it can be used either to give a representation of the system, given a set of resources R_k, or to identify a cost-effective set of resources given total expenditure Q.

A basic assumption is that the system will have the same priorities between resources and client groups even if the amounts of available resources change, and so the model can be used to estimate the likely consequences of such changes.

Usage of the Model

Three different types of calculation are particularly appropriate. The first is a 'base' calculation in which all the available data, including resource allocations between client groups and use of alternative packages of care for the current situation, are used in the model to calculate the prevailing standards. This provides a base against which the results of other calculations can be compared and also allows the inferred worth curves to be calibrated. The second type of calculation is an 'indicative' run in which the aim is to estimate the likely outcome (especially in terms of client group resource standards) of providing a given mix of resources. Figure 4.4 illustrates the input and output for this sort of calculation. The third type of calculation is an 'exploratory' one in which the model is allowed some freedom to choose resources and should therefore indicate which resources might be increased and which decreased, cost effectively. These calculations can thus be used by managers to describe their present situation, to examine the likely consequences of future plans for resource provision and to suggest possible changes to resource allocations. How this has been done in practice is considered later.

Input Data and Calibration

This section of the paper describes the types of data that are required for the model and outlines the work carried out to estimate the calibration parameters, defined in the previous section.

Data

The types of data required are as follows:

1. the number of patients in category i who receive care (D_i);
2. the maximum and minimum availability of the kth resource (R_k and R^*_k) and its unit cost (C_k);
3. the 'ideal' standards of allocation of resource k to patient category i in mode l (U_{ilk});
4. the available expenditure on health and social services (Q);
5. total actual allocation of resource k to client group j (e.g. elderly) (r_{jk});
6. the actual number of patients in category i assigned to mode l(d_{il});
7. the elasticity parameters (ϕ_{jk}), which may require information on the r_{jk} and d_{il}.

Figure 4.4: Model Input and Output for an Indicative Run

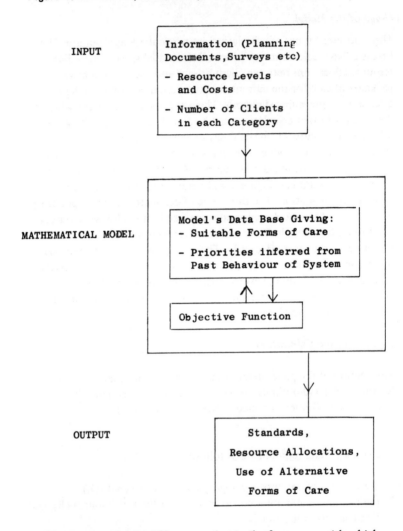

These types of data differ somewhat in the frequency with which they are updated. The data on available expenditure are those most likely to be changed between calculations, as in many cases a series of calculations is desirable in order to test the 'robustness' of recommended priorities under a variety of expenditure constraints. Expenditure is normally divided into capital and revenue and between health services and social services budgets.

The number of patients who are to receive care within the model and the availability of resources and their unit costs are specified for the particular year(s) represented. In the case of resource availability, it is usually worth while to explore the results of allowing the assumed rates of growth of resources to vary. The alternative modes of care, and the 'ideal' standards of receipt of resources in the modes, are usually constant within a series of calculations. These will need to be reviewed periodically, normally by a detailed study of the services available to a given client group.

The model is structured so that the basic allocation unit (mode) is a package of care. Such packages of care often involve a number of resources covering both health services and social services, which, as we have already mentioned, are generally funded and organised separately. However, the collection of regular statistical data on the services provided is traditionally based on a single resource and does not usually allow types of patient to be identified, nor their level of receipt. Hence, the calculation of patient numbers (d_{il}) and the use of resources by the various client groups (r_{jk}) is dependent upon special surveys.

The classification scheme which is applied to each client group is ultimately determined by the availability of data to support the scheme. A general principle applied to the development of classification schemes is that the classification should be as independent of the current resource allocation as possible, yet reasonably indicative of appropriate modes of care. For example, age and the severity of handicap might be desirable factors. The ability to wash and feed, to be aware of surroundings, the degree of support from family or friends and so on may be more desirable factors in relation to appropriate modes of care but may not be readily quantifiable. Whether patients/clients are currently in hospital or residential care is useful information, but clearly less desirable as factors for classifying patients within a resource allocation model which is designed to explore future policies regarding the desirable mix of different forms of care.

There are difficulties associated with what assumptions to make about the numbers of patients to receive care in the future. In the local application described later, demographic changes based on the latest population projection were applied to the current numbers. However, it is recognised that the numbers of patients receiving care are variables which depend upon the scarcity of resources.

Information on alternative modes of care and ideal standards is obtained via a series of discussions with professional advisers. This process has been undertaken separately for each client group because this is the way professionals are generally organised. A typical approach to these discussions is to describe the characteristics of a patient within a particular category, as determined by the classification scheme, and then to ask the advisers to discuss and prescribe the range of modes of care, covering both resources and their desirable levels, that might be applicable to such a patient. Each classification factor can then be varied in turn and the process repeated, until each type of patient has been covered.

The Estimation of the Elasticity Parameters (ϕ_{jk})

These parameters have been defined earlier in the description of the inferred worth formulation. The elasticity parameter for a resource serves to quantify the worth of sub-ideal levels of provision. The calibration of the parameters in a mathematical model is often carried out either by subjective estimates or by comparing outputs from the model with actual data from the system being modelled. The subjective approach has the difficulty of deciding from which set of managers the opinions should be sought. The balance of care in real life is the result of a compromise between many conflicting views on what should happen. In effect, estimates of field workers' collective values are required (see Gibbs for a more detailed discussion on this point[2]).

The method of estimating the elasticity parameters aims to match the model's mathematical optimum to observed resource allocations. The object is to achieve a model allocation which simulates the actual standards of care, the actual balance of allocation of each resource between and within different client groups and the allocation of patients between alternative modes of care. Two ways of doing this have been tried:

1. Constraints are added to the formulation representing the actual resource allocation and the model is run with a trial set of elasticity parameters. This yields shadow prices on the constraints. The parameters are then adjusted so as to reduce the difference between these shadow prices and the model rerun. This iterative procedure continues until a satisfactory set of parameters is obtained. However, this method presented technical difficulties with the algorithm for adjusting the parameters and was computationally expensive, so a different method has been adopted.
2. The analytic properties of the objective function are used to obtain conditions holding at an optimum which relate the elasticity parameters to the variables.

As an example of this approach, consider the distribution of a resource between client groups. For a model optimum the marginal benefit of any increase in a resource for a client group must be the same for each client group.

i.e.:

$$\frac{\partial(h_{jk} - C_k r_{jk})}{\partial r_{jk}} = \frac{\partial(h_{j'k} - C_k r_{j'k})}{\partial r_{j'k}} \text{ for all } j, j'$$

but

$$\frac{\partial(h_{jk} - C_k r_{jk})}{\partial r_{jk}} = C_k \left[s_{jk}^{-(1 + \phi_{jk})} - 1 \right]$$

therefore:

$$s_{jk}^{-(1 + \phi_{jk})} = s_{j'k}^{-(1 + \phi_{j'k})}$$

But it is desired to equate this to the real situation and so for a resource k, if the actual standards s_{jk} for all the client groups j are known and ϕ_{jk} is set arbitrarily for one client group, the values of ϕ_{jk} for that resource for the other groups can be determined using the above equation.

Further calibration quotations can be obtained by a similar examination of $\dfrac{\partial(h_{jk} - C_k r_{jk})}{\partial d_{il}}$; even so there is always one parameter that has to be arbitrarily set so that the calibration is relative rather than absolute, but this is all that is required to enable the model to reproduce the field workers' priorities successfully.

A numerical example of the use of the between-client group calibration using the above relationship is given in Table 4.2.

Talbe 4.2: Example of the Calibration of Between-client Group Elasticities for Home Helps

Client group	Observed % standard (s_{jk})	Inferred elasticity parameter (ϕ_{jk})
Elderly	34	1.50 (preset)
Physically handicapped	18	0.57
Mentally ill	57	3.80
Maternity	34	1.50

A Local Application of the Model

The resource allocation model as described was developed as an aid to national planning. However, the problems faced in planning health and social services for a region or a subregion are similar in many respects to those faced when planning nationally. Hence, in late 1975, a pilot project was undertaken in Devon (population about 1m) to demonstrate the potential contribution of the balance-of-care approach to the joint strategic planning of the Area Health Authority (AHA) and the Social Services Department. This pilot project was carried out by the Institute of Biometry and Community Medicine (IBCM) of the University of Exeter in co-operation with the Operational Research Service of the Department of Health and Social Security. The pilot project proved to be successful and the approach has continued to be used in Devon and is now also in use in Cornwall, Dudley, Wiltshire and East Sussex.

Management

In Devon, to provide a forum to discuss the joint planning issues considered by the balance-of-care model, senior officials of the AHA and of the Social Services Department have formed a Joint Management Team (JMT). This is a sub-group of the Joint Care Planning Team which is responsible for the joint planning of all health and social services in the county. The management structure is shown in Figure 4.5.

The task of the officials in the JMT is to set the planning horizon (typically five to ten years); to agree the policies to be examined and the constraints on the growth of resources (the physical constraints); to decide what will be the likely budgets – or more usually the range within which the budgets might fall (the financial constraints). They also agree the population projections and other assumptions concerned with the use of resources.

Professional Advice

Professional guidance about the forms of care appropriate for specified types of patient is provided by advisers nominated by the JMT. These teams of client group advisers (CGAs) consist of consultants, senior nurses, senior social workers and the like for each included client group. In addition, a team of operational research scientists provides the technical support for carrying out the necessary data collection and preparation and carrying out the calculations using the model. The relationships of both these groups to the JMT and to one another are illustrated in Figure 4.5.

Figure 4.5: Management Structure of the Balance of Care Approach to Joint Planning in Devon

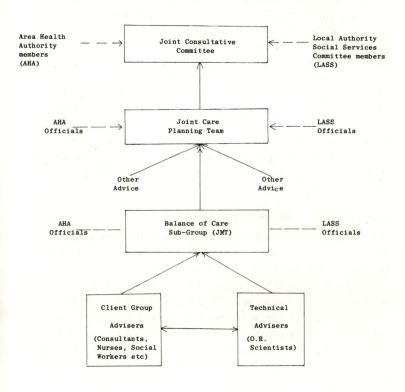

From the experience gained in Devon, it has become clear that the advisers for each client group must be seen to represent the general views of their colleagues. On the other hand, the number of advisers should not become such that the consultation process becomes unmanageable. In practice, we have found that between five and eight advisers satisfies these criteria, provided that two safeguards are incorporated into the advisory process. One is that at the end of each series of calculations the main assumptions and the corresponding model results should be discussed by those concerned with each client group. This provides the advisers, and the JMT, with an opportunity of taking account of a wider spectrum of opinion for future series of calculations. The other safeguard is that the client group advisers should be given the opportunity of reviewing the resource implications of their advice, with the opportunity of modifying that advice, before the JMT is appraised of the model results. This advisory and review process is illustrated in Figure 4.6.

Example of One Series of Calculations

Having agreed with the client group advisers on the appropriate forms of care and desirable amounts of each resource to be provided, the process of using the model is a cyclical one. For each set of calculations, the model is first used to simulate the known provision of resources in a recent year in order to provide a base against which to judge later exploratory calculations and to enable the model to be calibrated for the local area. Then the first set of assumptions is agreed and the resource and service consequences are calculated using the model. These results are reviewed and changes made to the assumptions in order to answer questions of the 'What if we . . .?' type. This process is repeated until the managers are satisfied that they have explored the feasible options. In a typical series of calculations the JMT agreed that a run of the model simulating the provision of resources in 1975 should be performed to provide the base against which to judge a number of exploratory runs for 1981. These exploratory calculations incorporated several assumptions about available finances, which are summarised in Table 4.3. Since the rate of future growth of available finances is unknown, the approach adopted was to consider the effects of the likely best (Opt. 1) and the likely worst (zero) rates of growth.

In the light of these two calculations, two further ones were made. In the first, the two authorities' capital budgets were pooled and increased to £4 million and made available to either authority. In addition, the facility for the AHA to transfer up to 1 per cent of its

Figure 4.6: Advisory and Review Process

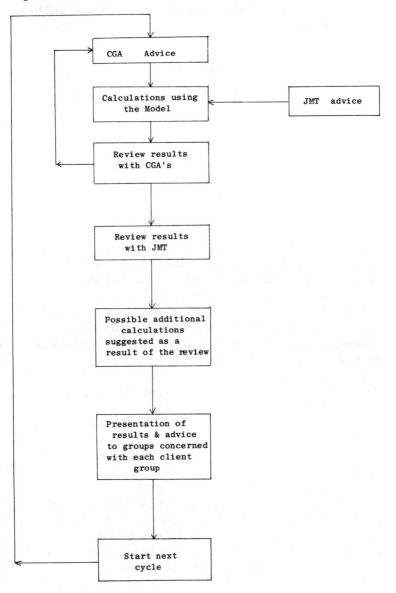

Table 4.3: Summary of Financial Assumptions in a Typical Series of Planning Calculations Using the Balance of Care Model for Devon

Run	Total assumed revenue budget £ million		Assumed 'capital budget' 1975-81 for 6 care groups £ million	
	Health services	Social services	Health services	Social services
1975 Base	77.1	14.3	—	—
1981 Zero growth	77.1	14.3	0.0	0.0
1981 Opt. 1	86.4	15.8	2.0	1.0
1981 Opt. 2	86.4	15.8	4.0	
1981 Opt. 3	102.2		4.0	

revenue to capital or up to 10 per cent of its capital to revenue was assumed. This was termed the Opt. 2 run. In the second additional calculation, Opt. 3, both the revenue and the capital budgets of the two authorities were pooled, with the facility for transfer between revenue and capital as in Opt. 2. In addition, constraints on the rates of increase of resources were relaxed, so that the ultimate logical consequences of the advice given by the advisers (within the over-all financial constraints) could be demonstrated.

For these calculations the JMT agreed that the assumed number of clients to be cared for in 1981 should represent the same proportion of the appropriate populations as were cared for in 1975 and that inferred worth net of cost should be maximised, subject to financial and physical constraints.

Typical results showing the amounts of resources required for the elderly client group under the Opt. 1 calculation assumptions, compared with the actual provision in the base year, are shown in Table 4.4. This shows an expansion in the long-stay geriatric beds and a slight reduction in other institutional resources matched by a growth in domiciliary and day care resources, especially in geriatric day hospital places. The provision of these is limited by the assumed rate at which they can be introduced; day centre places are similarly constrained.

Even with the increase in resources for day and domiciliary care, the standards of provision compared with those desirable will still be relatively low. This is shown in the last column of Table 4.4. Results such as these can prompt an investigation into ways of introducing these

Table 4.4: Estimated Provision of Key Resources Required in Devon
for the Elderly in 1975 and in 1981 under the Assumptions
of Optimistic Growth in Finances (Opt. 1)

Key resources	Provision		% of desirable standards of provision in 1981 (s_{jk})
	1975 actual	1981 Opt. 1 calculation	
Long-stay geriatric beds	870	1,280	—
Psychiatric beds for dementia	480	460	—
Residential home places	4,650	4,620	—
Geriatric day hospital places	100	380U	32
Psychiatric day hospital places for dementia	80	80	41
Day centre places	220	290U	30
Home nurses (whole-time equivalent)	180	220	64
Home helps (whole-time equivalent)	570	750	51
Meals (in thousands)	430	560	61
Number of elderly clients cared for	21,620	23,970	—

Note: U indicates that this resource was constrained not to be greater than this
value. If this constraint were removed then the indicated allocation would
be greater.

and/or alternative resources more rapidly.

Results of the Opt. 3 calculation give an interesting insight into the
financial requirements of the two services, confirming that capital should
be spent by the Social Services Department in order to generate the
capability of spending revenue. The calculated proportion of the capital
proposed for allocation to social services resources, at 33 per cent of
the total, is the same as the proportion the officers optimistically
consider could be available in 1981 (for Opt. 1). On the other hand, the
calculated revenue expenditure in 1981 by the Social Services
Department amounts to 16.5 per cent of the total compared with 15.6
per cent that actually occurred in 1975: this represents an increase of
£1 million in 1981.

To date, a number of operational calculations, similar to those
outlined above but with widely different assumptions, have been
performed. The results of these are now being debated widely within

the two authorities with a view to incorporating the conclusions within general policy guidelines.

Scope and Developments of the Model

One or Several Client Groups?

Most domiciliary resources and some institutional resources are shared by several care groups; for example, home helps are provided for the elderly, the younger physically handicapped and some patients who are discharged home early from acute hospitals. Therefore, an increase in the provision of a resource to one client group has implications for another client group competing for the same resource. All client groups compete for capital and revenue. So, there is a particular advantage in including all the client groups in the model, in order to allow the movement of resources between them to be explored, as well as the balance of resources within each client group.

However, it is possible to consider only one client group and forgo the advantage of examining the interaction between the groups. This loss can be minimised to a certain extent by testing the sensitivity of the calculated allocation of resources to the availability of revenue and capital and possibly certain other key resources.

Experience in Devon and Cornwall has shown that, when several client groups are considered, it is not easy for managers to comprehend the complex interactions that may take place, and so the value may be lost. Nevertheless, with experience, it is possible to take advantage of the facility to explore across client groups. On the other hand, the consideration of only one client group does allow a more detailed exploration of the options concerning that group.

How Local?

The balance-of-care approach was originally designed in the context of national planning, but in practice it has probably made a greater contribution to local planning. A possible explanation lies not so much in the similarities of the problems faced in national and local planning but rather in the differences between the two management structures. At the national level, the planning structure is large with relatively weak links between the health and the personal social services, and weaker links still between those planning different care groups. Locally, however, the system is more compact, with joint planning arrangements between the health and personal social services. National control is through finance, more than through those using or providing the resources. Local control is strong over finance and resource provision, and sometimes over its usage. Representative data about resources and resource usage are more readily available locally than nationally. Furthermore, local professional advice, in contrast to national advice, comes from those who actually provide the service in that locality and who are in close contact with their colleagues.

Thus, the local structure of the health and personal social services provides an environment which is more attuned to the balance-of-care approach, while local control over resources provides the ability to respond positively to the resource choices considered in the balance-of-care model.

Most of the local applications of the balance-of-care approach have been at AHA/Social Services Department level. The argument for this has been that the AHA and the Social Services Department produce the joint strategic plan for their area. In addition, the Social Services Department has a hierarchical management structure which has a tendency more towards central planning within the local authority.

However, health districts, with delegated responsibility from the AHA, have considerable autonomy with respect of planning their services, and this is likely to increase in the future. There is also the problem of translating an area strategic plan into the constituent district plans when each district has a present balance of resources often quite different from its neighbour; therefore, each district is likely to require a different future balance of resources.

It was with these considerations that it was decided to apply the balance of care approach to a health district in Devon. This has necessitated taking account of the health district overlapping several social services areas, but this is a general problem also associated with some AHAs.

Since a district has considerable autonomy in its planning, the model is calibrated for the particular district concerned. No difficulty has been experienced in using the approach for a district; indeed, the arguments above about the management structure and the representativeness of the professional advice are stronger for a district than for an area. The argument could indeed be taken further and the approach considered for a locality within a district. Using the present model, this involves the carrying out of several calculations, one for each locality within the district. Recent developments of the model, however, will allow geographical differences or constraints to be accounted for in one calculation.

A Management Tool

The purpose of strategic planning is to set achievable targets in the light of current wisdom and knowledge. Because knowledge (especially) and wisdom change with time, these plans must be reviewed and renewed regularly. Thus it is desirable for those planning the service to be able to use the balance-of-care approach routinely. Therefore, the local managers must be able to use the approach with the minimum of support from operational research scientists — in other words, it must become a management tool.

The application in Devon was initially more in the form of testing out the prototype under real life conditions, with operational research scientists carrying out all the data collection and preparation, as well as running the model. The application in Dudley is following similar lines. In Cornwall, however, the AHA and the Social Services Department have appointed a Joint Planning Officer whose role is to organise the data collection and preparation, using the facilities of the two authorities, and to learn to use the model and to interpret the output to the JMT. The lessons learned here will facilitate the preparation of a manual or code of practice for using the approach anywhere.

Unfortunately, the complexity and size of the current model virtually preclude it from being run on a local computer by local managers or by Joint Planning Officers. However, development work carried out by operational research scientists of the DHSS has been aimed at simplifying the model technically (and conceptually) while retaining the essentials of the approach, for example the matching of alternative modes of care to categories and the ability to explore ways of rationing limited resources.

There have been two main thrusts to this work. One, by Gibbs, Hughes and Aspden, carried out whilst at the International Institute for Applied Systems Analysis (IIASA), has led to a different formulation, capable of analytical solution. This enables an allocation of resources to be arrived at more simply and rapidly. The model so produced, called DRAM (Disaggregated Resource Allocation Model), is described in outline by Shigan, Hughes and Kitsul and it has already been used in projects to plan the allocation of acute beds to several specialties.[3]

Secondly, a radical attempt is being made by the DHSS Operational Research Service, in conjunction with Arthur Anderson and Company, to separate out and simplify the different functions of the current model. This includes retaining such concepts as inferring field workers' priorities from their observed behaviour and identifying cost-effective resource mixes, but without requiring respectively the complex utility functions or the mathematical programming algorithm that the current model uses.

The basic segments, which are intended to be used in a step-by-step manner, are as follows:

1. A segment to summarise the current levels of provision.
2. A segment to give an estimate of the resource needs in some specified future year in order to maintain current rates of provision to the projected population. This will give the managers an indication of the pressures on the service.
3. A segment to forecast the patterns of care in a specified future year, assuming the continuance of field workers' current priorities in the use of resources.
4. A segment to allow the testing of alternative assumptions about field workers' use of resources. These alternative assumptions might be considered desirable and achievable or of interest as extremes at which to aim. Any patterns of care indicated by this segment will be achieved only if specific action is taken to ensure that the field workers adopt the appropriate allocation rules. Hence it is considered important to keep this segment separate from the third segment so that a conscious effort is made to examine the feasibility of the changes assumed.
5. A segment to calculate more cost-effective mixes of resources.
6. A segment to calculate more cost-effective ways of distributing clients between alternative forms of care.

In addition, a facility to take account of geographical differences in the distribution of resources within the area under consideration is to be introduced. As already indicated, this will allow 'locality planning' to be carried out relatively simply, without necessitating a separate set of calculations for each locality. Data and information requirements for this version of the model will be the same as for the original version but with extra data being necessary for the locality planning component (as they would be, of course, if the original version were used for this purpose).

Value of the Balance of Care Approach

In this concluding section, we summarise the various factors which we believe have contributed to the favourable reception of the balance of care approach as an aid to the joint planning of health and social services at a local level within the UK.

1. The balance-of-care model encompasses the major health and social

services and provides a framework within which joint discussion between the officers of both authorities can be conducted.

2. The model enables the officers to explore the resource consequences of the many courses of action open to them and to set this information within the context of their experience to decide which is the most appropriate course of action to take.

3. The model can be used (indeed *should* be used) in an interrogatory manner ('what if we . . .?') by the officers, as they explore the consequences of various courses of action in the light of previous calculations using the model.

4. The model is not restricted to the consideration of forms of care currently in use, but can estimate the resource requirements and implications of proposed new forms of care for defined categories of patient/client.

5. By the use of classification structures linked to alternative modes or forms of care, officers and researchers are forced into a more analytical approach to the planning and provision of services; as a result, they have to make their assumptions much more explicit, thus allowing a more objective and wide-ranging debate concerning policy issues to take place.

Notes

1. © Crown Copyright 1980.

2. R.J. Gibbs, 'The Use of a Strategic Planning Model for Health and Personal Social Services', *Journal of the Operational Research Society,* vol. 29, no. 9 (1978), pp. 875-83.

3. E.N. Shigan, D.J. Hughes, P.I. Kitsul, *Health Care Systems Modeling at IIASA: A Status Report* (International Institute for Applied Systems Analysis, Laxenburg, Austria, 1979).

Geoffrey Royston acknowledges with thanks the help he received from colleagues in preparing his contribution; however, he alone is responsible for the views expressed, which should not necessarily be ascribed to the Department of Health and Social Security.

5 ON THE OPTIMISATION OF HOSPITALS[1]

Dietrich Fischer

Introduction

While in 1973 health system costs in West Germany were estimated at
about 110 billion DM, this had roughly doubled by 1978; 25 per cent
of this amount was believed to be due to hospital patient care.[2] If public
health policy is to gain control over the growth of hospital costs —
labelled 'cost explosion' in recent years[3] — appropriate strategic and
tactical measures will have to be taken to meet the given demand for
in-patient care: strategic measures involve the improvement of the
structure of the total hospital system, with its respective impacts on
individual hospitals; tactical measures involve the improvement of
hospital efficiency within a given structure.

In the past, the emphasis has been placed on tactical measures.
Architects, hospital authorities and management have tried, by the
appropriate layout and equipment of individual hospitals and by suitable
personnel and organisational measures, to stem the tide of rising hospital
operating costs and to increase operating efficiency. As one consequence
of this view on priorities, the application of operational research and
systems science has concentrated mainly on operational hospital
problems.[4]

How to determine the appropriate structure of a total hospital
system, however, may still be considered unsolved. The reasons for this
lie in the fragmentation of authority among a multitude of decision
makers and in the complexity of the problem itself.

The basic questions to be answered, when attempting to develop a
feasible hospital structure, may, in a simplified way, be specified as
follows:

1. What is the total capacity required?
2. What is the optimum operational hospital size?
3. What is the optimum allocation of functions?

Simplifying again, and referring to the number of beds as one of the
central parameters of the hospital system, the first question aims at
assessing the total bed requirements.[5] The answer to the second question

109

may be reduced to determining the optimum number of beds per hospital and the answer to the third question could be interpreted as the optimum centralisation and specialisation of functions in a hierarchical hospital system.

All three questions are strongly interrelated by their impacts, in terms of place and time, on hospital care requirements with respect to demand. As will be shown, the search for the 'optimum' hospital size cannot be isolated from the other two problems.[6]

Attempts to Determine the Optimal Hospital Size

Before deciding on the methodological approach to the problem, it is appropriate to consider the reasons why the manifold attempts — as revealed in the literature — over the past 20 years have generally had only limited success.

Most of the publications dealing with the subject of hospital size restrict themselves to a discussion of the pros and cons of certain hospital sizes, often unsupported by quantitative evidence. The influential factors cited most often have been listed by Gibbs, as in Table 5.1.[7]

Table 5.1: Factors Likely to Influence Hospital Size

Influential factors	Impact on hospital size
Quantitative	
Accessibility	−
Capital requirement	+/−
Economies of scale	+
Management	−
Quantitative/qualitative	
Functional capabilities	+
Relationship with community & GP services	−
Equal workload	+
Staff management	−
Training	+
Qualitative	
Decision risk	−
Patient well-being	−
Attractiveness/prestige	+

The greatest value of this type of publication is in the generally competent and enlightening description it provides of the hospital environment.

An interesting quantitative approach to determining the optimum hospital size is characterised by the endeavour to define the relationships between cost and the relevant service parameters by a regression analysis of the cost data reported by the hospital system; for example, Feldstein[8] in his dissertation, which Berki considered 'the most inventive and exhaustive analysis in the literature'[9] has taken advantage of the standard cost reporting system used by UK hospitals and analysed the data of 177 acute hospitals with capacities ranging from 72 to 1,069 beds. But neither he nor later authors have succeeded in arriving at convincing conclusions. So Berki, commenting on a tabular survey of typical results, arrived at the sarcastic conclusion:

> In summary, then, the question can be posed: What are the shapes of the short-run and long-run cost functions of hospitals? Are there economies of scale? The answer from the literature is clear: The exact general form of the function is unimportant, but whatever its exact shape, and depending on the methodologies and definitions used, economies of scale exist, may exist, or do not exist, but in any case, according to theory, they ought to exist.[10]

However, as early as 1968, Mann and Yett argued that the outcomes of the various investigations are less contradictory than they may seem at first glance, since the various authors have tested different hypotheses based on a different interpretation of the relationship between the measures 'output' and 'scale'.[11] Their comprehension of the difficulties — to be overcome by analysis — is indicated by the comment that 'it should not be supposed that the authors are solely responsible for the lack of uniformity in their respective interpretations of cost theory; at least part of the blame is attributable to the ambiguous state of cost theory itself'. They conclude: 'As important as these issues are, they will remain unsolved until a consistent and definite cost model has been developed.'

The derivation of production functions, as suggested, for example, by M.S. Feldstein[12] or P.J. Feldstein,[13] was bound to fail for basically the same reasons that have limited the success of regression analysis. A specific problem results from the fact that hospital output, often defined as the number of patients or patient days, consists in reality of a great number of 'products', i.e. a variety of cases consuming the inputs at rather different rates. With one known exception, consistent cost models, as requested by Mann and Yett,[14] used as standard tools in, for example, defence planning, have been undertaken and published for simple hospital functions only,[15] probably because the relevant data were not available.

The known exception relates to a fairly comprehensive study of the question of optimum hospital size carried out by an OR team in the Department of Health and Social Security in the UK.[16] The study concentrated mainly upon the *costs* of building and operating hospitals of different sizes although there was some examination of other factors. It concluded by recommending a size range of about 700-900 beds for a district general hospital with an urban catchment population and a rather smaller size range for rural situations. Policy documents reveal that this study has had a considerable influence on the policy towards hospital building in the UK.[17] The differences between the results of the UK study and that discussed later stress the fact that Mann and Yett, when assessing the reasons for contradictory results of various investigations, forgot one important aspect: the differences in the impact factors which shape the diverse national hospital systems under analysis.[18]

The application of simulation methods has, because of their resource requirements, been limited to hospital sub-models.[19] More comprehensive models, sometimes considering the total hospital or even health system, generally make use of linear programming.[20] However, no findings from such approaches, with respect to optimum hospital size, are known to the author, though this type of application has been suggested.[21]

The Approach Chosen

Model Family

From a consideration of previous approaches, the development of a parametric cost model for the derivation of heuristic results and of LP models for finding optimum sulutions appeared to be the most promising. In response to the three basic questions posed in the introduction, bearing in mind feasible data requirements, three models have been developed:

1. PARK – a parametric cost model, which allows for a relative assessment of cost resulting from hospital size and function, i.e. patient mix, and which can be applied to calculating the objective function values for the two following LP models;
2. OPTIK – an LP model for determining the optimum resource allocation within a hospital of a certain size and function, under consideration of well-defined restrictions;
3. FLINK – an LP model for determining the optimum size of a hospital forming part of a regional, integrated and hierarchically structured

hospital system.

Basic Assumptions

Two sets of assumptions are relevant for all three models and are therefore discussed first. One concerns the number of hospital types, differing by capability and size, to be considered; the second the number and types of patients who are to be taken care of by the hospital system. Both sets are closely interconnected by the required allocation of patients to hospitals. The first set of assumptions to be discussed are those on hospital types.

In the Federal Republic of Germany (FRG), a system of so-called 'care levels' has been developed for patient care by general hospitals, with the higher level generally including the capabilities of the lower levels. The attachment of a hospital to a specific care level depends on its functional capabilities and/or equipment, which at the same time determines — within a certain range — the number of beds to be provided. Use was made of the classification developed by a committee of the German Hospital Society in co-operation with a number of professional organisations.[22] This specifies five care levels, which are congruent with the requirements as defined by the German Federal Hospital Act (KHG); these are shown in Figure 5.1.

However, the modelling of this five-level structure appears to be neither feasible nor sensible. Feasibility is impaired by the data base, as it generally distinguishes demand and service data by three levels only:

B = basic care according to care level I;
S = standard care according to care levels II + III;
C = central care according to care levels IV + V.

We also wish to consider the situation of an integrated regional hospital system, in which — under the hypothesis of homogeneous population density — the catchment area of a higher care level comprises, for its additional specialties, a specific multiple of the lower-level area, the services of the respective lower level, however, always being limited to the corresponding catchment area around the hospital's location.

Figure 5.2 illustrates such an integrated regional three-level system in the suitable pattern of a honeycomb structure, which has been used as a basis for the ensuing calculations.[23]

The essential datum relevant to the structure of the hospital system, however, is the patient demand, defined by the annual frequency of

Figure 5.1: Hospital Care Levels, Departments, Beds and Facilities

Care Levels (also Requirement Levels KHG, in brackets previous denomination) i =	1 General Medicine	2 Gynaecology/Obstetrics	3 General Surgery	Traumatic Surgery	Anaesthesia	4 Radiotherapy	Radiology	5 Neurology	6 Neurosurgery	7 Paediatrics	Pathology	8 Ophthalmology	9 E.N.T.	10 Urology	11 Orthopaedics	12 Psychiatry	13 Dermatology	14 Dental Surgery	Paed. Surgery	No. Beds	X-Ray Diagnostics	Medical Stand-By	Emergency Admission	Intensive Care	Physical Therapy	Central Pharmacy	Blood Depot	Laboratories	Isolation Ward	Histology	Emergency Care with	Central Admission	Nuclear Medicine	Hospital Pharmacy	Blood Bank	Haemodialysis	Dept. for Intensive Care	Training Facilities
I (basic care)	X	X	X																	< 250	X	X	X	X	X	X	X	X										
II (ord. standard care)	X	X	X	X	X	X	X	•	•	•	•	•	•							< 350	X	X	X	X	X	X	X	X	X	X	X							
III (diff. standard care)	X	X	X	X	X	X	X	X	X	X	X	•	•	•	•	•	•			< 650	X	X	X	X	X	X	X	X	X	X	X	X	X	X	X	X		
IV (central care)	X	X	X	X	X	X	X	X	X	X	X	X	X	X	X	X				> 650	X	X	X	X	X	X	X	X	X	X	X	X	X	X	X	X	X	
V (max. care)	X	X	X	X	X	X	X	X	X	X	X	X	X	X	X	X	X	X	X	> 1000	X	X	X	X	X	X	X	X	X	X	X	X	X	X	X	X	X	X

patients entering the system and specified by the main diagnosis, which — probably in conjunction with one or more sub-diagnoses — determines the allocation of the patient to that department of a hospital which provides a certain minimum care level. The main diagnosis will generally also determine, depending on the care level, the duration of the patient's stay and the hospital (staff and material) resource requirements.

Figure 5.2: Illustrative Catchment Areas of an Integrated Hospital System

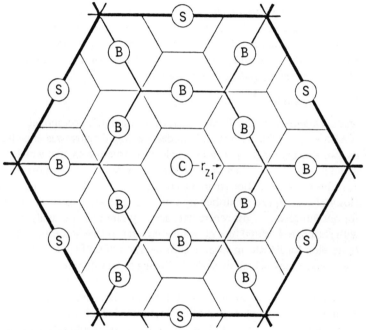

B = basic care; S = standard care; C = central care

Because of a collection of patient-related data made possible in the German Armed Forces hospital system, the Bundeswehr three-digit diagnosis coding system was selected.[24] It largely corresponds to the International Classification of Diseases and summarises approximately 500 diagnoses under 17 categories. Accordingly, the models consider a mix of 17 types of patients.

The most representative survey of patient demand in the FRG, broken down by diagnostic categories, is provided by the yearly statistics of the German social insurance system, which in 1970 covered 28 million inhabitants.[25] Unfortunately, the number of diseases requiring hospital care is reported rather than the number of hospital stays, thus neccessitating a conversion based on an estimate of the average number of hospital stays per disease. A further estimate is required to determine the percentage of patients of type j, who may be expected to be treated by a hospital department or ward of type i. Figure 5.1 shows that 15 departments/wards were considered (including intensive care). Because the data available from the accessible literature were insufficient, the estimates were based on data collected on 8,542 patients in the Bundeswehr Central Hospital at Koblenz. But, although both male and female patients are treated in the hospital, the figures concerning the load on gynaecological, obstetric and paediatric wards had to be derived from data published in the Northrhine-Westphalia state hospital plan.[26] At the same time, estimates were derived for the average length of stay of patient j in department/ward i.

The PARK Model

Model Description. The development of a parametric cost model (PARK) compatible with the LP models described below was impeded by two shortcomings: first, no suitable cost structure existed which could be readily modelled; second, there is even less information available on cost functions than on patient-related production functions. Hospital cost reports published by various organisations are not suitable for our purposes.[27] Cost centre data are very rare and cost analyses with respect to hospital functions are even rarer. Hence, it was necessary to develop for PARK, in specific consideration of OPTIK, a system of cost equations which allowed the following to be estimated:

1. capital costs as determined by hospital size, i.e. number of beds;
2. running costs as a function of services provided, i.e. the patient mix;
3. patient transportation and visitors' travel costs as a function of accessibility, i.e. catchment area size.

For the questions to be answered by OPTIK and consequently FLINK it was of primary importance to provide a sound *relative* estimate of costs as a function of number of beds, patient mix and catchment area, rather than striving for a reliable *absolute* cost prediction.

The latter would only be of interest for a given specific project, as some hospital functions do not lend themselves to general parametric description. A typical example is catering, the cost of which is mainly dependent on the layout and organisation of the kitchen, and less on hospital size. Nor was there any information available on the impact of patient mix on catering cost; therefore, this cost category was omitted from PARK.

If patient transportation and visitors' travel costs are added to the hospital running costs, the total yearly hospital cost C_{tot} may be expressed as a function of the care level z, i.e. the services provided and the size of the catchment area, by a two-sum equation:

(1) $C_{tot} = C_1 (BC) + \sum\limits_{j} (C_{Bj} \cdot x_j) = f(z)$

The first term defines the capital costs per year, which depend primarily on hospital size, i.e. the bed capacity BC. However, because of the different relationship between short, medium and long-lived assets and the consequently differing depreciation rates A_z, an impact of care level z on capital costs will also have to be considered. As a consequence, the cost-estimating relationship for C_1 (BC) also consists of two terms:

(2) $C_1 (BC) = BC.A_z. (81959.5 + 16.34 \, BC + 0.00041 \, BC^2)$
$+ BC.121. (3.0 + 1.1 \sin \dfrac{\pi}{2} (\dfrac{BC}{450} - 1) \, (100 < BC \leqslant 900)$

While the first sum (based on data collection performed by the German Hospital Institute (DHI) in co-operation with Düsseldorf University and Berlin Technical University[28]) determines the total capital costs per year according to German industrial standard DIN 276,[29] the second includes yearly capital cost for X-ray and radiological equipment. Data collected showed that hospitals tend to increase per bed investment in such equipment with size and care level. This trend, passing a point of inflexion at about 450 beds and reaching a saturation level of approximately 900 beds, is fairly well depicted by a sine curve.

The term C_{Bj} in Equation (1) represents the average cost (excluding capital) per patient of type j, which — multipled by the total number of patients j treated per year, x_j, and summed over all diagnostic categories j — gives the total yearly (relative) running costs of the hospital. As the bed costs have already been included in the capital cost, these remaining case costs reflect all patient-type-related resource consumption, which is also depicted in OPTIK:

1. the four basic types of laboratory tests (i.e. chemistry, haematology, bacteriology/serology/immunology, histology/cytology);
2. the workload on the seven basic types of staff (i.e. doctors, nurses, medical/technical services, housekeeping, maintenance, administration, special services);

3. the material costs for operations; laundry; X-ray and isotope diagnostics X-ray, radiology and physiotherapy; ECGs and EEGs;
4. patient transportation and visitors' travel costs.

Discussion of Results. Figure 5.3 illustrates cost per case as a function of hospital size for three of the 17 disease categories. It appears that, in general, costs per case tend to increase in proportion to number of beds. The discrete jumps at the transition from one care level to the next (at 250 and 650 beds — see Figure 5.1) are caused by changing depreciation rates, service standards and average duration of stay. As shown for diagnosis category 'diseases of urinary and genital organs', jumps in the cost curve may also be directed downwards.

Figure 5.3: Costs per Case for Three Disease Categories, by Hospital Size

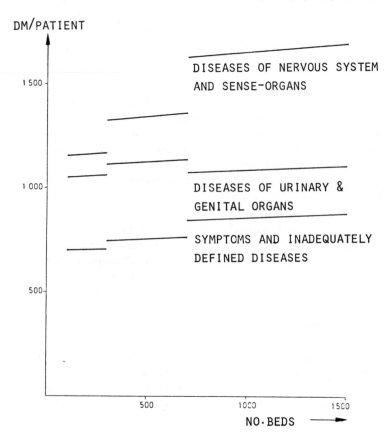

A critical evaluation of the results confirms that, in spite of the uncertainties implicit in the inputs and assumptions, yearly total hospital costs are essentially determined by diseconomies of scale; hence the most efficient hospital size should be expected at the lower end of the scale determined by medical and organisational considerations.[30]

Comparing the 1970 running cost results from PARK with estimates made by the town of Nürnberg for several large community hospital systems, it was found that the PARK model accounted for about 90 per cent of the gross total costs (BSK). Not considered by PARK are food, administrative supply, rents, taxes, insurance fees and other duties, all of which amounts to approximately 6-7 per cent of the average BSK; only partially considered by PARK are the water-energy-fuel cost categories and general operating supplies with a BSK quota of about 5 per cent. All these cost categories are determined mainly by local conditions and are of little relevance in the search for economies of scale. But, even if economies of scale might be expected here, they would be far outweighed by the yearly capital cost increase with hospital size as defined in Equation (2) and illustrated in Figure 5.4 and by the staff per bed rising in proportion to the number of beds, as shown in Figure 5.5. In addition, it is generally accepted that medical supplies per patient increase with increasing care level.

The OPTIK Model

Objective Functions. In principle, the PARK model has already answered the question as to the optimum size of a hospital forming part of a three-level hierarchical system. The remaining problem to be solved by a single hospital model is the optimum allocation of resources within a hospital of a specific size and function within given restrictions. Such an application may include an analysis of the relationships between hospital size and structure, between input and output within the framework of a parametric sensitivity analysis. This purpose is served by OPTIK.

As to what the objective function for such an optimisation should be, quite different answers may be expected, depending on the type of decision maker we are dealing with and the decision level. Meyer offers a range of such objectives in his hospital management game.[31] For the application of OPTIK, three alternative objective functions were defined, which cover a range of public and private welfare and economic objectives:

(3) $S_1 \quad \sum_j x_j \rightarrow max$ (social welfare objective)

120   *On the Optimisation of Hospitals*

Figure 5.4: Capital Cost per Bed — Total and Illustrative Additional

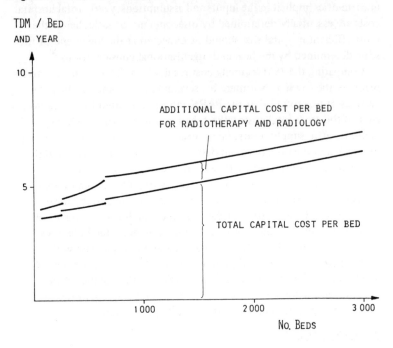

TDM / BED AND YEAR

ADDITIONAL CAPITAL COST PER BED
FOR RADIOTHERAPY AND RADIOLOGY

TOTAL CAPITAL COST PER BED

No. BEDS

(4) S_2 $\sum\limits_{j} (E_j \text{-} A_j). \ x_j \to$ max (private ownership objective)

(5) S_3 $\dfrac{\sum\limits_{j} A_j.x_j}{\sum\limits_{j} x_j} \to$ min (efficiency objective)

The first function reflects the welfare objective of maximising the number of patients (per year) belonging to the various diagnosis categories that can be cared for with the given resources. The second function reflects an economic objective, i.e. the maximisation of profit for a private hospital (or the minimisation of the subsidies required for a community or charity hospital, when case costs A_j — together with capital costs — exceed the income per patient). For equal fixed *per diem* rates, the objective function is reduced to cost minimisation, i.e. $\sum A_j. \ x_j \to$ min. As a third objective function, the impact of efficiency, i.e. minimising the average cost per patient, was also investigated. As

Figure 5.5: Relationship of Staff per Bed and Hospital Size

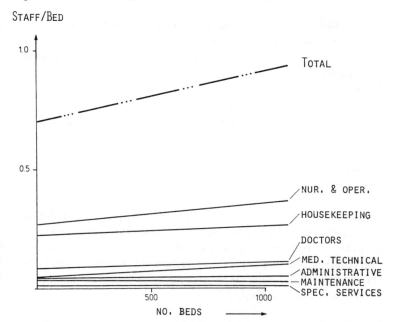

will be shown later, all three objective functions — and this applies to any other objective function as well — amount to a selection of the patient mix to be treated or, if bed capacity is unlimited, will require at least an allocation of patients to hospitals.

Restrictions or Constraints. The care that can be provided by a hospital is limited in various ways; its efficiency is further reduced by the general imbalance of these restrictions or constraints. If a_{ij} represents the average number of services of type i — e.g. X-ray exposures — required per patient of diagnostic category j, then the sum of these services must be less than or equal to the capacity of the respective service facility k; (e.g. the X-ray department):

$$(6) \quad \sum_{j} a_{ij}.x_j \leqslant K_i$$

In some cases a lower limit also has to be taken into account: for example, there may be a policy not to drop below a certain ward size.

Given data availability on both the service and cost sides, the following restrictions turned out to be reproducible by OPTIK:

1. the minimum number of beds in the 15 departments/wards;
2. the maximum total bed capacity of the hospital;
3. the maximum number of the four basic types of laboratory tests to be performed by one technician;
4. the man-hour capacity of the seven basic staff categories;
5. the capacity of operating theatres, laundry, X-ray and isotope diagnostics, X-ray and radiology therapy, physiotherapy, and ECG and EEG equipment.

The resulting set of constraints for a central care level amounts to 85, with 51 variables.

An Illustrative Application. Figure 5.6 illustrates the results of OPTIK when applied to a 150-bed hospital of the basic care level making use of all three objective functions discussed above. As already mentioned, each objective function implies the selection of a different patient mix. The results achieved using the three objective functions are summarised under four headings in Table 5.2.

Table 5.2: Summary Results from OPTIK According to Various Criteria

Objective function		Criterion			
		Patients total	TDM/year running cost	TDM/year total cost	DM/patient total
Max. no. of patients	S_1	2,736	3,115	3,735	1,365
Min. cost	S_2	2,408	2,755	3,374	1,401
Max. efficiency	S_3	2,703	2,928	3,546	1,312

Strategy S_1 is in total more expensive by about 10 per cent and strategy S_3 by about 5 per cent than the cost minimisation strategy S_2. The latter strategy at the same time results in the minimum number of patients treated, which is exceeded by 14 per cent under strategy S_1, and by 12 per cent under strategy S_3, which minimises the average cost per patient.

Figure 5.6: Illustrative Results of OPT|K using Different Objective Functions

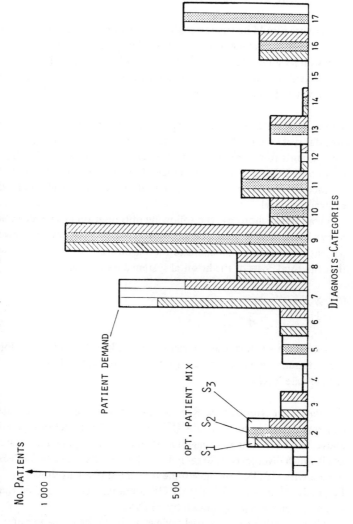

The FLINK Model

Objective Function. The answers given by PARK with respect to the relationship between capital cost, case cost and hospital size are certainly not sufficient. In fact, they tell nothing more than that:

1. patients should be treated at the lowest care level that is still capable of providing the medical service considered necessary;
2. hospitals should have the smallest possible size that still allows for an efficient operation of the required or planned departments, which are yet to be investigated by micro-studies.

This general statement is consistent with the present tendency to reduce hospital system costs by, among other measures, the allocation of low-care patients to hostels or nursing homes. On the other hand, it has to be accepted that a certain percentage of any diagnostic category will, for medical reasons, require treatment at at least the standard or even central care level.

From this dichotomy, the following optimisation problem can be derived: in a closed, hierarchically structured hospital system, a given patient mix has to be allocated to the various care levels in such a way that the total costs of the hospital system are minimised, i.e.:

$$(7) \quad \sum_j A_j x_j \rightarrow min$$

This problem statement at the same time leads to the determination of the optimum, i.e. minimum, cost size of the individual hospitals at the various care levels.

An Illustrative Application. Regarding the basic assumptions discussed earlier and making use of the PARK results and the restrictions specified above, the FLINK model suggested an allocation of patients to care levels which diverges considerably from the data that had been collected for use with OPTIK from government hospital plans, as shown in Figure 5.7.[32] In Table 5.3, the OPTIK input data are set against the system parameters as optimised by FLINK.

When assessing the potential savings, it should be borne in mind that, after the FLINK optimisation and as a result of the care-level-dependent durations of stay, the hospital system will provide a bed inventory that is higher by as much as 5 per cent. Of course, FLINK results should

Figure 5.7: Optimum Allocation to Care Levels (FLINK) compared with Government Hospital Plans (OPTIK)

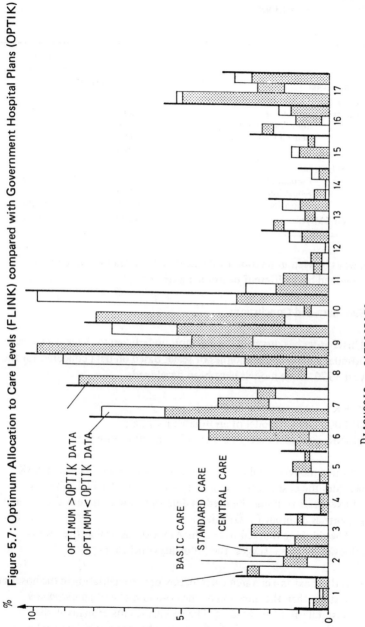

Table 5.3: OPTIK Input Data and System Parameters as Optimised
         by FLINK

			OPTIK input data	FLINK optimisation
Patients/year			110,860	
treated by				
Hospital of Basic Care	(%)		39.8	47.1
Standard Care	(%)		14.4	27.4
Central Care	(%)		45.8	25.5
No. of beds in system			6,106	6,431
No. of beds per				
B-hospital			218	262
S-hospital			288	586
C-hospital			2,626	1,525
Million DM/year			180.088	173.619

always be seen in relation to the assumed constraints, which may be
redefined by a different decision maker.

Summary and Conclusions

This chapter has surveyed the attempts undertaken to check the German
hospital system for economies of scale. Based on data collected for the
year 1970, three models have been developed:

PARK: a parametric cost model;
OPTIK: an LP model of an isolated hospital;
FLINK: an LP model of a hierarchic hospital system.

All three models should be seen as part of one model family. PARK
provides the cost inputs required by FLINK and OPTIK, whereas
FLINK in its turn may be used to determine the optimum allocation of
patients as an input for OPTIK.
     The thinking that led to the three models, as well as the results
achieved by them, suggest the following conclusions:

1. If there exists a hierarchical structure or a specialisation in the hospital
   system, then the question of the optimum size of an *individual*
   hospital can be misleading. The varying results of many earlier
   investigations, in which the interaction between an individual hospital

and the total hospital system was neglected, may at least be partly attributed to this omission.

2. Within the investigated range, costs per bed or case increase with hospital size. This also holds true if visitors' costs — counted as a social cost — are excluded from consideration.

3. For a closed hierarchical system it can be shown that there is an optimum hospital size, depending on the care level.

4. A hospital structure of more than three care levels appears to be impracticable, since it precludes the reasonable description of an integrated regional structure.

5. In a hospital system with limited capacity, the specification of a particular objective function will inevitably result in a particular patient case mix selection.

Notes

1. Translated and adapted from D. Fischer, 'Zur optimalen Grösse von Krankenhäusern', in M. Meyer, *Krankenhausplanung* (Stuttgart-New York, 1979), with kind permission by Gustav Fischer Verlag.

2. J. Schmucker and K. Szameitert, 'Was kostet die Gesundheit', in J. Schlemmer (ed.), *Haben wir die richtige Medizin* (R. Piper and Company, München, 1975), p. 106.

3. H. Adam and K.D. Henke, *'Das aktuelle Stichwort: Kostenexplosion im Gesundheitswesen'*, Manuscript, Techn. Universität, Hannover, 1977.

4. D. Fischer, 'Zum gegenwärtigen Stand der Anwendung von Operations Research und Systemanalyse im Krankenhaus- und Gesundheitswesen', *Schweizer Spitalzeitschrift*, 37 (1973), p. 274.

5. M.D. Fottler, 'Some Correlates of Hospital Costs in Public and Private Hospital Systems', *Quarterly Review of Economics and Business* (1975), p. 101.

6. For a complete description of the analysis see D. Fischer, 'Zur Dimensionierung eines mehrstufigen Krankenhaussystems', PhD thesis, Nürnberg, 1978.

7. R.J. Gibbs, *Factors Affecting Hospital Size* (Memorandum, Department of Health and Social Security, London, 1972), p. 2.

8. M.S. Feldstein, *Economic Analysis of Health Service Efficiency* (North Holland Publishing Company, Amsterdam, 1967).

9. S.E. Berki, *Hospital Economics* (Lexington Books, London, 1972), p. 112.

10. Ibid., p. 111.

11. J.K. Mann and D.E. Yett, 'The Analysis of Hospital Costs: a Review Article', *Journal of Business*, 41 (1968), p. 191.

12. Feldstein, *Economic Analysis of Health Service Efficiency*.

13. P.J. Feldstein, *An Empirical Investigation of the Marginal Cost of Hospital Services* (University of Chicago, 1961).

14. Mann and Yett, 'The Analysis of Hospital Costs'.

15. W.G. Sullivan, 'A Cost Evaluation Model for Radiology Departments', *Engineering Economist*, 20 (1975), p. 70.

16. C.R. Tristem, R.J. Gibbs, M. Belchamber, R. Swan, D.J. Browning and G.C. Watt, 'Optimum Size of District General Hospitals', paper given at EURO 1

(First European Congress on Operations Research) Brussels, January 1975.
   17. E.g. *Review of Health Capital* (Department of Health and Social Security, London, 1979).
   18. Mann and Yett, 'The Analysis of Hospital Costs'.
   19. R.B. Fetter and J.D. Thompson, 'The Simulation of Hospital Systems', *Operations Research* (September/October 1965), p. 689.
   20. A.G. McDonald, G.C. Cuddeford and E.M. Beale, 'Some Mathematical Models of the National Health Service', *British Medical Bulletin*, 30 (1974), p. 262.
   21. R.M. Gurfield and J.C. Clayton Jr, *Analytical Hospital Planning, A Pilot Study of Resource Allocation using Mathematical Programming in a Cardiac Unit* (RAND RM-5893-RC, Santa Monica, 1969).
   22. Strukturkommission der Deutschen Krankenhaus-Gesellschaft (ed.), *Moderne Krankenhausstrukturen* (Deutsche Krankenhausgesellschaft, Düsseldorf, 1973).
   23. W. Christaller, *Die Zentralen Orte in Süddeutschland* (Wissenschaftliche Buchgesellschaft, Darmstadt, 1968).
   24. Bundesministerium der Verteidigung (ed.), *Gesundheitsbericht der Bundeswehr* (Heft 25 der Beiträge zur Wehrmedizinalstatistik, Institut für Wehrmedizinalstatistik und Berichtswesen, Remagen, 1971).
   25. To guarantee the consistency of model inputs, all demand, cost and service data were collected for, or at least related to, the year 1970.
   26. Der Innenminister des Landes NRW (ed.), *Bericht der Kommission zur Erstellung eines Krankenhausplanes für das Land NRW 1968-1980* (Reckinger and Company, Siegburg, 1969).
   27. Stadt Nürnberg, Krankenanstalten, *Betriebsvergleich kommunaler Grosskrankenanstalten* (Bayerische Krankenhausgesellschaft e. V., München, 1971).
   28. DKI Düsseldorf, UNI Düsseldorf, Institut für Krankenhausbau der TU Berlin (eds), 'Kosten für die Wiederbeschaffung der mittel- und kurzfristig nutzbaren Anlagegüter sowie der Instandhaltung und der Instandsetzung von Krankenhäusern', *Das Krankenhaus*, vol. 63 (W. Kohlhammer Verlag, Stuttgart, 1971), p. 385.
   29. Fachnormenausschuss Bauwesen im Deutschen Normenausschuss (ed.), *DIN 276: Kosten von Hochbauten* (Beuth Vertrieb GmbH, Berlin, 1971).
   30. This will certainly not apply to hospitals with less than 100 beds, as for them the investigations discussed earlier have proved beyond any doubt the existence of economies of scale.
   31. R. Meyer, 'Entwicklung und Testeinsätze eines Planspiels 'Klinik-Management (KLIMA)' ', PhD thesis, Nürnberg, 1978.
   32. OPTIK and FLINK solutions were computed on a CDC 6500, making use of the APEX I system. CPU time was 4 sec for the OPTIK example, 4.7 sec for the FLINK example.

6 PLANNING THE CARE OF THE ELDERLY

Richard M. Burton and David C. Dellinger

Introduction

Strategic applications of operational research are few when compared to tactical applications (see Boldy[1]). The reasons are numerous and varied. Strategic problems are much more difficult to define, solutions more difficult to implement and results more difficult to measure. Strategic problems are in the domain of top management or political representatives who are appropriately reluctant to turn strategic problems over to operational researchers for 'solution'. Hence, successful strategic applications are characterised by co-operative efforts by top officials and operational researchers. Strategic decisions are likely to take the form of a series of decisions made by groups of leaders in an atmosphere of compromise and trade-off. The impact of the operational researchers on the decisions actually made may be limited to influencing the way officials think about the problem or to selecting the information upon which the decision is based. Strategic problems require that a great deal of technical information from a variety of experts be integrated in an appropriate manner so as to guide the decision makers. Successful applications to strategic problems are likely to involve directly not only the strategic decision makers but also a variety of technical experts.

Finally, strategic problems can rarely, if ever, be structured in a closed form so that unambiguous optimal solutions can be found. Either the closed form optimisation model constructed for the analysis captures only a part of the problem and its use requires the direct participation of the decision makers, or the closed form model is not operational, i.e. it is used only to ensure logical consistency of the problem structure, not to generate optimal solutions. The Duke OARS (Older Americans Resources and Services) model described herein is an example of the latter.

In spite of these difficulties and risks, the potential for significant contribution to society by strategic applications of operational research makes them worth while. The contribution of operational research to strategic decisions related to military force structures has been well documented by Enthoven and McNamara.[2] Also, the popularity of

129

strategic planning models in the corporate world attests to such potential (see Naylor[3]). In the area of health, where government expenditures are skyrocketing and strategic public policy issues are being addressed throughout most of the Western world, the potential contribution of operational researchers can be estimated in billions of dollars or, perhaps, in better health and/or care for millions of people.

Strategic applications of operational research must be planned to overcome the difficulties mentioned above. There must be direct involvement of the individuals who have a major role in the strategic decisions. The problem must be structured to reflect the situation as perceived by these individuals. The analysis must lead to the collection of technical information, probably through the involvement of experts from many fields, in a form which can be integrated into a unified analysis of the strategic problem at hand. Finally, the results of the analysis must be presented in a form which permits the decision makers to use it in the political atmosphere of compromise where strategic decisions are made. The decision makers should be helped to understand the total problem, the uncertainties involved and the options open to them; they should not expect, or be presented with, a simple single recommended course of action.

This chapter presents an account of a strategic application of operational research which meets most of these standards. The work began in 1972 with a request to the Duke University Center for the Study of Aging and Human Development from government policy makers faced with strategic choices regarding government programmes for the elderly. (See Maddox for a discussion of the formation and early days of OARS.[4]) The Duke Center found that the methodology for a proper investigation of this problem was not available. The Center thus responded to the request by organising a long-term effort to develop a methodology to address the basic issue. Among others, the US General Accounting Office (GAO) adopted the methodology and conducted a series of studies for the US Congress which led to reports to congressional and administrative policy makers.

The Problem

In 1972 the US Congress expressed the view that the current situation of the nation's elderly was intolerable. There had been a great deal of adverse publicity regarding the well-being of the elderly, especially those in nursing homes, privately operated at federal expense. About one million older Americans were 'relegated' to these institutions at an annual cost of over $8 billion. The public was deluged with reports of inadequate care and, in some cases, neglect. Moreover, it was projected that the elderly population in the United States would increase dramatically over the next 20 years, so some alternative approaches to caring for the elderly were needed for the long term, as well as short-term action to improve the current situation.

The Administration on Aging (AOA), an agency of the then Health, Education and Welfare Department (HEW), turned to the Duke University Center for the study of Aging and Human Development for help on the long-term issue of finding alternatives to institutional care. The AOA was created in 1965 by the Older Americans Act and serves as a focal point for the administration on policy regarding the elderly. The head of the AOA also acts as a special assistant to the President on ageing. The 1973 amendments to the Older Americans Act broadened the AOA's scope of activities and it began to channel funds into developmental programmes for the elderly, such as meals on wheels, home care, co-ordination of services, senior centres, etc. However, most federal expenditures on programmes for the elderly were managed by other agencies, such as the Social Security Administration. Nevertheless, while only a small portion of the federal monies being spent on the elderly were directly controlled by the AOA, it was in a position significantly to influence administrative policy on the care of the elderly.[5] Moreover, the AOA maintained liaison with the committees in the US Congress which develop specific legislative proposals establishing federal policy pertaining to older citizens. Hence the AOA's request represented an opportunity to influence the thinking of the principal players in the political game which would eventually lead to strategic decisions defining federal policy on the care of the elderly.

In initial discussions with the officials of the AOA, their perception of the problem emerged. They felt that the institutionalisation of the elderly was an unsatisfactory method of care. It was not only too costly; it did not provide quality care. They wanted to investigate alternatives which included the provision of a broader array of services in the home (nutritional, health services, personal care, etc.), other 'semi-institutional' alternatives such as the elderly housing arrangements in the United Kingdom, or perhaps the strengthening of family support for the elderly.

Information on the status of the elderly was limited to demographic census data on the entire population and to a variety of specific studies of small sub-groups of the population. There was almost no evidence on the effect of government-sponsored programmes on the well-being of the elderly. Yet piecemeal data suggested that the elderly suffered from a variety of problems. A disproportionate share subsisted on incomes well below the established poverty level. Expenditures on health care for the elderly were two and a half to three times those for the rest of the population, yet the elderly constituted only 10 per cent of the population. Depression and other mental diseases were markedly more prevalent among the elderly. The elderly suffered from social isolation to a much greater degree than did the rest of the population. Total expenditures on existing programmes for the elderly were expected to grow significantly in the next few years. It was felt that expenditures of that magnitude should yield more in terms of social benefits, and the problem was to find ways to accomplish this goal.

Preliminary investigation by the Duke Center, which had more than 15 years of experience investigating problems of the elderly, confirmed the belief that the information needed for the analysis was not available. Moreover, the methodology for collecting it did not exist. A procedure was needed for making comparisons among alternative ways of caring for the elderly based upon effects, or outcomes, as well as costs. The alternatives must consist of integrated packages of care which cut across the traditional departmentalisation by specialty, e.g. health care, mental health care, personal services, financial aid, etc. The measure of effect on the elderly must reflect the multidimensional nature of the problems they encountered. A method must be developed for collecting the necessary information in an economical, yet reliable and valid way. An efficient procedure must be developed to process the information gathered such that it would be understood and viewed as relevant by the policy makers.

It was clear to the Duke Center that such a project would require an interdisciplinary effort over an extended period of time. A carefully co-ordinated, co-operative effort would be required to integrate the bits of relevant information currently fragmented into disciplines and specialties. Such an undertaking would be difficult. The project required that fundamental definitional and measurement problems be solved and it was not clear that solutions existed. On the other hand, the Duke Center was uniquely qualified to undertake such a project: it had an extensive background studying the problems of the elderly and strong ties with scholars in the array of disciplines and specialties involved, it operated a clinic which could be used for experimentation, and it had good relationships with the many agencies providing services for the elderly in the area. Moreover, this request from the AOA represented an opportunity for the Center to make a major contribution to the solution of a strategic problem. So the Duke Center agreed to undertake the methodological work required but not the major data collection and processing work. The AOA planned to make other arrangements for testing the results of the Duke project. The project was expected to last three years.

The Approach

A team representing a variety of disciplines and specialties was organised to undertake the project. Operational researchers, administrators, chaplains, economists, lawyers, nurses, psychiatrists, sociologists and social workers made up the team. The operational researchers were asked to participate as their research approach to problem formulation and resource allocation was deemed by the Center Director as a potentially useful way to view this problem. As the team began its work on the development of a conceptual framework for the project, the expected variety of points of view among the members began to surface. For example, some members of the team viewed the elderly as individuals with unique needs, while others viewed them as members of the population whose status could be modified by the provision of services. Some identified services by their providers, for example nursing services. Others saw services as unique sets of activities independent of their providers. The status of elderly individuals was identified in terms of diseases by some team members, in terms of needs by others, and in terms of legal entitlement by others. Various researchers viewed costs as charges, as allocated historical costs, or as forgone opportunities. Obviously, if the group were to become a team, in fact, it must reconcile these legitimate, but contradictory, points of view and reach a common understanding of the problem. Maddox discusses the team-building issue in some detail.[6]

It was at this point that the operational research members made their most significant contribution to the team. By focusing on the central task of developing a formal structure for the problem, they were able to lead the team in the development of its own conceptual framework for the problem.

Quite simply, we were able to convince the team that it would be useful to view the issue in the following terms:

1. with money, we buy personnel services, equipment and facilities;
2. with personnel services, equipment and facilities, we provide services to the target population;

3. with services, we change, or affect, the target population, which is the result, or benefit.

This framework was sufficiently basic and intuitive to appeal to a broad group of specialists. Individual team members were able to look beyond their own disciplines and specialties and see the larger problem. The result was a conceptual framework which the entire team claimed as its own, not one imposed by the project director or the operational researchers. The individual team members understood the conceptual framework and were willing and able to make continuing contributions from their unique specialties in the ways which permitted the integration of their individual contributions. This made it possible for the project to become a truly interdisciplinary effort.

The further development of the framework in an initial series of meetings of the team led to the following features:

1. The appropriate basis for preparing alternative programmes for the elderly was the impact the programmes would have on the elderly population to be served. This agreement was not easy to obtain.
2. The appropriate measure of impact was the change in the capacity of the elderly for independent living. A number of policy documents, including the Older Americans Act, enunciated this as the principal objective of federal programmes for the elderly.
3. The measure of capacity for independent living must be multidimensional accurately to reflect the nature of the problems of the elderly. It could not be limited to the measure of a single characteristic such as physical health, for example. The team eventually settled on five specific dimensions: physical, mental, social and economic well-being and a measure of an individual's ability to perform routine activities of daily living.
4. The team would not attempt to define a specific utility measure of the five dimensions. This would require team members to go beyond their areas of expertise to impose social preferences. Moreover, it was believed that the five-dimensional capacity for independent living status definition was an adequate description for the policy makers to use in making social preference judgements. That is, policy makers could distinguish between any two populations described in these terms and, more importantly, be able to indicate which was socially preferred.
5. The entire set of services received by an individual must be considered in determining the impact the services have on a person's capacity for independent living. That is, the interaction of sets of services must be

considered as well as individual services. This led to the concept of a service package, i.e. the entire set of services received by an individual regardless of source.

6. A set of basic generic services must be defined which would serve as building blocks for any service package existing or proposed. It was important to be able to define service packages without reference to the source of the service. Only in this way could the alternative means of providing services be compared.

7. Generic service definitions must be such that quantities of services could be observed and measured.

8. A system must be devised for linking the cost of alternative service programmes for the elderly to the impact the programmes have or are expected to have on the elderly population to be served. This is the key specification of the system to be developed as given in the conceptual framework discussed earlier.

Few of these specifications of the conceptual model came easily. There was a great deal of controversy among team members regarding the appropriate form of the measure of impact. A number of team members believed that 'need' was the appropriate basis for determining which service programmes to fund. But the operationalisation of 'need' incorporates social preferences and subsequent resource allocations. We wanted to avoid the elimination of alternatives in this fashion. The five-dimensional status measure was also a subject of controversy. Some team members believed that only the activities of daily living index provided a true measure of status and that the other dimensions should be dropped. Others believed that there should be three dimensions to status — activities of daily living, physical health and mental health — and that the social and economic resources were environmental measures which could be changed directly and would, in turn, influence the true status as measured by the other three dimensions. (This is also the view adopted by Wright in a similar project at York University in the UK.[7]) The five-dimensional form was finally adopted as it was argued that the number of dimensions could always be reduced if later experience proved this to be necessary, whereas it would not be possible to add dimensions later.

The Conceptual Model Operationalised[8]

A schematic of the conceptual model as it finally evolved is shown in Figure 6.1. The specifics of the model are based on its application to

Figure 6.1: Schematic Diagram of Model

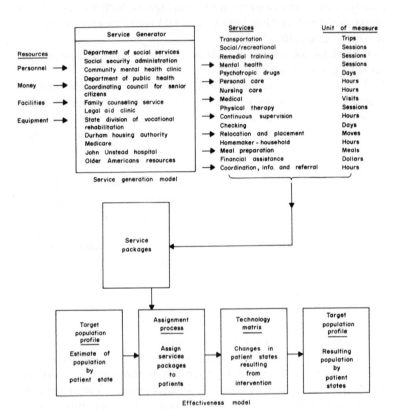

Source: reproduced with permission from the *Journal of the Operational Research Society,* vol. 29, no. 7 (1978), p. 636.

Durham County, North Carolina, which was used by the team to test
most of its ideas and concepts. Beginning at the upper left, Figure 6.1
shows a sample of the more than 25 organisations which serve the elderly
in Durham County. Since these organisations consume resources and
generate services it is possible to state relationships between costs and
the services generated. To do so, however, requires that services be
defined in measurable terms, e.g. number of trips, number of hours of
personal care, etc. Figure 6.1 shows a sample of the 24 generic services
defined from the OARS model and their units of measure.

The total set of services produced for Durham County is allocated
among individuals in the target population. The particular set of services
assigned to any particular individual we defined as a service package.
For example, the service package received by an individual might consist
of three trips, five hours of nursing and six hours of personal care a
week. The notion of the service package completes the conceptual part
of the model dealing with the generation of services. It is the conceptual
link which unifies the service provision component with the effectiveness
or impact component of the model. For this project it was the crucial
conceptual idea which also brought unity to the team itself.

The lower portion of Figure 6.1 depicts the concept for estimating
the impact a particular set of service packages will have on the target
population. Beginning with the known or estimated status of the
members of the target population, the available service packages are
assigned to individuals. The technology matrix, or impact function, is
a summary statement which indicates the probability distribution on
the patient's new state, given his current state and specific service
package. The technology matrix is modelled as a matrix of transition
probabilities in a Markov chain. Thus, the changes in the target
population can be predicted as a function of the service packages
available, which in turn is a function of the service generation system
chosen and, ultimately, the cost of producing the service. The
technology matrix requires that a method be developed for
characterising the states of the individuals in the target population. We
refer to these states as patient states. This conceptual model, then, links
the cost of producing services to the estimated impact of these services
on the target population.

A Mathematical Model

Concurrent with the development of the conceptual framework by the
team, the operational research members constructed a sequence of

mathematical models which constituted formal statements of the team's evolving conceptual model. This permitted the operational researchers to test the concepts for internal consistency, completeness and specificity, and to feed back to the team the need for redirection or refinements in the conceptual framework.

Many of the important characteristics of the conceptual framework were the result of this behind-the-scenes activity. For example, the properties of service definitions and service packages discussed above were derived from the model-building exercises. The clinicians who, because of their experience in providing services, possessed the knowledge necessary to define services were convinced by arguements based on the model that generic definitions suitable for quantification were necessary for the over-all analysis, and hence were willing to work on this important aspect of the problem. The necessity for a functional rather than a disease-based status measure was also a result of work on the mathematical model, as was the idea of estimating costs on the basis of services rather than the disease status of individuals. The model also revealed that there was an ultimate need for developing a framework for observing how service packages are, as a matter of practice, assigned to individuals through the box labelled 'assignment process' in Figure 6.1. The clinicians confirmed that little was known about how the 'system' currently assigned services. This reinforced the need for generic service definitions and patient state definitions to provide a basis for observing this process.

The mathematical model also revealed that there must be some inexpensive, systematic, yet reliable and valid, method for determining or estimating the status of populations of elderly persons targeted for service programmes and, more importantly, determining how the status of the population would change over time with the provision of services.

Finally, the model made it clear that either the team must take on the task of defining a social preference function on the defined patient states or the patient states must be defined in such a way that policy makers could define their own versions of social preferences. That is, the patient states must define the status of individuals in non-technical, common terms, recognisable and understood by laymen. For example, a person in patient state 43232 (one of the 6^5 possible states) can be described as a person whose:

> Social relationships are unsatisfactory, of poor quality and few. Income is adequate but who has no reserve assets. Handles both routine and major problems in his life satisfactorily and he is

intellectually intact and free of psychiatric symptoms. Has only minor illnesses and/or disabilities which might benefit from medical treatment for corrective measures, and who can perform all the activities of daily living without assistance.

The mathematical model, as it finally evolved, accurately represented the team's concept of the problem facing the AOA and other policy makers. The mathematical version of the model, like the schematic version, has two components linked by service packages.

The first, the service generation component, links the generation of services with their cost. Since the services are generated by particular facilities, e.g. hospitals, nursing homes, legal aid clinics, etc., and the number of different types of facilities is a major planning variable, the model is formulated around this variable.

Let
Y_l be the number of lth type facility available (a decision variable);
μ_{kl} be the quantity of the kth service produced by the lth type facility;
C_l be the cost of an lth type facility (personnel, materials and capital costs);
S_k be the total quantity of the kth service produced.

The cost for all facilities is: $\Sigma_l C_l Y_l$ and the quantity of each type of service produced is: $\Sigma_l \mu_{kl} Y_l = S_k$.

Secondly, the effectiveness component links the services assigned to the target population to the expected impact on that population. At the heart of the effectiveness model is the stochastic technology matrix.

Let T^i be the technology matrix for service package i in which an element $q^i_{jj'}$ is the probability that a patient initially in state j assigned service package i will emerge in state j'

$$\Sigma_j q^i_{jj'} = 1. \; - \; \forall i$$

Let X^i be a service assignment vector in which an element x_{ij} is the number of patients initially in state j assigned service package i and $\Sigma_i x_{ij}$ is the total number of persons in the target population initially in state j. For any X^i, the impact on the target population can be determined in terms of a population profile vector

$$M = \Sigma_i X^i T^i,$$

in which an element m_j is the expected number of persons emerging in state j.

The service generation component and effectiveness component are linked by the relationship: $\Sigma_i \Sigma_j x_{ij} s_{ik} = S_k$ ∀k., where S_{ik} represents the quantity of the kth service in service package i.

The use of a Markov process to represent changes in status over time was the result of much debate among the operational researchers on the team. Several alternative models, based on suggestions by the clinicians on the team, were considered. But there appeared to be no evidence to support any of the clinicians' suggestions and all involved rather complex models. The Markov model (called the technology matrix in Figure 6.1) was selected because it was simple and it was believed to be adequate for the purpose of specifying the data to be collected. It was expected that empirical evidence on changes in status over time would either verify the Markov nature of the process or provide a basis for developing a more appropriate model. The important thing was to collect data on status changes of individuals over time simultaneously with data on the services received by the individuals between observations, and the Markov model required that data be collected in this manner.

The greatest potential problem with the model was the large number of possible patient states and service packages. The five-dimensional patient state definitions with six levels of functioning on each led to a possible 7,776 states which meant that each matrix of transition probabilities could be as large as 7,776 by 7,776. Moreover, the potential number of service packages was practically unlimited. With only 24 geriatric services and three levels of intensity for each service, there could be 280 billion possible individual service packages. When one considers that the model calls for a separate 7,776 by 7,776 matrix for each of the service packages, the data requirements for estimating the transition probabilities were overwhelming. Clearly, the model 'size' had to be reduced.

Fortunately, the number of patient states could be reduced dramatically by combining levels of functioning. For much of the experimental work on the project, only two levels of functioning were used. Levels 1, 2 and 3 were grouped for one level of functioning and levels 4, 5 and 6 grouped for the other. (The six-level status measures were retained in the basic data.) Additionally, reductions in the number of state definitions could be obtained if some of the five dimensions turned out to be inappropriate as status measures. It was therefore expected that appropriate reductions in the number of patient states could be made. Moreover, the clinicians involved in the project did not believe that all the potential states were actually possible. For example, it would be impossible, they argued, for a person to have a functional level 6 on the physical functioning dimension (the most severely impaired level of functioning) and a level of one (the highest level of functioning) on the activities of daily living dimension. So it was very likely that the number of states could be reduced to a manageable level.

Although there was no obvious way to reduce the large number of potential service packages, clinicians believed that only a very few of the potential service packages would actually be observed and preliminary investigation supported this belief. In addition, some reductions could be made by aggregating the levels of intensity for certain services. For example, the clinicians expected that the number of trips provided to older persons would cluster around one per week or one per day, so that only two levels of intensity would be needed for most cases. In summary, the dimensionality problem appeared to be solvable for particular applications of the model, but a general solution would have to await the collection of empirical data.

These dimensionality problems almost led to the abandonment of the model in the early stages of the project; however, no simpler alternative was proposed which captured the problem as well. Moreover, development of this model would produce components which would facilitate the analysis of a number of lesser but important problems regarding the care of the elderly. For example, the clinicians saw that a simple procedure for determining the functional status of individuals, which the model required, would also serve as a clinical evaluation procedure. It would permit clinicians in any specialty to assess the over-all status of individuals and systematically to determine and co-ordinate an appropriate package of care for the individual. This would be true even though some of the services in the package of care might be provided by members of other specialties. They believed that current practice led clinics to provide their own services to individuals who came to them, although the services of some other clinic might be more appropriate for the individual. In effect, they saw the assessment procedure as a means of improving the assignment process (see Figure 6.1). The operational researchers saw the definition of services as a means of quantifying the output of a service production system and the means for evaluating alternative processes for producing the same output. Studies which compared the cost of alternative forms of care were found generally to be comparing apples and oranges. Well-defined services avoided this problem. Administrators saw the functional assessment system as a survey instrument which would permit them to characterise their target population in a systematic way — something they saw as essential to good planning. Planning was then based on data from clients (case loads), which represented only a sub-set of the population to be served, and census or public health data, which did not reveal functional status. Planners also saw the MFAQ (the Multidimensional Functional Assessment Questionnaire) as a means of evaluating service programmes in a systematic way.[9] By observing the status of the population before and after a service programme was implemented, there was the possibility that they could, with appropriate statistical techniques, estimate the impact of the programme on the population. So, even if the research effort failed to produce a usable set of transition probabilities which were germane to the resource allocation problem of the project, completion of the other components of the project would result in major contributions to the solution of significant operational and evaluation problems relevant to the provision of services to the elderly. Hence, we elected to continue with the model in spite of these potential difficulties.

The Research

The research on this project included the initial modelling effort, which has already been discussed, and extended into developing and testing the specifics of the model and the information-gathering system. More specifically, the research project was decomposed into five major sub-projects as follows:

1. develop a set of patient state definitions;
2. develop a set of service definitions;
3. develop procedures for estimating the cost of generating specified service packages by alternative service-generating systems;
4. develop a system for determining the patient state of individual elderly persons and observing the services being received by the person;
5. develop procedures for estimating the transition probabilities in the technology matrix.

This particular decomposition of the work to be done, of course, followed naturally from the model. But without the model some other decomposition, probably along disciplinary lines, would have been used.[10] It is difficult to see how the results of such a decomposition could be integrated into an efficient method for addressing the strategic policy problem at hand. The decomposition based on the model is designed to ensure that the results of individual sub-projects will fit into an integrated whole when completed. Yet the sub-projects were of interest individually.

The model played an equally important role in co-ordinating the work on the sub-projects. It specified the relationships among the various sub-projects and, in turn, the form of the products each sub-group must produce. For example, the model made it clear that service packages played the key role of linking the service generation system and the effectiveness-measuring system and, consequently, the service definitions must be of a form to fit into both systems. They must be suitable for observation and measurement of the output of a production system in an economic sense, and must also be usable by the clinicians who prescribe or provide services. This task group could not arbitrarily select any one of the many incompatible service definitions used by government agencies, service providers or economists. Similarly, the model provided direction for the development of the Duke OARS questionnaire, the device developed to determine the status of elderly individuals and the service packages being received by them.[11] Every question considered for the questionnaire was put to the test, 'Will it help determine the status of the individual or the services he is receiving?' Throughout the project many issues which arose between sub-task groups or among members of the same sub-group regarding the specific forms of their products were resolved by reference to the model. The results of the five sub-task groups are now briefly described.

Patient State Definitions. The interdisciplinary team developed a set of patient state definitions which reflect the patient's ability to function independently with respect to five dimensions: physical health, mental health, social resources, economic resources and activities of daily living. Patients are rated on a scale of 1-6 on each of these dimensions according to the degree of impairment in each. (A '1' represents no impairment and a '6' represents severe impairment.) As already indicated, there are, in total, 7,776 possible patient states, but for much of the work on the Duke OARS project these have been reduced from six possible states on each scale to two (impaired and unimpaired), yielding 2^5 or 32 possible states. As an example, the six functional-level definitions for the activities of daily living scale are shown in Table 6.1.

Service Definitions. The definition and measurement of generic services turned out to be one of the most difficult tasks in the project. The definition task was accomplished by creating a small number of

Table 6.1: Performance Rating Scale for Activities of Daily Living

---

[Rate the current performance of the person being evaluated on the six-point scale presented below. Circle the *one* number which best describes the person's present performance. Activities of daily living questions are numbers 56-69.]

1. *Excellent ADL capacity.*
   Can perform all the activities of daily living without assistance and with ease.
2. *Good ADL capacity.*
   Can perform all the activities of daily living without assistance.
3. *Mildly impaired ADL capacity.*
   Can perform all but one to three of the activities of daily living. Some help is required with one to three, but not necessarily every day. Can get through any single day without help. Is able to prepare his/her own meals.
4. *Moderately impaired ADL capacity.*
   Regularly requires assistance with at least four activities of daily living but is able to get through any single day without help. Or regularly requires help with meal preparation.
5. *Severely impaired ADL capacity.*
   Needs help each day but not necessarily throughout the day or night with many of the activities of daily living.
6. *Completely impaired ADL capacity.*
   Needs help throughout the day and/or night to carry out the activities of daily living.

Source: reproduced with permission from Center for the Study of Aging and Human Development, *Multidimensional Functional Assessment,* p. 194.

equivalence classes from a large number of activities. For example, nursing care was defined as those activities required to co-ordinate, implement and monitor the plan of care prescribed by a health care professional, including administration of medication, health counselling and carrying out treatment routines. Nursing care does not include many of the activities in which nurses actually engage, e.g. feeding or bathing an impaired person (which fall under personal care). After many iterations which involved defining and testing the definitions in clinical and production settings, a usable set of definitions for 24 services was developed. The service definition for nursing care is shown in Table 6.2. Once defined in this manner, the services could be measured in terms of number of trips, hours of personal care, etc.[12]

Estimating the Cost of Service Packages. The cost of a service package depends on where, how and under what circumstances the package is produced. The team's task was to demonstrate that the definitions of

Table 6.2: Nursing Care Definition

Purpose:	To co-ordinate, implement and monitor the plan of care prescribed by a health care professional.
Activity:	Administration and/or monitoring of prescribed medication or treatment regimens; health counselling; communication with primary clinician and other health team personnel.
Relevant personnel:	RN, LPN, attendant, family member.
Unit of measure:	Contact hours.
Examples:	Administration of oral medications, intramuscular or intravenous therapy, catheter care, dressings, taking blood pressure.

Source: reproduced with permission from Center for the Study of Aging and Human Development, *Multidimensional Functional Assessment,* p. 204.

services were suitable for cost estimating. This demonstration consisted of identifying the service production system in Durham County and developing cost-estimating relationships based on data collected within the system. Based on this experience, a set of guidelines for estimating the cost of service packages was prepared.[13]

Determining the Patient State of Individuals and Service Packages Being Received. The task of developing an economically feasible procedure for classifying individuals into patient states was as difficult as the other sub-tasks, and more time consuming. A lengthy questionnaire was developed for use by an interviewer with minimum training.[14] The questionnaire was initially applied to over 1,200 subjects and was successfully tested for reliability and validity through repeated observations.[15] Questions are included which simultaneously determine the status of individuals and the service package received. This questionnaire, called 'The OARS Multidimensional Functional Assessment Questionnaire', or MFAG, is a key operational tool in the Duke OARS evaluation system.

Estimating Transition Probabilities. An element in the technology matrix is the probability that a person in a given state and assigned a particular service package will, after a specified period of time, be in any particular state. Using the simplified 33 (32 live states with two levels of functioning, plus death) patient states and some small number, say 25, service packages, it is obvious that a large number of observations would be required to estimate the transition probabilities based only on empirical data. This is true even when it is apparent that many of the elements will, *a priori*, be zero. (Some service packages would never be assigned to some patient states and many transitions are very unlikely.) A procedure was developed to augment empirical data with judgemental estimates of the transition probabilities made by the clinicians who worked with patients in the clinic. The procedure is a Bayesian technique for updating clinical judgement with observation and additional clinical judgement.[16]

Applications of the Method

The research on the initial project by the Duke OARS team produced a conceptual model, a set of operational definitions of the components of the model, an instrument for gathering the empirical data and a procedure for estimating the transition probabilities of the technology matrix. However, it had produced only a minuscule sample of the empirical evidence needed to affect significantly the strategic decisions regarding programmes for the elderly. By the time the methodology part of the research project was completed, general interest in completing the project as a whole waned for a variety of reasons.

One of these reasons was that the activities of the Duke OARS clinic were not sufficient to provide the data required to estimate the transition probabilities. It would require a large national sample. We did not have access to a large sample, nor the resources to generate one. Patient privacy was a major concern of many funding agencies and, although the required data could be impersonal, the data were not forthcoming. It was a practical concern and did cause a certain sense of frustration for the OARS team. A major breakthrough was the interest of the General Accounting Office (GAO). This was coupled with a burst of interest by local agencies. These events have changed the direction of the Duke OARS project from its original intent, but these applications are very much in the spirit of the goal of providing a general methodology which is useful in yielding better resource allocation.

Local Agency Studies

To date, there are about 80 documented applications of the Duke OARS methodology throughout the US.[17] The range of uses to which the approach has been applied includes initial clinical assessment of individual elderly persons, population assessment, programme evaluation and community surveys. We report a brief summary of a number of users to illustrate their variety and the type of applications.

The Benjamin Rose Institute in Cleveland, Ohio has used the OARS approach at the individual level to assess client needs and at the community level to assess whether the institute was meeting its goals as a service to the community.

The Wisconsin Community Care Organization used the MFAQ for client assessment. Following assessment, a specific plan of care is developed for each client and is approved by the Community Care Organization for reimbursement with funds. The Community Care Organization provides various services which are alternatives to institutional placement.

Staff of the Greene County Commission on Aging used the OARS approach in a federally funded systematic survey of the needs of the elderly population in Greene County, Ohio. The purpose of the survey was to obtain data on the characteristics of persons aged 60 years or older, their utilisation of existing services, and the need for services as stated by survey respondents. This will provide government and service organisations with the information needed to plan services and to minimise service duplication and gaps.

In 1978 the Community Service Planning Committee of the Cleveland Jewish Community Federation used the MFAQ in a survey of Cleveland's older Jewish population. The study emphasised the ways in which older persons function in basic areas of their lives and the ways they cope with their problems.

In Tallahassee, Florida, the Office of Education of the Department of Health and Rehabilitative Services used the OARS methodology in the evaluation of a legislatively mandated demonstration programme of various approaches to serving the community's elderly.

The Greene County (Ohio) Adult Foster Care programme is studying adult foster care under a demonstration grant from the AOA. It uses the MFAQ to assess clients prior to placement and for regular follow-up at six-month intervals thereafter.

Elder Services of the Merrimack Valley, Inc., an agency in Lawrence, Massachusetts, are using the OARS materials to train their case management staff in the multidimensional assessment of the aged person.

The questionnaire was used in a Waco, Texas Veteran's Administrative Hospital to identify the status and needs of veterans receiving a pension and special aid and attendance allowance. The study hopes to identify ways in which services could be provided to these veterans which would allow them to remain in the community rather than in contract nursing homes.

Data using the Duke OARS methodology form part of the information supplied by the 'Living Textbook of Geriatric Care' — an automated information system developed from a research base and applicable to research, training and patient care. The goal is to standardise the data on the status of the elderly, the types of care received and the evaluation of service delivery into a form which can be used by clinicians and researchers. It is an important step in creating a data base of national significance for the care of the elderly and the efficient allocation of resources.

The GAO Study

The most notable application of the Duke OARS methodology is found in a number of studies designed to evaluate the service programmes for the elderly population in Cleveland, Ohio, conducted by the US General Accounting Office. (The GAO is an investigative arm of the US Congress and has influence on the strategic policy decisions taken by Congress. In effect, the GAO picked up where the Administration on Aging left off in the development of a large-scale test of the model.) The GAO decided to adopt the OARS system to conduct studies for strategic policy decisions.

The GAO became aware of the OARS developmental work when, in 1975, a study group within the GAO was charged with evaluating the effectiveness of service programmes for the elderly funded by the federal government. They set out to:

1. evaluate the service programmes as a group, not as individual programmes;
2. base the evaluation on the degree to which the programmes facilitated improvement in the lives of individual elderly people;
3. reflect the broad array of problems encountered by the elderly.

In a general search for an approach and methodology, they found the Duke Center and the OARS system, decided it was more or less ready-made for their study, and quickly adopted it.

The GAO study would focus on the elderly population in Cleveland, Ohio, a city with some 80,000 elderly citizens who were served by some 118 agencies funded largely (90 per cent) by the federal government. The study would sample 1,500-2,000 elderly citizens living in the community. The MFAQ would be administered at two points in time — approximately one year apart. The OARS system would be modified so that the providers of the services could be identified for each individual and carefully cross-checked with the agencies which provided the services. Members of the OARS development team would be engaged as consultants on the project. It would be the first full-scale field test of the OARS concept; but it was more than simply a field test.

The GAO closely supports Congress and the congressional committees on the elderly. As information is gathered, significant findings are reported to Congress; the GAO does not wait for long-term studies to be completed before reporting. Neither does the congressional committee simply commission studies and await results. It continually raises policy questions and requests whatever relevant information might be available. In short, the necessary dialogue between the policy makers and analysts for an effective application of operational research to strategic issues existed between Congress and the GAO study team.

During the course of the study, which covered a period of approximately three years, the GAO study team produced three formal reports and responded to a large number of policy questions raised by the US Congress as legislative policy on the elderly was developed.[18] The more interesting and significant findings reported to Congress are summarised below.

Regarding the Status of the Elderly Population Served. About 20 per cent of the population over 65 years of age were found to be capable of living totally independently. About 17 per cent were extremely impaired. Of this 17 per cent, about one-third were living in institutions and the other two-thirds were living in the community. The distribution of elderly in the urban Cleveland area was not significantly different from the distribution in suburban and rural areas.

Regarding the Assignment of Services. The assignment of services to individuals was influenced as much by where they live (urban, suburban or rural) as by their status. The location of the service providers was based more on untested theories about who needed services than on hard evidence. Eligibility tests were found not to be an efficient means of distributing services. Large numbers of eligible persons (as high as 89 per cent) were not receiving the services for which they were eligible.

Regarding the Economics of Service Delivery. The services required by the most extremely impaired elderly, about 10 per cent of the population over 65, could be delivered more economically in institutions than in homes. Only about one-third of this group were actually in institutions and the remainder were able to remain outside institutions because services were supplied by an informal network of family and friends. Family and friends provided equivalent services of $673.00 per month and agencies supplied $172.00 for a total of $845.00. This service could be provided in an institution for $458.00.[19]

The family and friends network was extensive (providing more services to all groups of elderly than did federal programmes) and additional federal programmes might simply replace this network rather than augment it. Unless this was the intent of Congress, new service programmes must be carefully designed to avoid simple replacement and shifting of the cost of the services to the government. The family and friends network tended to deliver only certain types of services (non-medical home health, for example) and Congress could therefore authorise home health care services without increasing costs unnecessarily.

Regarding the Effectiveness of Service Programmes. Government programmes for the elderly were not being effectively co-ordinated. There was no unified system providing an integrated comprehensive co-ordinated package of health-related services for delivery in the home. Programmes which were more helpful than others to the elderly were identified. For example, medical care programmes were benefiting about 10 per cent of the elderly population, whereas social-recreational programmes were benefiting only about 3 per cent. Food stamps provided an example of a programme with high potential for benefiting the elderly, but this was ineffective because the elderly were reluctant to accept aid in the form being provided.

Regarding Resource Allocation. The GAO was unable to implement the OARS model exactly as it was originally designed, but it was able to use the MFAQ and, with some modifications to the model, develop a system to do essentially what the OARS project set out to do. Because the sample was relatively small and not representative of the US, the GAO was reluctant to extrapolate its results to the entire country. But for the Cleveland area it was able to estimate the impact in terms of the number of people helped and the cost of each of several classes of services. It also recommended that the system it used for collecting information and making such analysis be expanded nationwide so that Congress would be better able to evaluate the alternatives.

One of the principal problems encountered by the GAO was that it was unable to find a manageable number of naturally occurring service packages and, consequently, could not measure the impact of service packages on the over-all status of the elderly as specified in the OARS model. It was, howerver, able to develop rough surrogate measures of impact, e.g. numbers of people whose status on certain dimensions could be improved by a specific service.[20] With these measures, relations between the kind of help and the benefits and costs were developed, using the data collected with the MFAQ. The GAO was also able to make, for illustrative purposes, projections of the changing conditions of cohort groups of elderly over a 20-year horizon with alternative service programmes, using the Markov model, and demonstrate that corrective services, provided early in the life of the elderly, would more than pay for themselves by reducing the need for supportive services in later years.

The GAO analysts, then, were able to complete the job initiated by the OARS team some seven years earlier. While they were not able to implement the exact model developed by the OARS team, they were able to implement the conceptual model using their own status measures and the OARS data collection system. They demonstrated the feasibility of the approach and recommended that a national information system, based on the OARS model, be established.

The precise impact of the GAO studies on congressional policy making is, as expected, difficult to identify. Specific legislation always follows a formal hearing in which many interested persons and organisations, including the GAO, testify. Even when legislation which follows GAO recommendations is passed, it cannot necessarily be attributed to the GAO since the testimony of other persons may also have supported such legislation. On the other hand, it is clear from official correspondence between the congressional committees and the GAO that the GAO studies and reports had influenced the way the committees thought about the problem. Questions raised by the committees reflected an understanding of the underlying GAO model: e.g. 'Does the well-being (status) of older people differ between rural and urban areas?' or 'How does the cost of providing services in congregate housing compare to providing *similar services* in the community?' Moreover, the committee actively seeks information regarding service programmes for the elderly from the GAO on a continuing basis. We conclude that the studies have had an impact on the strategic decisions defining federal policy on the care of the elderly.

At the community and state level, the Cleveland studies have had a more directly observable impact. The Metropolitan Health Planning Corporation, a body responsible for health programmes and hospital construction in a five-county area including Cleveland, took account of the results of the first-phase report and placed a moratorium on hospital construction. The Ohio House and Senate are considering two bills to expand home health care as a result of the GAO studies. These activities suggest that data and information of appropriate dimensions for addressing policy questions can have an effect on how resources are allocated.

Conclusion

This description of the Duke OARS experience illustrates the difficulties and benefits of strategic applications of operational research. The principal difficulties in strategic applications centre around the problem of obtaining a co-operative and co-ordinated research effort by a team of mixed specialists and decision makers with diverse interests and points of view over a long period of time. Team projects have always characterised operational research efforts, but in strategic applications the diversity of the team membership is greater and their role more active than in tactical applications. In the Duke OARS project, a co-operative and co-ordinated effort was obtained by using the standard operational research approach of focusing on the development of a model from the outset, but with active participation by *all* team members in model development. There rarely is a single well-defined decision maker in any operational research project. But in strategic applications the diffusion of authority and diversity of interests are greater. In the OARS experience, the focus by the OARS team on the development of a clear, unambiguous explicit model independent of social values and the emphasis continually placed on the GAO's making the conceptual framework clear to the congressional committee helped overcome this diffusion of authority and interest. Since the conceptual framework was acceptable to all participants and permitted them to exercise their own social preferences, they were more willing to accept the information provided by the study group and to think about the problem within a common frame of reference. The problem of maintaining interest in a long-term operational research effort is not easily overcome, particularly when the decision makers frequently change. In the OARS experience, the original federal agency did not sustain its interest and funding, and terminated the project before its implementation phase. However, the problem was of significant social importance and had been addressed within a sufficiently general and acceptable conceptual framework that the work of the OARS team was adopted by the decision makers who eventually had to deal with the problem.

The Duke OARS experience is but one example of a strategic application of operational research to health problems. Other significant examples include the balance of care model, discussed in Chapter 4 of this book, and the Lipscomb, Berg, London and Nutting study of Arizona Indian tribes.[21] These applications are similar in that they require active participation by many specialists and groups of diverse decision makers, they are based on clearly defined mathematical programming models for which decision makers can exercise their own social preferences, and they are long-term, broad projects. There are also differences: the Duke OARS project utilised the model primarily for ensuring logical consistency and completeness of the conceptual framework and for decomposing the project into integratable sub-projects. It has not as yet included the development of an operational optimising model which could provide numerical solutions.[22] The balance-of-care model, on the other hand, is an operational, optimising model. However, as Chapter 4 makes clear, it is not used to generate a single optimal solution for implementation. Rather, it is used to project the future resource consequences of options of interest to decision makers in much the same way as models are used in corporate planning.[23] The Lipscomb *et al.* model is very similar to the OARS model in concept (a principal difference is that it utilises only physical health as a status measure in its current application) and has been used to help decision makers think through their problems.[24] It also includes operational models which help decision makers estimate the social preferences of the target population (by voting procedures) and allocate resources based on derived preferences. While these are differences, we would not argue that one model is inherently superior to another. All, in our view, have the essential ingredient — a conceptual framework which all the decision makers utilise to think through the problem and consider alternative courses of action.

The rewards from applications of operational research to strategic problems must eventually come from improved strategic decision making, which may take the form of bad choices rejected as well as good choices taken. The evidence is, by its very nature, inconclusive and difficult to obtain, but there is evidence, cited earlier, that the GAO applications of the OARS conceptual model have had a favourable influence on government decision makers. This is in spite of the difficulties the GAO analysts encountered in attempting to operationalise the effectiveness portion of the OARS model. The local agencies applications, documented by the Duke Center, have also had their impact.[25]

These applications have been successful because they have provided a broad group of interested individuals — administrators, social workers, medical doctors, legislators, etc. — with information that they deemed relevant to their problems. We believe that this relevancy is no accident. It is the result of the process adopted in developing a clear conceptual model by an interdisciplinary team. We believe that the Duke OARS project will continue to generate successful applications at the individual, institutional, community and national levels.

Acknowledgements

We wish to express our thanks to a number of individuals for their help on this chapter. Mary Ann Gough, our research assistant, was our partner in putting this chapter together. Her efforts were supported by the Center for the Study of Aging and Human Development. Gerda Fillenbaum, research psychologist, helped us with the Duke OARS users' surveys. George L. Maddox, Director, Center for the Study of Aging and Human Development, Duke University Medical Center, read an earlier draft and provided encouraging comments. William F. Laurie, Project Manager, United States Government Accounting Office, Cleveland, Ohio, commented extensively and provided corrections on an earlier draft. To each, we appreciate your generous support.

   Needless to say, we assume full responsibility for errors and omissions. The opinions and interpretations herein do not necessarily reflect those of the individuals who have aided us, not those of the sponsoring agencies.

Notes

   1. D. Boldy, 'A Review of the Application of Mathematical Programming to Tactical and Strategic Health and Social Services Problems' *Operational Research Quarterly*, vol. 27 (1976), pp. 439-48.

   2. S.A. Tucker (ed.), *A Modern Design for Defense Decisions, A McNamara-Hitch-Enthoven Anthology* (Industrial College of the Armed Forces, Washington, DC, 1966).

   3. Thomas Naylor, *Corporate Planning Models,* (Addison-Wesley, Reading, 1978).

   4. G. Maddox, 'Interventions and Outcomes: Notes on Designing and Implementing an Experiment in Health Care', *International Journal of Epidemiology* vol. 1 (1972), pp. 339-45.

   5. Later in the project two other agencies which controlled much larger portions of the federal funds earmarked for the elderly joined the AOA in

sponsoring this research project.

6. Maddox, 'Interventions and Outcomes'.

7. K.G. Wright, 'Alternative Measures of the Output of Social Programmes: the elderly', in A.J. Culyer (ed.), *Economic Policies and Social Goals* (St Martin's Press, New York, 1974), pp. 239-72.

8. Liberally adapted from Richard M. Burton, David C. Dellinger, William W. Damon and Eric A. Pfeiffer, 'A Role for Operational Research in Health Care Planning and Management Teams', *Journal of the Operational Research Society,* vol. 29, no. 7 (1978), pp. 633-41.

9. Center for the Study of Aging and Human Development, *Multidimensional Functional Assessment. The OARS Methodology,* 2nd edn (Duke University, Durham, NC, 1978).

10. In fact, suggestions at the outset of the project (before the conceptual framework was developed) were that the physicians would investigate the medical and mental health needs of the elderly, the sociologists would develop the questionnaire, the operational researchers and economists would investigate the cost of care, etc.

11. Center for the Study of Aging and Human Development, *Multidimensional Functional Assessment.*

12. Ibid, Appendix, gives a complete set of service definitions.

13. David C. Dellinger, 'Guidelines for Estimating the Cost of Service Packages for the Chronically Impaired', GSBA Paper no. 146 (Graduate School of Business Administration, Duke University, Durham, NC, 1975).

14. Center for the Study of Aging and Human Development, *Multidimensional Functional Assessment,* p. 151.

15. Gerda G. Fillenbaum, 'Validity and Reliability of the Multidimensional Functional Assessment Questionnaire', in note 9, pp. 25-35.

16. Richard M. Burton, William W. Damon and David C. Dellinger, 'Patient States and the Technology Matrix', *Interfaces,* vol. 5, no. 4 (August 1975), pp. 43-53; Richard M. Burton, William W. Damon and David C. Dellinger, 'Estimating the Impact of Health Services in a Community', *Behavioural Science,* vol. 21, no. 6 (November 1976), pp. 478-89.

17. These data are continually collected and updated in Program IOU administered by the Center. There is an annual users' conference at the Center for reporting various applications. Information concerning Program IOU and the users' conference can be obtained from the Center for the Study of Aging and Human Development, Duke University Medical Center, Durham, NC 27710, USA.

18. Comptroller General of the United States, *The Well-being of Older People in Cleveland, Ohio,* HRD-77-70 (US General Accounting Office, Washington, DC, 1977); Comptroller General of the United States, *Home Health – The Need for a National Policy to Better Provide For the Elderly,* HRD-78-19 (US General Accounting Office, Washington, DC, 1977); Comptroller General of the United States, *Conditions of Older People. National Information System Needed,* HRD-79-95 (US General Accounting Office, Washington, DC, 1979).

19. Comptroller General of the United States, *Home Health,* p. 16.

20. For specifics of their measures of impact, see Comptroller General of the United States, *Conditions of Older People.*

21. Joseph Lipscomb, Lawrence E. Berg, Virginia L. London and Paul A. Nutting, 'Health Status Maximisation and Manpower Allocation', *Research in Health Economics,* vol. 1 (JAI Press, Inc., 1979), pp. 301-401.

22. The OARS project would eventually lead to the development of an operational model to project the expected population profile, i.e. the technology matrix in Figure 6.1.

23. Naylor, *Corporate Planning Models.*

24. Lipscomb *et al.* 'Health Status Maximisation and Manpower Allocation'.
25. See note 17.

PART THREE

ASPECTS OF TACTICAL PLANNING

7 HOSPITAL STUDIES

P. Ciaran O'Kane

Introduction

Hospitals constituted the first large sector of the health services to be subjected to serious study by operations research scientists. Although operations research (OR) is now being applied to many other areas of these services, hospital studies continue to form a large part of the total corpus of OR work in this field. This chapter outlines, briefly, the history of the development of OR in the hospital field and discusses the particular features of hospital systems which make them not only an attractive area of study for management scientists but also one which presents very special difficulties. This will be followed by a brief outline description of some projects that have been carried out. It would be impossible, within the confines of a single chapter, adequately to review the immense literature on the subject of OR in hospitals. The examples chosen are meant to be neither exhaustive nor necessarily representative of this literature. They simply represent one author's choice of projects which illustrate a few of the many applications of the scientific approach to problem solving in the hospital context. Interested readers should consult some of the excellent surveys that have been published, if they wish to obtain a more comprehensive overview.[1] The chapter concludes with a detailed description of a case study with which the author was involved.

Development of Operations Research in Hospitals

Hospital studies began to appear in the OR literature in the early 1950s, much of the pioneering work being due to Bailey and his co-workers in Britain[2] and Flagle and his team in the United States.[3] For about ten years almost the entire OR effort devoted to health service studies was concerned with various aspects of hospital administration.

The resources devoted by the profession to such studies in those early years were, of course, minute compared to those today. OR interest in this field not only has expanded over the years but has grown at an ever-increasing rate. Fries noted that more articles on OR in the health

159

services appeared in the journals in the four years 1970-73 than had been published in the previous two decades.[4] In his bibliography of such work published up to March 1976, Fries provided 188 entries. The actual total of publications was probably greater than this, as Fries laid down strict criteria that each article had to meet before being included in his list. It is quite probable that a number of items which would be relevant to the subject of this chapter were excluded. However, Fries noted that the applications listed were predominantly concerned with hospital systems.

There has been a trend for more recent work to consider other aspects of health care delivery as well as hospitals. This is a desirable development, although hospital studies continue to be an area of major interest. In an update to his bibliography which includes work published to January 1978, Fries added a further 154 titles.[5] While hospital studies are not quite as predominant in this bibliography, they still represent a substantial proportion of the total. Boldy and Clayden's findings provide further evidence of this trend.[6] In comparing two registers of current OR work in the health services in the United Kingdom and Ireland prepared in 1972 and 1977, they note that, while the percentage of projects listed of which the main focus was hospital studies had fallen from 77 per cent in 1972, such projects still represent some two-thirds of the total in 1977.

The reasons for this emphasis on hospital studies are not difficult to find. To the layman, a large hospital complex is the most obvious and concrete manifestation of the magnitude of the health service in any developed country. To the administrators, hospitals represent the single, most expensive, element of a modern service. For example, in 1971, of the $75 billion of health expenditure in the United States, about 40 per cent was spent on hospital care,[7] while in Britain in the financial year 1976/77 the corresponding figure was almost 60 per cent.[8]

Thus, the magnitude of the hospital system makes it an obvious area of study to any group interested in improving the efficiency of the health service, but, in addition, the study of hospitals is professionally attractive to anyone trained in OR. By definition, this science is concerned with the study of complex systems and there are few industrial or commercial organisations which exhibit anything like the complexities of a modern hospital system.

There has been some criticism in recent years, not least from within the OR community itself, that excessive effort is being expended on studies in the hospital service. While it is both necessary and desirable that the recent trends of applying OR to as many facets of the health care field as possible should continue and expand, the hospital service must continue to attract a considerable amount of attention from OR workers if they are to make a real impact on the service as a whole. A host of problems remains to be solved in the hospital service.

A Hospital as a System

A hospital is an extremely complex system consisting of a large number of physical, human and technical elements, all of which are devoted to providing an output which is difficult, if not impossible, to measure in purely quantitative terms. In fact, any hospital may be visualised as a macro-system comprising a large number of sub-systems which are quite complex both within themselves and in their interactions with each other. These interactions occur in a wide variety of ways but the nett result is that the totality of a hospital is greater than the sum of its individual parts. This is one factor which makes a study of a hospital system so difficult.

It is also the case in most modern hospitals that, unlike many industrial systems, there is not one decision maker but many. A decision of any consequence requires the agreement of a number of people who, while they have a common over-all objective which is usually expressed in such general terms as 'to provide the best care possible for the patients', will also have a number of sub-objectives. It is frequently the case that these sub-objectives are in conflict and any 'solutions' proposed must thus take account of such conflict.

Many examples can be quoted. For instance, clinic time-tables will usually be arranged to meet the clinicians' immediate objectives but the result may be to place very uneven workloads on service facilities such as X-ray, laboratories, etc., thus conflicting with the immediate objectives of those responsible for the efficient running of such departments. Again, the allocation of resources is a frequent source of conflict. Many units can make a good case to be provided with extra resources to allow them to perform their task much better than at present. In many countries, all units are funded from a common source with a finite amount of resources, which are invariably insufficient to meet total demands. Hence an allocation which meets the objectives of one unit will prevent some other unit from meeting its objectives as seen by the unit staff. This is where OR can make a major contribution by attempting to explain the underlying structure of the system and by throwing an analytical light on the interactions which exist, thus going some way towards resolving the conflicts that exist.

It has, however, been argued that much of the OR effort in hospitals to date has concentrated on specific sub-systems rather than on the system as a whole, with the result that the total system may be performing below its potential. It is implied by some writers that no real progress can be made until a model has been developed which would accurately describe the entire hospital macro-system. Such a model would be invaluable and, although some work has been done in this area,[9] the magnitude of the problems has, to date, defeated all attempts to produce a fully operational model.

However, the failure to achieve this ideal should not be used as an argument against the current application of OR to individual parts of the hospital system. It is recognised that 'absolute perfection' cannot be attained in this way, but, as many of the studies described below show, it is possible to improve on the existing state and such improvements are worthwhile, even if they do include an element of sub-optimisation. No managerial problem exists in isolation and an important part of any system's study is to define the appropriate boundaries of the system being examined. These will always be arbitrary, to some extent, but a large element of the art of the OR practitioner is to define these boundaries so that they are neither so narrow as to exclude elements that have an important effect on the area of study, nor so broad as to make any detailed study impossible.

I hope to show in this chapter that, provided that the model builder realises that he is not dealing with an isolated system and that interactions between the sub-system which he is studying and other sub-systems exist, and provided he allows for such interactions which appear most relevant, then significant changes for the better can be brought about from the separate study of the sub-systems. It is also a reasonable assumption that our chances of eventually succeeding in constructing a 'total hospital' system must improve as we gain greater insight into the operations of its constituent sub-systems. Finally, it must not be forgotten that the total hospital is not, of course, the final level in the hierarchy of systems. It is itself part of the larger health care system which, in turn, is part of the social system, etc. The search for a 'total system' model can only end when it is possible to incorporate all the diverse factors which affect mankind.

Implementation of Operations Research in Hospitals

The extent of the literature on OR in the hospital service shows clearly that the profession has accepted the challenges presented by the management of such a complex entity. However, it would be pointless to deny that, despite considerable progress in some areas, many problems remain unsolved. The practical impact of OR on hospital administration has not, to date, been commensurate with the technical effort expended. Theoretical developments have outstripped practical applications.

The development of theories and of new approaches to existing problem areas which may have no immediate application are important parts of the growth of any science. This is as true in OR as it is in, for example, physics or engineering. Management scientists who discuss health service problems in purely theoretical terms can make an immensely valuable contribution in the long run through indicating the categories of problems that should be tackled, the type of data that should be collected, etc. Nevertheless, as has been pointed out by many writers, the all-important task of OR is not to try to evolve 'universal truths' from scientific experiment but to solve practical problems. No problem can be said to be fully solved until the proposed solution has been implemented and tested in the real world situation.

The general problems of implementation of OR in the health services have already been discussed in Chapter 2, but they deserve special mention in the hospital context. A number of authors have attempted to identify the barriers which have prevented fuller implementation of many of the OR studies that have been carried out in hospitals.[10] Ackoff has provided one of the most concise statements of the position, paraphrased by Stimson and Stimson who wrote:

> implementation is an integral part of Operations Research. The objective of OR is not simply to understand the organisation studied but to improve it and to enhance the organisation's ability to diagnose and prescribe for its ills. Hence one result of intervention in an organisation should be a strengthening of its ability to solve its own current and future ills.[11]

It is to be hoped that, as OR workers and, equally important, hospital decision makers, come to appreciate what the barriers to successful implementation are and how these can be overcome, a greater proportion of OR projects in hospitals will culminate in successful implementation, i.e. both to improve the organisation and to enhance its ability further to improve itself. I believe that this is starting to happen.

Many reasons have been suggested in the literature to explain why OR projects have not been implemented, but they all tend to fall into one or more of the following categories:

1. the special peculiarities of the hospital system;
2. the approach adopted by the OR team;
3. the attitude of the hospital staff who will be involved in any implementation process.

These are not, of course, mutually exclusive categories. The approach adopted by the OR team must, if its work is to have any chance of success, take account of the features peculiar to the hospital system. At the same time, its approach will be affected by the attitude of the staff and this attitude will, in turn, be affected by the team's approach. Any group of OR workers who think that their task is finished when they have produced and tested a model of the situation or who are not prepared to spend a large proportion, perhaps the greater part, of the total project time on the implementation of their findings will rarely discover that their work brings about any real change.

Probably the most important single requirement for successful implementation is the involvement, at every stage, of the staff likely to be affected. Most people's natural reaction is to resist change. This is especially true if such change is seen to be imposed by an outside source and when the reasons for it may not be fully understood. It has been shown, time and again, that real headway towards implementation has been achieved only when a proper rapport between the OR team and the hospital staff has been firmly established. This involvement of the hospital staff, at all levels, must begin at the very earliest stage of the project. Before any work is carried out, the OR analyst must ensure not only that the problem he proposes to examine is a real one but that it is perceived as being real and important by those affected. Failure to do this may lead to the work being regarded as an intellectual exercise with no practical significance. On the other hand, close involvement of those concerned will create a feeling of team effort and will ensure that the staff are made to feel part of the solution. No solution, irrespective of its merits, will be implemented unless the people involved wish to make it work. As Revans has said, in discussing the problems of organisation and management in hospitals, 'while help is available, salvation will not be by outside experts'.[12]

In proposing any change, OR workers must be fully aware of the
criteria and constraints imposed by the organisation under study. In the
hospital environment there are many decision makers, but all have
limited powers. Thus, any organisational change, beyond the most
trivial, cannot be implemented by edict but only through the consensus
of a number of such decision makers. It must also be remembered that
the criteria of desirability used by the decision makers may differ and
that their assessment of the potential outcomes of proposed changes
will frequently have moral, social and ethical dimensions. It is also
important that the analyst makes himself aware of the financial,
administrative and political constraints which operate on the hospital,
so that he can distinguish clearly between what can readily be changed
and what cannot.

It can sometimes happen that, given the proper involvement of
hospital staff, the solution to the problem will be produced by the staff
themselves when the OR worker has persuaded them to consider the
situation from a different point of view and to try to identify the real
underlying causes rather than simply to look at its effects. (Gorman
describes a situation where this process took place.[13]) More often, the
OR worker will have to build some type of model of the situation,
frequently mathematical, in order to derive a 'solution'. In such cases it
remains essential that the hospital staff are kept fully involved, that the
model is explained to them, that the validity of any assumptions made
is tested against their judgement and that the correctness of any data
used is verified. In general, the model used should be as 'credible,
flexible and simple' as possible.[14]

While implementation of OR requires a great deal of effort from
the specialists in that field, it also requires an input from the hospital
staff themselves, especially, but not exclusively, from professionals
such as doctors and nurses. This may involve a change in how these
people view their job. They must realise that, although they have been
trained in the care of the sick and this is their basic vocation, the
carrying out of this vocation involves a management function. Those
in the caring profession are frequently responsible for expensive
resources and they must realise that it is in their interests and in the
interest of their patients that these resources are used as effectively
and efficiently as possible. It is necessary for them to appreciate that
no group is better placed than they to identify the basic problems which
exist and that they are the people who must be involved in arriving at
a solution to these problems.

Thus it is necessary, if OR is to play its full part in improving the effectiveness of the hospital service, that the professionals within that service have some appreciation of how this science can help to solve some of their problems. OR does not provide an easy road to problem solving but it is hoped that the examples given below of its applications in the hospital field will help, in some small way, in making hospital staff aware of the potential it has for assisting them to overcome at least some of their particular organisational difficulties and will encourage them to consider its use in their own organisations.

Review of Operations Research Applications in Hospitals

There is no such thing as an 'OR problem'; almost any organisational problem may be regarded as a potential area for the application of the problem-solving approach of operations research. Hence, it is difficult to construct a fully satisfactory classification system for OR projects which have been applied in the hospital context. Some writers have classified projects by the type of technique used but it is considered that such an approach would be inappropriate in the context of this book, where the main concern is to discuss the uses of OR rather than the technical details of the methods used.

Other authors have classified projects according to the areas of the hospital system in which they were applied. Stimson and Stimson, for instance, classify the projects that they discuss under seven headings:

1. scheduling in out-patient clinics;
2. staffing studies;
3. admissions, discharges and utilisation of in-patient facilities;
4. blood banking;
5. inventory control and menu planning;
6. computer applications and total hospital information system;
7. models of hospitals.[15]

Boldy and Clayden categorise the projects they have considered under six headings which have many similarities with the above list:

1. hospitals, general;
2. in-patient specialties;
3. out-patients;
4. hospital staff;
5. hospital support services;
6. discharge/admission policies, appointment systems, etc.

All such lists are to some extent arbitrary. While they help to show
the wide spectrum of hospital activities that have been investigated,
there have been a number of studies which do not fit exactly into any of
the above classifications. Also, such lists may imply that the majority of
OR studies concentrate on a single part of the system when, in fact,
much of the published work concentrates on the relationships between
some of the sections listed separately above, e.g. the influence of out-
patient scheduling on the support services, the effect of various staffing
policies on the utilisation of both in-patient and out-patient facilities, etc.

In what follows, no attempt has been made to use any formal
system of categorisation. I have chosen, in a fairly arbitrary fashion, a
few of the projects carried out in recent years where it appeared that
the OR teams provided information that was of real practical value to
the hospital staff. Emphasis has been placed on applied work, which
can be considered as falling into one of three groups:

1. projects which set out to solve a given problem in a given area, e.g.
   how to reduce a particular consultant's waiting list;
2. projects which are concerned with evaluating the effect of a proposed
   change prior to its implementation, e.g. the effect of increasing
   operating theatre facilities;
3. projects which develop systems models which allow the effect of
   various changes, some of which may not yet be under consideration,
   to be evaluated, e.g. models of maternity suites or X-ray departments.

Out-patient Scheduling

Much of the early work of operations research in hospitals was
concerned with scheduling attendances at out-patient clinics.[16] The
mathematical techniques of queuing theory were used to estimate the
effect on patient waiting time and on the idle time of medical staff of
various scheduling and appointment systems. More recent studies have
added to our knowledge of how these systems behave and have
demonstrated how an equitable balance may be struck which eliminates
excessive patient delays while ensuring that professional time is not
wasted. Generally, this can be achieved with minimal changes in the
operations of the clinic. However, long patient delays remain a feature
of many clinics today. This is one area which demonstrates clearly that
change will only come about with an alteration in the attitudes of
hospital staff.

Welch gives data from nine different hospitals covering 34 separate
clinics which demonstrate that in almost every one the doctor

commenced his clinic later than the scheduled time.[17] Yet, patients were given appointments as if the clinic commenced at the proper time and their appointments were given in blocks according to fixed rules which paid little attention to the probable length of consultation. There is some evidence to suggest that average waiting times have decreased somewhat since Welch's original work. However, a study carried out by the Nuffield Provincial Hospitals Trust commented that the difference in waiting times between clinics depended to a large extent on the degree of interest shown by physicians in the managerial affairs of the clinic.[18] This study showed that those clinics in which the medical staff recognised the importance of organisational matters had fewer long waits and less overcrowding than those where an OR study had demonstrated the technical feasibility of improving matters but where full implementation was thwarted by the lack of interest of the staff concerned.

Some of the improvements that can be achieved, using only the most rudimentary techniques, but given the full involvement of staff, have been described by Henderson.[19] This doctor, over a short period of time, recorded what was actually happening in his clinic and, on the basis of the results of these observations, he made some minor alterations in routine which resulted in a considerable improvement in the performance of his clinic. A comment from this paper is worth quoting: 'a doctor will obtain professional and emotional satisfaction from the effective clinical management of his patients . . . whoever does the organising needs to know rather than only to feel that things are going right'.

Wiseman describes another successful project which concentrated not on the time a patient spends in the clinic, but on the time he has to wait to get an appointment to attend.[20] This is one of the many projects carried out in the hospital service by the Institute for Operational Research (now renamed the Centre for Organisational and Operational Research). This project was concerned with the allocation of appointment dates for a surgical clinic, and again underlines the importance of the co-operation of the medical staff.

The traditional method used in this clinic was to divide referrals into three categories: high urgency (HU), medium urgency (MU) and low urgency (LU). This division was usually based on the information contained in the referral letter from the GP. Appointments were then made, taking account of those already given, so that HU patients were seen within the next week, MU patients as soon as possible after about three weeks and LU patients after about six weeks. The consultant was unhappy with this system because of the length of time some patients had to wait for an appointment and also because it led to large variations in clinic workload. A computer model was developed and tested which allowed the effects of various decision rules to be tried out. One rule which emerged and which was eventually put into use was to specify a maximum period rather than a minimum period within which each category of patient would be seen. When these periods were set at one, four and eight weeks for the three categories of patients, it was found that not only did the delay in seeing patients decrease but the clinic workload was much more even. In addition, the system was very easy to operate.

In-patient Scheduling

Admissions of patients to hospitals as in-patients fall into two categories:

1. emergency admissions;
2. scheduled admissions.

Hospital staff have no control over the first of these but must arrange the admission policies for the second group and the discharge policy for both so that, while medical criteria are satisfied, there will be the necessary capacity to deal with the unpredictable level of emergency admissions. They must also ensure that expensive hospital facilities are utilised as fully as possible. Milsum, Turban and Vertinsky identify three interacting control variables in this process, i.e. bed occupancy levels, stability of patient flows and patient mix selection.[21] High bed occupancy rates are often taken as an indicator that the hospital is using its 'plant' effectively but this mitigates against the ability of the hospital to meet the demand for emergency admission. Stability of patient flow is an obvious ideal to aim for, while a proper patient mix is desirable if the many diverse resources within the hospital are to be properly utilised.

Most of the studies that have been carried out concentrate on bed occupancy, as this is the variable most easily controlled by any individual hospital. This is affected by a number of factors, such as average length of stay, demand from emergency admissions, and patient mix, but the bed occupancy rate, actual and predicted, will be a decisive factor in deciding on the policy for scheduled admissions.

Webb, Stevens and Bramson have discussed the difficulties of accurately forecasting the actual bed occupancy for any reasonable period into the future.[22] Their investigations indicate that the errors in forecasting admissions and discharges beyond about two days are so great that scheduled admissions can seldom be used as a control mechanism, except perhaps in the cancellation of admissions already arranged.

Kao and Pokladnik, however, have proposed a relatively simple forecasting method which allows for exogenous factors such as holidays, capacity changes and other exceptional factors to be incorporated with the minimum of effort.[23] Since such exceptional factors are neglected by most of the standard forecasting techniques, they claim that their model must improve forecast accuracy. Their method is an adaptive forecasting technique with the exogenous factors included by making simple changes to a few parameters. They illustrate their method applied to the bed census in a hospital in Texas and the figures quoted for a one-year period show close agreement between actual data and short-term forecasts. The authors claim that the method also gives satisfactory forecasts for longer terms.

A number of OR approaches have been used in an effort to control the admission of non-emergency patients to hospitals, or at least to estimate the effect of various policies. Many of these have been theoretical in nature but some serve a useful purpose in providing an insight into how the daily census would react to various policies. For instance, Young used queuing theory and simulation to estimate the differences that would result from a policy of admitting a fixed number of non-emergency patients each day irrespective of the daily census and a policy which admitted whatever number of patients was necessary to bring the census to a fixed, pre-determined level.[24] Kolster,[25] Smith and Solomon[26] and Bithell,[27] among others, have tested a variety of policies using a number of different measures of effectiveness.

Perhaps results which are of more immediate, but less general, applicability are those produced by Fetter and Thompson as a result of experiments with a simulation model of a maternity suite.[28] Using actual hospital data, they investigated the effect of increasing the rate of admissions. They found in one hospital that a 25 per cent increase in the number of admissions could be dealt with using existing labour and delivery facilities but that, unless the number of other beds available could also be increased, the percentage of patients who would not find facilities available immediately on admission would increase from 1 per cent to 8 per cent. They also investigated the effect of increasing the number of scheduled admissions, i.e. elective inductions, from its current level of zero. Their results indicated that the method of scheduling, rather than the number of such admissions, was the most important parameter. If 10 per cent of admissions were scheduled with one or two inputs per day, an increase in beds provided would probably be necessary. However, if a number of admissions per day is used with fewer patients per admissions, an important smoothing effect is achieved and up to 20 per cent of patients for elective inductions could be handled with a slight decrease in the number of beds required.

Luckman and Murray describe another study carried out by the Institute for Operational Research concerning the best admissions policy for a gynaecology department in a hospital in Portsmouth, England.[29] This study was carried out in collaboration with a group of surgeons and was prompted by the decision to pool beds between different consultant teams. Although bed occupancy rate was taken as the main measure of workload, it was recognised that the admissions policy of any surgical unit depends upon the time-table of operating theatre sessions. The study showed how the peak occupancy of beds could be reduced and less variability in rates of bed occupancy through the week could be achieved by relatively minor changes in the operating theatre schedule. This project also showed how, by a formal but simple analysis of patient data, the day-to-day control of the unit could be improved and also how it could assist with longer-term planning.

Organisation of Hospital In-patient Facilities

The efficient use of in-patient facilities is of obvious importance in improving the over-all effectiveness of the service provided by any hospital. OR studies have been applied to many such facilities.

Perhaps one of the most interesting applications is that described by Gorman, not only because of the rather unique role played by the OR worker but also because it shows how the hospital staff themselves can arrive at methods of improving the use of facilities.[30] In this case the role of the OR scientist was that of educator and guide rather than that of problem solver.

During the rebuilding of the existing Sydney Hospital in Australia the opportunity was taken to examine the traditional methods and procedures of operation being used. The OR consultant employed to assist with this task decided to involve all staff as deeply as possible in the study from the initial stages. His philosophy was that any ideas and/or solutions which came from the staff themselves stood a better chance of being implemented than any suggested by him.

He began with the ward sisters and, after some weeks of informal discussions and introductory talks, a more structured series of seminars was held which attempted to identify the practical problems in running a ward — these ranged from the trivial to the fundamental. Under the guidance of the OR consultant, the sisters were then encouraged to concentrate on the underlying causes of these problems. Gradually, the participants identified examples of conflicting objectives, poor delegation, planning weaknesses, etc. From this, it was a relatively short step for the sisters to suggest improved management processes to deal with specific situations. The nett result was the introduction of a number of innovations which included a ward accounting system for items such as linen, food, dressings, etc. and a system of assessing quality of nursing care to improve staff utilisation. Not only did this involvement improve the morale of the sisters but it had other practical results, such as allowing an extra ward to be opened without employing any additional staff, simply by removing imbalances in existing staffing levels.

The same approach was adopted with other groups of staff, with beneficial results. Better communications between the different levels of management and different disciplines were achieved, nursing turnover fell by nearly 50 per cent, the number of patients treated rose by over 50 per cent and the cost per patient treated fell, despite high inflation rates. This project, which lasted some three years, illustrates how OR intervention can assist an organisation to diagnose and cure its own ills.

Another study which emphasises the importance of the involvement of hospital staff but which entailed some more sophisticated OR models is reported by Barber[31] and by Sharatt, Jennings and Barber.[32] This was carried out in the London Hospital and was undertaken at the request of the anaesthetists who were worried about the ability of existing staff levels to provide a satisfactory service in the face of growing demands on the hospital's anaesthetic services, arising from developments of intensive therapy units and cardiac arrest services. It was found that the anaesthetic emergency service could be represented as a multi-channel, non-pre-emptive priority queuing system. The solution of this model allowed various duty rotas to be compared and one which gave the best service level under the conditions imposed to be chosen. It was found that a better emergency service could be provided by pooling all staff at the main hospital site instead of dispersing them among a number of annexes and also that, by means of a slight rearranging of rotas, the day-time cover could be greatly improved at the expense of a slight worsening of the night cover. The authors of these papers also comment on the less tangible results of this study which included an increased awareness by the staff of the effects of their decisions, not only on a particular department but throughout the hospital system as a whole.

Bryers and Collings have also used queuing theory to estimate the number of maternity beds that would be required over the next decade in a Scottish hospital.[33] This was a city hospital situated in an area with an increasing population and in which two existing small rural hospitals were scheduled for closing. Given that no more than 5 per cent of patients should find the maternity ward full on admission, the authors showed that it would be necessary to increase the number of labour beds from the existing level of five to nine. This finding was accepted by management. In addition, the authors showed that the number of post-natal beds would have to be increased from 65 to at least 90 and possibly to 100.

The same team was asked to examine the situation in another maternity hospital where the staff felt that they were short of beds. A method similar to that used in the previous project confirmed that there was an inadequate number of beds, but only in the post-natal ward; the labour ward had sufficient capacity to cope with an increase in demand of 16 per cent.

At the same hospital, consultants complained about the delay in admitting inductions into the labour ward. By using simulation, a number of policies were examined, but in each case it was shown that the number of beds was more than adequate. Eventually, the problem was identified to be one of staff shortage rather than bed shortage.

Hospital Support Services

The efficient operation of any hospital depends on a large number of support services which range from the paramedical departments such as X-ray and laboratory through 'hotel' services such as catering, cleaning and laundry to 'commercial' services like the purchasing and storing of supplies. These areas have not been neglected by OR scientists.

The case study which concludes this chapter describes in some detail an investigation of an X-ray department; other aspects of the management of such departments have been discussed elsewhere.[34]

Hospitals carry large amounts of a vast variety of items and, since scientific inventory management has been relatively common in industry for many years, it is to be expected that some effort would have been devoted to transferring these methods to the management of hospital stocks. There are, however, a number of problems in directly transferring the techniques developed in industry to the control of inventory in hospitals. While it may make financially sound sense for an industrialist to plan for a service level somewhat less than 100 per cent, a hospital must be certain that it has particular products, such as drugs, always available when requested. Thus, the level of 'safety stock' of many items tends to be relatively high. In one area in which the author has worked, there is a general policy that a minimum of two months' supply of all pharmaceutical products will be held.

Another major problem is that in many countries where hospitals are financed from the public purse, such as Britain, there is no explicit 'cost of capital' shown in any accounts, i.e. units suffer no financial penalty for keeping excessive amounts of money tied up in inventory. Since traditional inventory models are designed to minimise the total inventory cost, of which cost of capital is a major component, it has been argued that these models are not applicable in the health services.

Duncan and Norwich have proposed a method which takes direct cognisance of this fact and simply determines the inventory policy which minimises ordering costs only subject to a maximum allowable stock level.[35] This approach has been criticised by a number of people, including hospital supplies officers, mainly on the basis that, irrespective of what the formal accounts show, money tied up in inventory does represent a real cost.[36] Therefore, prudent management should strive to keep stocks at the level that incurs minimum costs consistent with providing the desired level of service.

Flagle[37] used regression analysis to show how the total linen inventory in a hospital could be reduced, while Kilpatrick and Freund[38] investigated the problem of how many oxygen tanks should be kept to meet different demand patterns.

Smith, Gregory and Maguire, who were among the critics of the Duncan and Norwich approach, developed a simple stock control system based on traditional ideas of inventory control and applied it in the hospital context.[39] This was implemented in some 20 hospital stores in Britain and showed average savings in space of the order of 10 per cent and estimated total achievable savings of some £1 million per annum (at 1975 prices). Other, less quantifiable advantages of the implementation of their approach were noted, such as improved control, and the enhanced quality of the data was of assistance in arranging supply contracts.

In the same paper the authors discuss a large-scale project concerned with the best type of stores system for hospitals. They showed that considerable cost savings could be achieved by having a central store for an area serving a number of hospitals. At the time of publication of this paper, the basic concept has been accepted but has been implemented only at local level. In an example quoted by Smith, an incomplete centralised system is estimated to have produced savings of about 7 per cent of the total cost of the supplies handled.

Luck, Luckman, Smith and Stringer report an application of OR to a different aspect of support services.[40] This work was concerned with the uneven workload forced on some of the paramedical departments because of the way out-patient clinics were organised. Not only does this project examine the interactions which exist between different parts of the hospital system, but it again shows how effective a relatively unsophisticated approach can be. The measure of variability of workload used was the coefficient of variation (CV), i.e. the mean number of requests per day received by a given department divided into the standard deviation. The workload on each of a number of service departments arising from each of the clinics was measured and a computer programme written which allowed the changes in this load, caused by various proposed changes in the clinic time-table, to be demonstrated. Examples are given of how the CV in all service departments but one was reduced by amounts varying from 13 per cent to 30 per cent by such simple expedients as a consultant moving his clinic from one half-day to another or a consultant reversing the days on which he saw old and new patients. The single service department where CV was not improved suffered an increase from 18 per cent to nearly 19 per cent.

An interesting application of OR to the problems of the physical location of clinics is described by Elshafei.[41] This work was implemented in a Cairo hospital where the out-patient department consisted of 17 clinics. The demand on these clinics had been increasing and, since there was a considerable movement of patients from the reception area to individual clinics and also between clinics, considerable congestion was occurring. The problem was to find a way to relocate these clinics within the existing building so that the total distance travelled by patients would be minimised, thus reducing the congestion.

The problem was formulated as a quadratic assignment model with the objective of minimising the total over-all flow, measured in patient metres. Elshafei's solution not only produced a reallocation of clinics which reduced the total patient metres travelled per year by 19 per cent but also succeeded in meeting certain medical objectives which management were keen to satisfy in the new layout.

Modelling a Diagnostic X-Ray Department — a Case Study

Introduction

The previous section was designed to illustrate the range of OR applications in hospitals. This section describes, in rather more detail, part of a study of the organisation of an X-ray department in a general hospital in which the author was involved.[42]

The diagnostic X-ray department is one of the major sub-systems of any hospital and also one of the most complex. This complexity arises both from the type of service provided, i.e. a wide variety of types of examinations, and from the extent of its interactions with other parts of the hospital system. A larger proportion of all classes of patient who enter the hospital system utilises the services of this department than those of any other medical or paramedical department. Thus, such a department is highly sensitive to changes in other parts of the hospital, while internal organisational changes within an X-ray department can have considerable effects throughout the hospital. However, both the internal and external interactions are so complex that the effects of such changes are difficult to assess in advance without some idea of how the department operates as a system.

A simulation model, called SIMRAD, was constructed in an attempt to provide such information. The model can deal with a stochastic flow of patients from a number of different sources, such as different wards, various out-patient clinics, etc., each of which will require different types of service. It also allows for a combination of different types of machines and a varying number of staff. Facilities exist to deal with patients both with and without appointments.

The model also makes an attempt to include some of the human factors that can have such an important effect on the smooth running of a department. It allows not only for such obvious elements as staff rest and meal periods but also for such factors as the natural tendency for staff to prefer to use certain machines rather than others, although all may be equally efficient. The model was tested using data from one particular hospital in Ireland but has been written so that it can be applied to other hospitals with the minimum of alteration.

The radiography department in any general hospital is essentially a waiting line system with patients forming the inputs and one or more X-ray examinations representing the service provided. The service facilities consist of examination rooms manned by trained radiographers. However, even a cursory examination of the operation of such a department demonstrates the existence of a number of factors which would invalidate any attempt to represent the system by a simple analytical model.

The inputs do not form a single stream, as patients come from a number of unrelated sources and thus generate a number of parallel and independent input streams, each with its own characteristics and subject to different levels of control. For instance, the arrival of casualty patients, which, because of hospital policy, is not subject to any control, demonstrates a random, but quite stable pattern. At the other end of the spectrum, there are patients with appointments whose rate of arrival is rigidly controlled. Between these extremes are patients from out-patient clinics and those from the wards of the hospital itself. Arrivals of the former group are basically random but occur only within certain periods dictated by clinic time-tables, while the rate of arrival of the latter groups can be controlled, but only to a limited extent, by the radiology department itself.

The main service required by the arrivals consist of one or more X-ray examinations. In addition, some arrivals will require a subsidiary service facility in the form of changing cubicles. All patients enter a single waiting line. In theory, the queue discipline is first-in-first-out but this order is more frequently broken than adhered to. Before a service can commence, an examination room (and a cubicle if required), together with a radiographer, must be available. Typically, a trained radiographer can perform any examination. However, examination rooms are not all equipped in the same way, so that only a sub-set of the rooms is suitable for any given patient's requirements. While the model can assign the first radiographer who is free to the patient at the head of the queue, this patient cannot be examined unless one of the rooms which is available suits his examination requirements. Therefore, a particular patient may be served out of turn if a room suitable for his requirements, but not for those ahead of him in the waiting line, becomes available. The suitability of the room is a function of the examination required which, in turn, is a function of the source of the patient. It has also been observed, in practice, that a radiographer, if faced with a choice of suitable rooms, will have a 'favourite room'. A realistic model must take cognisance of this fact.

Another factor often ignored in models of this type is that the time at which a radiographer or a room becomes available does not necessarily coincide with the end of an examination. When an examination is completed, the patient can be dismissed from the system, but frequently certain work has to be performed in the room before another patient can use it. Similarly, each radiographer has certain duties to perform in relation to the last patient she has examined, such as checking films, dealing with records, etc., before she is free to deal with another patient. Only when these operations have been completed is either the room or the radiographer free to accept another patient.

Input to the Model

From a detailed study of one particular department,[43] it was concluded that the following input data were the minimum required by the model if an acceptable level of realism was to be achieved:

1. a description of the arrival pattern of patients;
2. the distribution of examination requirements;
3. the distribution of durations of each type of examination;
4. the availability and suitability of examination rooms;
5. the number of radiographers and a time-table giving their availability.

The values these data take vary from department to department. Hence, before the model can be applied in any given situation, an empirical investigation of the operations of that particular department will be necessary.

Patients can be divided into separate streams, depending on the source from which they come, i.e. different out-patient clinics, casualty, in-patients, etc. The model describes the rate of arrival of patients by means of statistical distributions derived from an analysis of the data relating to the particular department being studied. This rate can be varied as required by using a number of sessions for each source and any source can be shut down at any time if, for instance, a particular out-patient clinic is not operating on a given day or part of a day. In this way the model can be informed of changes in other parts of the hospital. Information can also be supplied about the appointments that have been made for any particular day.

The probability of a patient requiring a given type of examination is a function of the source from which he comes. These probabilities are provided to the model, together with statistical distributions of the time required to complete any given examination, which is also a random variable. Finally, information is provided on which rooms are suitable for which type of examination and what the 'popularity rating' of each room is in the eyes of the staff. Any number of radiographers can be supplied and for each a time-table of scheduled breaks is input to the model.

Structure of the Model

The model increments time from event to event, where an event is defined as any set of conditions which may change the current state of any of the status variables.

The two main events in the system are:

1. the arrival of a new patient;
2. the departure of a patient on completion of an examination.

However, the occurrence of either of these main events depends on a number of subsidiary events which are as follows:

3. a source comes into operation;
4. a session ends;
5. an examination room becomes available;
6. a radiographer becomes available;
7. a radiographer's rest period commences.

Arrivals are generated from each source independently and hence the over-all rate of arrival depends on the number of sources in operation at any given time. Different sources come into operation at different times and the model will not generate an arrival from a particular source until a preset time is reached. Similarly, if during the time that a source is in operation a session ends, then the mean inter-arrival time will change and the generation of arrivals takes account of this. If any arrival is generated at a time outside of a current session, the model suppresses this arrival.

As already indicated, a room cannot generally be used for another patient as soon as it is vacated by the previous patient. A certain amount of time must be allowed for preparation and so on (referred to as LAG in the model). Thus event (5) above will not occur until LAG minutes after event (2).

Similarly, a radiographer who has finished one examination will have certain duties to perform in respect to that patient's records, films, etc., and so will not be available until CHECK minutes after event (2). Thus, the time that a patient's examination begins depends on the occurrence of both events (5) and (6) above. Finally, in order to simulate the availability of the radiographers as realistically as possible, the model makes allowances for radiographers' lunch breaks and other rest periods. Hence a radiographer may not be engaged in examinations but will still be unavailable for allocation because she is on a scheduled rest period. Event (7) above allows the correct action to be taken in this situation.

The model can be used to simulate as many days of operation as required and at the end of a run outputs a wide variety of statistics relating to the number of patients, patient waiting time, utilisation of facilities, etc. The validity of the model was checked against some data collected in the particular department being studied. While perfect correspondence between simulated and actual data was not, of course, found, the results indicated that the model did replicate reality reasonably well and with sufficient accuracy to allow it to be used for planning purposes.

Model Experiments

This model was designed not to test any one particular theory but to provide planners with a tool which would allow them to assess the probable impact of a large variety of possible changes. Many experiments are possible and the results of a few of these are outlined below.

Effect of Changing the Number of Radiographers. It seems intuitively obvious that patient mean waiting time (MWT) will decrease as the number of radiographers (RAD) is increased. However, the model showed that the relationship is by no means straightforward. The marginal effect of a change in RAD depends not only on the absolute number of staff on duty but also, of course, on the length of time that a radiographer spends between examinations checking records, etc. (CHECK) and, to a lesser extent, on the length of time an examination room is unavailable between examinations (LAG). Figures 7.1 and 7.2 illustrate the results of some experiments.

If CHECK = 2 minutes and LAG = 3 minutes, an addition of one radiographer to a staff of three will decrease MWT by about 45 per cent but the addition of the same radiographer to a staff of six will have virtually no effect. The difference is even greater if CHECK = 4 minutes, when increasing the staff level from three to four will decrease MWT by approximately two-thirds. The percentage decrease of MWT due to an increase in the number of radiographers is constant for any fixed value of LAG but the absolute value of MWT is affected by a change in LAG. For instance, four radiographers, with a lag time of one minute, will achieve a 16 per cent improvement in MWT compared with that of five radiographers, with a lag time of three minutes. Even greater reductions in MWT can be achieved by reducing the value of CHECK. Four radiographers can achieve a decrease in MWT in excess of 40 per cent

Figure 7.1: Patient Mean Waiting Time (MWT) According to Number of
Radiographers and CHECK, for LAG = 1 Minute

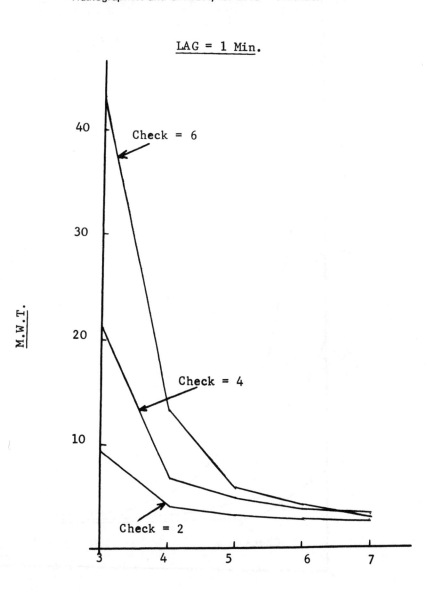

LAG = 1 Min.

M.W.T.

Check = 6

Check = 4

Check = 2

NUMBER OF RADIOGRAPHERS

Figure 7.2: Patient Mean Waiting Time (MWT) According to Number of
Radiographers and CHECK, for LAG = 3 Minutes

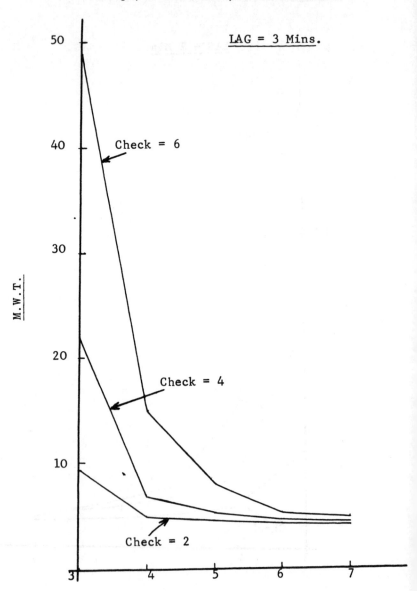

by decreasing CHECK from four to two minutes. Thus the model demonstrates the extent to which a decrease in the mean waiting time of patients can be achieved by actions other than providing additional staff.

'Optimum' Number of Radiographers. Whilst it is obvious that an increase in the staffing level will decrease patient waiting time, it will also increase staff idle time. Thus some balance must be struck between these factors. For the purpose of this experiment, the 'optimum' number of radiographers was defined as the number which minimised the total of patient waiting time and the time during which radiographers are not engaged in examinations. Again, it was found that this depended on the values given to LAG and CHECK but, using values of three and four minutes for these two parameters, it was found that four radiographers gave the best balance. Figure 7.3 illustrates the results.

Effect of Room Usage on Patient Mean Waiting Time. As already mentioned, it had been observed that staff had preferences for certain rooms for a given examination. While SIMRAD allowed staff to use the 'most popular' room if it was available, it always ensured that a patient was allocated to a suitable room that was free, even if this happened to be the least 'popular'. There was some suggestion that this did not happen in reality. A run was made which output, for each of the rooms, the numbers of patients who had one examination only and no repeats. This output was compared with some of the survey data collected. For a number of technical reasons, these data were not exactly comparable with the simulated data, since the survey figures included weekend arrivals which are not included in the model. However, despite the limitations, the results show that the model does allocate patients to rooms more evenly than occurred in reality. For instance, chest X-rays could be performed in Rooms 1, 2 or 3. In the survey, 74 per cent of such examinations were performed in Room 3, 24 per cent in Room 2 and 2 per cent in Room 1; the corresponding figures from the model were 43 per cent, 42 per cent and 15 per cent. In a similar manner, examinations of an extremity could be performed in either Room 3 or Room 4, the breakdown in reality being 12 per cent and 86 per cent, while the model allocated the examinations in the ratio 45:55.

Similar results were obtained for other examinations and the over-all conclusion was that patients were being asked to wait unnecessarily until the more popular rooms became available, although other viable rooms were free. Thus MWT could be decreased by a change of attitude on the part of the staff.

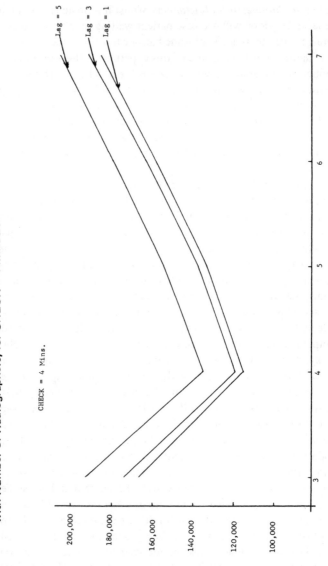

Figure 7.3: Variation in Radiographers' Non-examination Time plus Patients' Waiting Time, with Number of Radiographers, for CHECK = 4 Minutes

Sensitivity of the System to Changes in Demand. The model was run with various decreases and increases in the number of patients examined and the effect on various parameters noted. While, obviously, fewer numbers of patients improved the system performance from the patients' point of view, the 'gain' from a percentage decrease in the number of patients is much less than the relative 'loss' from a corresponding increase. For instance, an 8 per cent decrease in patient numbers decreased MWT by 18 per cent but a 9 per cent growth in the number of patients increased this by about 39 per cent. The introduction of one extra radiographer will result in a 13 per cent decrease in MWT even with an increase of 11 per cent in the number of patients. However, when radiographer idle time is taken into account, the employment of an extra radiographer is not really justified until the increase in patient numbers is of the order of 20 per cent. At this stage, the extra radiographer can keep the MWT to a value only slightly in excess of its value with the current patient load.

Conclusion. The above examples represent only a small selection of the possible experiments that can be performed with this model. Not only does it provide management with a means of assessing the impact of future developments, but it increases their understanding of the impact of the complex interactions which currently exist. Some of the conclusions may be intuitively obvious to professionals in the field, but only with a model such as this can their effects be readily quantified.

Notes

1. D. Clayden and D. Boldy (eds.), *Current Operational Research Projects in Health and Welfare Services in the United Kingdom and Ireland* (Operational Research Society, Birmingham, 1977); R.A. Denison, R. Wild and M.J.C. Martin, *A Bibliography of Operations Research in Hospitals and Health Services* (Management Centre, University of Bradford, 1969); B.E. Fries, *The Application of Operations Research to the Hospital Complex*, Technical Report no. 92 (Department of OR, College of Engineering, Cornell University, 1969); D.H. Stimson and R.H. Stimson, *Operations Research in Hospitals, Diagnosis and Prognosis* (Hospital Research and Educational Trust, Chicago, 1972).
2. N.T.J. Bailey, 'A Study of Queues and Appointment Systems in Hospital Outpatient Departments with Special Reference to Waiting Times', *Journal of the Royal Statistical Society*, Series B (1952), p. 185; N.T.J. Bailey, 'Queueing for Medical Care', *Applied Statistics*, 3 (November 1954), p. 137; N.T.J. Bailey, 'Operational Research in Hospital Planning and Design', *Operational Research Quarterly*, 8 (September 1957), p. 149; J.D. Welch, 'Hospital Applications', *Operational Research Quarterly*, 3 (March 1952), p. 8; J.D. Welch, 'Some Research into the Organisation and Design of Hospital Outpatients Departments', *Journal of the Royal Sanitary Institute*, 72 (July 1952), p. 298; J.D. Welch and N.T.J. Bailey,

'Appointment Systems in Hospital Outpatient Departments', *Lancet* 1 (May 1952), p. 1105.

3.   C.D. Flagle, *Optimal Organisation and Facility for a Nursing Unit*, Progress Report (Operations Research Department, Johns Hopkins Hospital, Baltimore, 1960); C.D. Flagle, 'The Problem of Organisation for Inpatient Care', in C.W. Churchman and M. Verhulst (eds.), *Management Science; Models and Techniques*, vol. 2 (Pergamon Press, New York, 1960); C.D. Flagle, *The Progressive Care Hospital; Estimating Bed Needs*, Public Health Service Publications, no. 930 -c -2 (Government Printing Office, Washington, 1963).

4.   B.E. Fries, 'Bibliography of Operations Research in Health Care Systems', *Operations Research*, 25, 5 (September-October 1976), p. 801.

5.   B.E. Fries, 'Bibliography of Operations Research in Health Care Systems; An Update', *Operations Research*, 27, 2 (March-April 1979), p. 408.

6.   D. Boldy and D. Clayden, 'Operational Research Projects in Health and Welfare Services in the United Kingdom and Ireland', *Journal of the Operational Research Society*, 30, 6 (June 1979), p. 505.

7.   D.P. Rice and B.S. Cooper, 'National Health Expenditure 1929-1971', *Social Security Bulletin*, 35 (January 1972), p. 3.

8.   A . Merrison (Chairman), *Report of the Royal Commission on the National Health Service* (HMSO, London, 1979).

9.   H.H. Baligh and D.J. Laughhunn, 'An Economic and Linear Model of the Hospital', *Health Services Research*, 4 (Winter 1969), p. 293; R.B. Fetter and J.D. Thompson, 'A Decision Model for the Design and Operation of a Progressive Patient Care Hospital', *Medical Care*, 7 (November-December 1969), p. 450; M.D. Nasta, J.K. Beddow and R.A. Shapiro, 'A Deterministic Input-Output Model to Facilitate Management of a Hospital System', *Journal of the Operations Research Society of Japan*, 15 (March 1972), p. 19.

10.   B. Barber, 'Operational Research and Implementation at the London Hospital − Part I', *European Journal of Operational Research*, 1 (March 1977), p. 79; M.G. Simpson, 'Health', *Operational Research Quarterly*, 27 1(ii) (1976), p. 209; A.J. Singh and P.R.A. May, 'Acceptance of Operations Research/Systems Analysis in the Health Care Field', *Interfaces*, 7, 4 (August 1977), p. 79; Stimson and Stimson, *Operations Research in Hospitals*.

11.   Ibid., p. 67.

12.   R.W. Revans, 'Research into Hospital Management and Organisation', *Millbank Memorial Fund Quarterly*, Part 2, 44 (July 1964), p. 207.

13.   M.C. Gorman, 'The Sydney Hospital Experience', in B. Barber (ed.), *Selected Papers on Operational Research in the Health Services* (Operational Research Society, Birmingham, 1976), p. 89.

14.   E.P.C. Kao and F.M. Pokladnik, 'Incorporating Exogenous Factors in Adaptive Forecasting of Hospital Census', *Management Science*, 24, 6 (1978), p. 1677.

15.   Stimson and Stimson, *Operations Research in Hospitals*.

16.   See note 2.

17.   J.D. Welch, 'Appointment Systems in Hospital Outpatient Departments', *Operational Research Quarterly*, 15 (1964).

18.   Nuffield Provincial Hospitals Trust, *Waiting in Outpatient Departments* (Oxford University Press, London, 1965).

19.   K.M. Henderson, 'Some Aspects of Clinic Management', in Barber (ed.), *Selected Papers on Operational Research in the Health Services*, p. 161.

20.   H.C. Wiseman, 'Allocation of Outpatient Appointment Dates', in Barber (ed.), *Selected Papers on Operational Research in the Health Services*, p. 127.

21.   J.H. Milsum, E. Turban and I. Vertinsky, 'Hospital Admission Systems: Their Evaluation and Management', *Management Science*, 19, 6 (February 1973),

p. 646.

22. M. Webb, G. Stevens and C. Bramson, 'An Approach to Bed Occupancy in a General Hospital', *Operational Research Quarterly*, 28, 2(ii) (1977), p. 391.

23. Kao and Pokladnik, 'Exogenous Factors in Adaptive Forecasting of Hospital Census'.

24. J.P. Young, 'A Queueing Theory Approach to the Control of Hospital Inpatient Census', unpublished PhD thesis (n.d.), Johns Hopkins University.

25. P. Kolster, 'A Markovian Model for Hospital Admission Scheduling', *Management Science*, 16, 6 (1970).

26. W.C. Smith and M.B. Solomon, 'A Simulation of Hospital Admission Policy', *Communication of ACM*, 9, 5 (May 1966).

27. J.F. Bithell, 'A Class of Discrete Time Models for the Study of Hospital Admissions System', *Operations Research*, 17 (January–February 1969), p. 48.

28. R.B. Fetter and J.D. Thompson, 'The Simulation of Hospital Systems', *Operations Research*, 13 (September–October 1965), p. 689.

29. J. Luckman and F.A. Murray, 'Organising Inpatient Admission', in Barber (ed.), *Selected Papers on Operational Research in the Health Services*, p. 111.

30. Gorman, 'The Sydney Hospital Experience'.

31. Barber, 'Operational Research and Implementation at the London Hospital – Part 1'.

32. M. Sharat, A.M.C. Jennings and B. Barber, 'Staffing Levels for Emergency Anaesthetic Services', in Barber (ed.), *Selected Papers on Operational Research in the Health Services*, p. 195.

33. F. Bryers and T. Collings, 'Maternity Hospital Bed Requirements', paper presented to EURO Working Group, 'O.R. Applied to Health Services' (Dublin, 1979).

34. W.D. Jeans, S.R. Berget and R. Gibb, 'Computer Simulation Model of an X-ray Department', *British Medical Journal*, 1 (1972), p. 675; B. Lev, B.S. Caltagirone and F.J. Shee, 'Patient Flow and Utilisation of Resources in a Diagnostic Radiology Department', *Investigative Radiology* (1975), p. 517; P.C. O'Kane and A.D. Gough, 'An Evaluation of Patient Demand in a Hospital Radiology Department', *Hospital and Health Services Review*, 74, 7 (July 1978), p. 226.

35. I.B. Duncan and H.S. Norwich, 'Opportunity Costs and Inventory Theory in the Hospital Services', *Operational Research Quarterly*, 24 (i) (1973), p. 27.

36. Viewpoints, *Operational Research Quarterly*, 24, 4 (1973), p. 627.

37. Flagle, 'The Problem of Organisation for Inpatient Care'.

38. K.E. Kilpatrick and L.E. Freund, 'A Simulation of Tank Oxygen Inventory at a Community General Hospital', *Health Services Research*, 2 (1967), p. 298.

39. A.G. Smith, K. Gregory and J.D. Maguire, 'Operational Research for the Hospital Supply Service', *Operational Research Quarterly*, 2 (ii) (1975), p. 375.

40. G.M. Luck, J. Luckman, B.W. Smith and J. Stringer, *Patients, Hospitals and Operational Research* (Tavistock Publications, London, 1971).

41. A.H. Elshafei, 'Hospital Layout as a Quadratic Assignment Problem', *Operational Research Quarterly*, 28, 1(ii) (1977), p. 167.

42. Further details of this study may be found in P.C. O'Kane, *A Statistical Analysis of the Operation of a Hospital Radiology Department*, Occasional Paper (Department of Business Studies, Queens University, Belfast, 1974); P.C. O'Kane, 'A Planning Model in a General Hospital', paper presented to TIMS/EURO Conference, Athens, 1977; P.C. O'Kane, 'A Simulation Model of A Diagnostic Radiology Department', paper accepted for publication by *European Journal of Operational Research* (1980); O'Kane and Gough, 'An Evaluation of Patient Demand in a Hospital Radiology Department'.

43. See notes 34 and 42.

References

Balmforth, G.V. 'Clinician's Viewpoint', in B. Barber (ed.), *Selected Papers on Operational Research in the Health Service* (Operational Research Society, Birmingham, 1976), p. 171

Curnow, R.N. and D.G. Neal. *Report on the Work of the Unit — May 1967-June 1971* (OR (Health Services) Unit, Department of Applied Statistics, Reading, 1971)

Davies, R., D. Johnson and S. Farrow. 'Planning Patient Care with a Markov Model', *Operational Research Quarterly,* 26, 3 (1975), p. 599

Fetter, R.B. and J.D. Thompson. 'Patients' Waiting Time and Doctors' Idle Time in the Outpatient Setting', *Health Services Research,* 1 (Summer 1966), p. 66

Hosios, A.J., C.A. Laslo and M.D. Levine. 'A Model to Support Radiographic Equipment Allocation Decisions', *Journal of the Operational Research Society,* 29, 3 (1978), p. 204

Rockart, J.F. and P.B. Hofmann. 'Physician and Patient Behaviour under Different Scheduling Systems in a Hospital Outpatient Department', *Medical Care,* 7 (November-December 1969), p. 463

8 NURSE STAFFING MANAGEMENT

John Hershey, William Pierskalla and Sten Wandel

A great deal of attention has been given by operations researchers and industrial engineers during the past several decades to the nurse staffing problem — how to assign nursing staff to provide a desired level of patient care. This has been a natural area for research, because of the extent and high cost of nursing activities and the range of seemingly applicable operations research techniques available.

This area will become even more important in the future as hospital costs are subject to increasingly tighter public regulation. New reimbursement methods, which provide incentives to halt the escalation of costs, are being instituted. Output and process performance, rather than input resources, are increasingly being used as a basis for both reimbursement and inter-hospital comparison. Clearly, hospitals will continue to be under increasing pressure to bring about improved cost control. We believe that the development of innovative approaches to the organisation and management of nursing resources holds great promise for cost savings in the delivery of hospital services.

In this chapter we discuss quantitative procedures that have been developed to support nurse staffing activities. The strengths and deficiencies of these techniques are analysed, and extensions of certain techniques are suggested. A major difference between this review and those of Stimson and Stimson[1] and Aydelotte[2] is that the suggested procedures are viewed in the context of a conceptual framework of nurse staffing management. In addition, successfully applied procedures and methodologies are presented for those who wish to undertake further applications as well as those who wish to extend current knowledge.

The framework we propose includes five areas of management activity:

1. activity analysis and workload prediction;
2. tactical nurse staffing decisions — corrective allocations, shift scheduling and manpower planning;
3. performance monitoring;
4. strategic planning;
5. co-ordination with other hospital activities.

This framework provides a basis for pinpointing those activities and

189

aspects which have been largely overlooked by operations researchers and industrial engineers but which are potentially important for improving over-all nurse staff utilisation and performance.

After the framework is presented, we review studies which have analysed nursing activities and how the workload varies with the numbers and types of patients to be served. Methods developed to provide forecasts and demand and use rates are also discussed. The next section reviews quantitative procedures that have been developed to assist in making tactical nurse staffing decisions, and describes how these procedures can be integrated with performance monitoring, strategic planning and other hospital activities as well. The final section summarises our major conclusions and suggests areas where more research and development seem desirable.

We have found that the great bulk of nurse staffing research has concentrated on activity analysis and workload prediction, and on two of the three levels of tactical nurse staffing decisions − corrective allocations and shift scheduling. There has been little examination of potential improvements in the third tactical decision level − manpower planning − or of the interrelationships among the three levels. Finally, minimal attention has been given to improving performance monitoring, strategic planning, or co-ordination with other hospital activities such as admission and treatment scheduling.

It is our hope that this chapter will serve several purposes:

1. it should guide future nurse staffing research toward more comprehensive and fruitful problem-solving approaches;
2. it should give hospital systems analysts a good appreciation of the state-of-the-art and help them select procedures which might be applicable in their own setting;
3. it should help hospital administrators identify areas where, although no ready-made solutions are currently available, they might want to support specific studies in their own hospitals;
4. because it focuses on a major manpower administration aspect of health care, it should provide a basis for developing comprehensive plans for the care of patients and for determining the most effective facilities in which to provide patient care.

The Nurse Staffing Process

The nurse staffing process can be conceptualised as a hierarchy of three tactical decision levels which operate over different time horizons and with different precision. These three decision levels will be called corrective allocations, shift scheduling and manpower planning.

Within a shift, the staff capacities among units may be adjusted to unpredicted demand fluctuations and absenteeism by using float, part-time, relief, pulling, overtime and voluntary absenteeism. ('Float' refers to a pool of cross-trained nurses who are floated among units to smooth demand fluctuations; 'pulling' refers to the temporary reallocation of a nurse to a unit other than the one where she normally works.) These 'corrective allocations' should be based upon the individual's preferences and capabilities, and they are restricted by shift schedules and the employees' capabilities.

The second decision level is 'shift scheduling', i.e. uniform and smooth matching between expected workload and staff capacity among units on a week-to-week and day-to-day basis. For each employee days on and off, as well as shift rotation and time for classes, are determined. The individual's preferences should be considered to bring about high personnel satisfaction and one should ensure that personal capabilities are made use of in the best way.

These two 'scheduling' levels concern the utilisation of personnel already existing within the organisation; they have a known mix of specialisation and experience. However, the long-term balance of numbers and capability of nursing personnel among units is obtained by hiring, training, transferring between jobs and discharging. We call this decision level 'manpower planning'. Because of the time-lags involved, manpower-planning actions should be taken early to meet anticipated long-term fluctuations in demand and supply. As we shall see, very few studies have addressed this decision level.

The vital interdependence of the three levels must be recognised in order to bring about systematic nurse staffing improvements. Each level is constrained by available resources, by previous commitments made at higher levels and by the degree of flexibility for later correction at lower levels. Therefore, each decision level is strongly dependent on the other two; one level should not simply be considered in isolation.

In general, the later a decision is made the more reliable the available information is, but the alternatives that remain are fewer in number and generally more expensive. Hence, there is a trade-off between early and inexpensive actions based upon unreliable information (e.g. transferring) *v*. late and expensive corrections made when more reliable information is available (e.g. using overtime). This trade-off can be likened to the balance between fire prevention and fire-fighting capability.

Furthermore, decisions at each level should be co-ordinated not only with decisions at the other two levels, but also with future and past events within the level itself. Co-ordination with the future should be accomplished through the planning stages: forecasting, tentative planning, action planning and execution. All of the uncontrollable or partially controllable variables that have a major influence on the staffing process have to be forecast. Examples of these variables are workloads for each skill category, hiring prospects, turnover and absenteeism. However, the planning process at each level should be dependent on the other two. The plans can be said to be 'gliding' or 'rolling'. That is, an action plan for one level should be the basis for a tentative plan for the level below, and they should be updated and made firmer as execution is approached and more information becomes available.

These three decision levels are depicted in Figure 8.1. It can be seen from this figure that there are important interactions between these tactical nurse staffing decision levels and other management activities. As shown in the box at the left of Figure 8.1, co-ordination with the past should be accomplished through a monitoring system, which should: (a) take an inventory — number and capabilities — of employed personnel; (b) measure, control, evaluate and correct staffing performance ;and (c) gather statistics to be used as a basis for forecasting.

There are also important strategic policy and design decisions taken in a hospital that restrict the number of alternatives available at each of the three tactical decision levels. This aspect is depicted in the box at the top of Figure 8.1. Examples might include policies about the use of float personnel, the control of admissions, the skill mix of the nursing personnel, or the number of nurses in the training pool at any one point in time. These policies should be part of any investigation into new methods to improve productivity. The impact upon cost, quality and satisfaction of the policies in use should be recognised by the administrator; only then can the long-run value of maintaining them be intelligently assessed. Hence, the strategic planning level forms a decision level of its own which (a) dictates the range of options available in each of the three tactical decision levels, (b) sets the standards to be used for performance evaluation, and (c) makes policy and design decisions for all hospital functions.

We have stressed the importance of recognising the interdependence among the three tactical decision levels as well as among strategic, tactical, forecasting and monitoring activities. However, it is equally important to consider the interdependence between nurse staffing and the other hospital activities, shown at the right of Figure 8.1. Each

Figure 8.1: The Nurse Staffing System

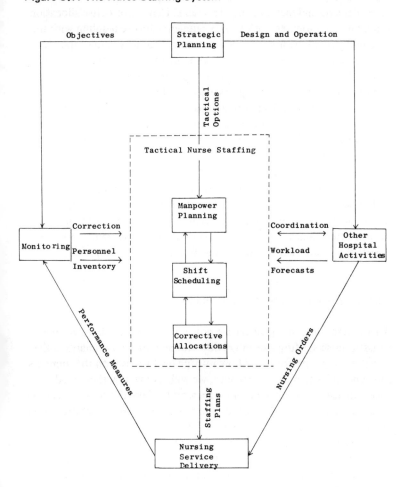

nurse staffing level should co-operate with equivalent and related levels in the demand and facility control systems. That is, corrective allocation should be co-ordinated with task assignment; shift scheduling with the scheduling of admissions, operation rooms, treatment and supportive services; and manpower planning with budgeting, recruitment, training and facility planning. Gross imbalances among these activities are common, due to a lack of organisational and motivational incentives for co-ordination. This reflects ambiguous and sometimes conflicting objectives based on traditional and strong value systems. Unfortunately, most studies have omitted these crucial horizontal interdependencies.

In summary, the nurse staffing process can be conceptualised as a hierarchy of three highly interdependent tactical decision levels that are restricted by strategic decisions. Staffing decisions should be co-ordinated with other hospital activities and the performance of the staffing process should be measured and evaluated frequently in order to obtain over-all staffing effectiveness. (For greater elaboration of this framework, see Abernathy, Baloff and Hershey[3] and Wandel and Hershey.[4])

Activity Analysis and Workload Prediction

Before examining the quantitative procedures that have been proposed to assist nurse staffing, we will review studies which have analysed the activities nurses perform and how nursing load varies with the numbers and types of patients. In particular, we will review how these studies have been used to develop methods for workload prediction — a necessary input into any planning or scheduling procedure. (See Aydelotte for an extensive discussion of this literature.[5])

For each tactical decision level — corrective allocation, shift scheduling and manpower planning — the activity analysis and workload prediction needs vary with respect to the amount of detail required and the corresponding accuracy of the workload measures given by skill level on each nursing unit. On a shift basis, the actual patient mix and illness severity along the many dimensions which affect staffing needs must be accurately predicted at the beginning of the shift in order to allocate available personnel appropriately. On a daily and weekly basis, the average workload and minimum staffing needs on each shift must be predicted with cyclic and/or seasonal patterns in order to build 2, 4, 6 or 8-week work schedules for the personnel on each unit. Finally, on a monthly, quarterly, semi-annual and annual basis, the average workload and minimum staff by skill levels must be predicted, based on trends, seasonal patterns and other hospital activities, in order to follow appropriate hiring, training and staffing policies.

Staffing Based upon Average Patient Requirements

For many years, it was assumed that nursing units should make staffing decisions for each specialty unit (e.g. medicine, surgery and obstetrics) by multiplying the average number of nursing hours required per patient by the number of patients (see Stimson and Stimson[6]). As early as 1940, Pfefferkorn and Rovetta used this approach[7] and similar procedures were developed by the American Hospital Association[8] and George and Kuehn.[9]

In 1947, the National League of Nursing Education developed a patient classification scheme for the care of pediatric patients.[10] An attempt was made to relate the amount of nursing time required to this classification but the times were not sufficiently refined to provide a sensitive tool for staffing needs.

Bernstein *et al.*,[11] Binhammer *et al.*[12] and Claussen[13] assigned patients to categories according to their individual needs for direct nursing care, and the time requirements for direct nursing care per patient in each category were also established. Then the average mix of patients was determined for each unit and average staffing requirements were also calculated. These requirements were assumed to remain constant overtime when used as a basis for staffing.

In the 1950s, work sampling and time study were introduced to clarify the various functions that nurses of different categories perform and to determine the skill levels required to perform these tasks, and, for each personnel category, the proportion of time devoted to tasks above or below the category's skill level. If there were striking deviations from what was expected, changes could be made in the organisation and operation of the nursing units.[14]

Activity Studies Based on Direct Care Indices

In the late 1950s and early 1960s, a group at Johns Hopkins University revealed wide swings in demand for nursing care within each unit from day to day, even when the total number of patients remained the same, because of variations in the distribution of patients in various 'need' categories.[15] Three need categories – total care, partial care and self-care – were defined through checklists of observable patient characteristics. Work sampling studies were then used to determine the means and standard deviations of minutes per day spent on direct nursing care for patients in each category. It was also shown that the distribution of direct care times could be approximated well with normal distributions (Connor[16]). By multiplying the number of patients in each care category by the average direct care times for that category, and then summing over all categories, a 'direct care index' was obtained. This index could be used to estimate the number of hours of direct nursing care required in each unit and each shift to meet existing standards of care for a given patient load.

Some of the advantages of this approach are its simplicity, objectivity and reliability. As to simplicity, it is easy to train personnel (such as a charge nurse) to fill out the data collection form quickly and consistently. On a thirty-bed unit it can be done in about five minutes. The approach is objective and reliable since it consists of evaluating the status of patients with regard to physical and hygienic needs so that evaluation bias is kept to a minimum.

However, a criticism of this approach is the strong emphasis on physical and hygienic needs and the exclusion of instructional, observational and emotional support needs of patients. For some patients the intensity of these latter needs correlate highly with physical and hygienic needs but for others they do not.

Based on the definitions developed at Johns Hopkins, the direct care load comprised only about 30 per cent of the total workload. Therefore, Connor made further work sampling studies to determine the relationships between the time nursing personnel spent in productive activities (direct patient care, indirect patient care, paper-work, communications, etc.) and the following three independent variables:

1. the amount of direct care to be given (direct care index);
2. the total number of patients (i.e. 'census');
3. personnel hours available.[17]

Using a step-wise linear regression analysis, he concluded that the time spent in productive activities varied significantly with both the index and the personnel hours available, but not with the census.

Connor also noticed that, when hours available increased beyond a level required to give adequate care, the extra time was not used for increasing the level of direct care administered. Instead, it became mainly idle time, with a small percentage for communication, paper-work and indirect care. One important implication is that, if labour-saving equipment is introduced, the number of nursing hours should be reduced simultaneously. Otherwise, the personnel time saved will not go into direct care but into increased idle time. Another finding important to nurse staffing was that the workloads among the units were statistically independent and only some 20 per cent of the total staff needed to be 'floaters' in order to smooth the daily fluctuations.[18]

The average time requirements used for calculating the direct care index and the coefficients in the regression equations were based on historical care patterns, not patient needs. To improve the standard of care, the content of patient care should be examined to evaluate the levels of skill and times required before a direct care index and regression equations are used to predict workloads.

Connor's regression analyses were extended to several variables by Jelinek.[19] He included four categories of nursing personnel (professional nurses, practical nurses, nursing aides and student nurses), whereas Connor studied only professional nurses. He verified Connor's conclusions, as well as the following important hypotheses:

1. marginal productivity decreased as staff increased, for all personnel except nursing aides;
2. contributions to direct care made by increases in staff were greatest for nursing aides, followed by practical nurses, student nurses and professional nurses respectively;
3. staff shortages in a given category were at least partially corrected by substituting nurses from other categories.

The regression analysis approach used by Connor and Jelinek is an important tool, not only to increase the understanding of the existing nursing system, but also to establish ratios and standards for planning and control purposes, obtain models for workload predictions and forecast effects of changes in the organisation or operation of the nursing system.

Workload Predictions Based Directly on Nursing Activities

Besides the patient classification methods of estimating workloads, several methods have been developed that use nursing activities directly. The alleged advantage of this direct method is that the workload for each individual patient is estimated separately, instead of using average workload estimates for patient categories. The most complete method would be to use time standards for all tasks on each nursing order to predict direct care time for each patient. The same method could also be used to calculate time requirements for indirect care and non-patient-related activities. Through summation, a total care time could be predicted. The major shortcomings are that (a) nursing orders and care plans are generally not accurate enough, (b) some tasks are mutually dependent, (c) time standards are difficult to estimate and, above all, (d) the method is very cumbersome.

In order to circumvent some of these problems, several methods have been developed that use samples of nursing activities instead of all activities. They use either the most frequent activities of a unit, the most time-consuming activities, the activities that require the least skill, the activities that require the most skill, or some combination of the above. A time standard is established for each activity and, by studying the frequency of occurrence for each activity, an index of workload is established for each unit.

One example is the study of White, Quade and White.[20] They used five activity areas — diet, vital signs, respiratory aids, suction and cleanliness — to make estimates of care needs. Clark and Diggs added toileting and turning and/or assisted activity to the list of activity areas and showed that the time required for these activities made up 76 per cent of the total direct care time.[21] The staff utilisation and control programme developed by CASH also uses direct activity analysis.[22] It gives normative data on how occupancy levels should be translated into number of personnel in each category for each of the three shifts of a unit's operation.

SPRI used step-wise regression analysis to determine the relationship between patient characteristics and patient-dependent workload for each personnel category.[23] Using from five to eight patient characteristics, each with its own scale for measurement, nearly 60 per cent of the total workload, both direct and indirect care, for individual patients could be explained.

Markovian Workload Predictors

One major disadvantage with all the methods reviewed above is that they can be used to predict workloads only one or two shifts in advance, since the status and number of patients on each unit changes rapidly. Thomas tried to overcome this by using a Markov model that utilised four phases of patient recovery, each subdivided into three categories.[24] These twelve states, together with entry and exit states, are linked with a matrix of transition probabilities. But since different diagnoses have different length-of-stay distributions, a separate matrix has to be established for each possible diagnosis. This makes the method extremely cumbersome to apply. Balintfy,[25] Kolesar,[26] Meredith,[27] Singer,[28] Warner,[29] and Wendell and Wright[30] also used Markovian analysis.

Offensend[31] and Smallwood, Sondik and Offensend[32] developed a semi-Markov model. This semi-Markov model was used to calculate the mean and variance of the amount of nursing time required during each hour of the day in each nursing unit for each category of nursing personnel. It should be noted that both the index and the direct methods could also be extended to predict variance in workload. This would be valuable for calculating the accuracy of workload predictions and as a basis for establishing desired reserve staff capacity.

Forecasting Monthly Workloads

Since the length of stay in short-term hospitals is normally much less than one month, the movements of patients inside the hospital need not be followed in order to forecast monthly workloads. Average requirements for nursing hours from each category of personnel in each unit per patient in each admission category during the total length of stay would be sufficient information to translate expected admissions to expected workloads. However, the expected variance of the workload during a month is much more difficult to predict.

Several methods for making forecasts of demand and use rates have been developed, but few methods for translating these forecasts into workloads have been reported.[33] Kaplan used historical monthly average data in a linear regression model to determine the relationship between the number of professional nursing hours and patient days for each individual unit.[34] This is an improvement over the commonly used statistic — average number of nursing hours per patient day — since a fixed component is added.

The regression model was tested over a seven-month period to translate patient days into nursing hours. Most of the variations could be explained by the model and larger deviations were due to inconsistent staffing or transient effects. This information, which represented an evaluation of the staffing process, was not fed back to the decision makers for correction and adaptation. Kaplan remarked that providing supervisors with such information might reduce the number of extreme deviations.

Conclusions

The purpose of having accurate workload predictions is to be certain that the best possible data are available as an input to allocating personnel efficiently and effectively to the appropriate nursing unit to provide a comprehensive plan of care for each patient. In most hospitals workload measurement utilises data gathered by the head nurse based on each patient's needs. The data are estimated either subjectively through her knowledge of the patients or formally using direct and indirect care activities on patient classification forms. Markovian workload predictions are not widely used.

More and more hospitals are adopting formal patient classification systems. Based on the above studies and our own experience, we recommend the following practical methodology for the implementation of a patient classification and nurse workload measurement system:

1. Establish good quality control on the nursing units in order to measure the impact of any changes in staffing levels, reassignment, or modified organisational structures. This will establish a 'base-line' against which to measure any changes. Ideally, this quality of nursing care measure will involve outcome as well as process criteria.
2. Initiate Patient Classification System (PCS)
   (a) Define *objective* categories which measure: (i) physical needs of patients, (ii) hygienic needs of patients, (iii) instructional needs of patients, (iv) observational needs of patients, (v) emotional support of patients, (vi) medications and treatments, and which classify patients by age, degree of self-help, and other items useful in assessing nursing needs. These categories will vary by medical services; however, some attempt to achieve parallel categories across such services is worth while in order to provide a consistent system for the hospital.
   (b) It is desirable to keep the total number of categories to around 20-30 for most units. More categories yield greater accuracy, but result in more resistance from the persons completing the forms; hence a balance must be struck. On a 25-bed unit, the time required to complete the form for *all* patients should not exceed ten minutes by a person with experience in using the form.
3. Initiate nursing unit work factors study.
   (a) Relate the direct patient care to the particular class of patient defined by the PCS. 'Direct patient care' is loosely defined as 'care provided at the patient's bedside in direct support of that patient'.
   (b) 'Indirect or non-direct patient care' must also be measured. This workload is usually expressed as a constant amount of time which depends on the number of patients and not on the PCS.
   (c) Before beginning the study the distinction between direct and indirect care must be made clear, otherwise much confusion will result.
   (d) The data on direct and indirect care should be gathered (i) over

a two- to three-week time period when the unit is at a reasonably stable capacity, (ii) by each shift, (iii) by PCS (for direct care), (iv) by skill level (RN, LPN, aide, other), and (v) by hour of day.

(e) This data can be gathered by (i) self-recording time forms completed by each person, or (ii) work sampling by a disinterested third party.

(f) Data so collected must then be analysed. Times for each skill level to do the daily PCS tasks for each category of patient must be computed. Averages are needed and variances are useful.

4. After the workload factors are computed as in (3) above, they can then be incorporated into a computer programme.

5. Generally, the PCS is undertaken on a unit prior to the day shift and nursing workload is computed for the next three shifts. Unusual PCS events, happening later in the day, are then allowed for as they occur.

6. Allocations of personnel can be made based on the workloads computed in (5) above and the supply of available nurses. Methods for corrective allocations are described in the next section.

The above approach to workload measurement is useful for the daily allocation of available staff. For forecasting daily and weekly unit staffing needs in order to construct two, four, six or eight-week schedules, a practical methodology is to use time series or regression methods which utilise the daily workloads collected over the past three to twelve months.

Quantitative Procedures for Nurse Staffing

This section reviews quantitative procedures that have been proposed to assist in the management of nurse staffing activities in each of the three tactical decision levels — corrective allocations, shift scheduling and manpower planning. In our framework of Figure 8.1, staffing activities include not only the planning and co-ordination of staffing actions but also the monitoring of outcomes and the analysis of alternative policies and designs. Throughout the discussion, we shall point out those elements and aspects within this framework which have been largely neglected, but which are nevertheless important for over-all system effectiveness.

Corrective Allocations

The main purpose of the corrective allocation system is to smooth the workload to staff ratios among the units by using float, pulling, part-time, relief, overtime, voluntary absenteeism and patient reallocation.

Connor *et al.* reported the use of the direct care index as a basis for the assignment of overtime and float pool.[35] Temporary shifting of personnel among wards has long been a common practice, and many hospitals have implemented some procedure for predicting workloads — often merely based on a census — to bring about more systematic and equitable personnel allocations.

In order to make the allocations more specific and objective, though often less individualised and flexible, computers have been programmed with heuristic decision-making procedures that evaluate the available information and suggest personnel allocations. For example, Jelinek *et al.* have developed a 'Personnel Allocation and Scheduling Control System for Patient Care Services' that has the following three interrelated but separate computer-based functions: personnel scheduling, personnel allocation and management reporting.[36] The allocation function is a heuristic procedure based on pre-established priorities that balance the trade-off between employee dissatisfaction and the workload to staff balance. Another example is Medinet's time-sharing programme.[37]

Wolfe[38] and Wolfe and Young[39] used a linear programming model to assess existing nursing personnel of different categories to match given demands from nine groups of tasks. The objective function value for a task from group i assigned to personnel category j is $x_{ij} w_j + v_{ij}$, where x_{ij} is the number of minutes required, w_j the wage per minute, and v_{ij} the intangible costs of having category j perform a task in group i. These intangible costs were assigned by a panel of nurses. Since personnel were assigned only for a full eight-hour shift, integer solutions were required and undistributed idle time had to be evaluated. However, a non-integar solution procedure was used. The difficulties of obtaining input data and integer solutions, the fact that the model covers only a single period, and the neglect of preferences and capabilities of individual nurses, indicate that more development is needed before the model can be successfully applied.

Warner[40] and Warner and Prawda[41] formulated the allocation problem as a mixed integer quadratic programme. Demand is assumed to be known and the objective function value for personnel category n in ward i during shift t is the quadratic 'cost'

$$W_{int} \left(R_{int} - \sum_m Q_{imnt} U_{imnt} \right)^2$$

where R_{int} is the demand, U_{imnt} the number of nurses of category m who are working in category n, Q_{imnt} the associated substitution ratio, and W_{int} the relative seriousness of shortage. The problem was decomposed by a primal resource-directive approach into a multiple-choice programming master problem, with quadratic programming sub-problems. As with Wolfe's model, additional work is required, particularly in estimating the subjective parameters.

Another mathematical programming model has been formulated by Liebman.[42] She used a psychometric technique called the Q-sort to measure quantitatively the existing nursing concepts of effective utilisation of personnel in an extended care facility. This was the basis for the objective function of a model that generated personnel allocations, given a set of patient requirements and a nursing team configuration. Actual assignments and computer-generated assignments were compared, and the model was found to produce a good fit.

A stochastic allocation model was developed by Miller and Pierskalla.[43] The objective was to minimise the cost of allocating nurses among nursing classes and units subject to constraints on the demand for, and the supply of, nursing services. Because the number of nurses reporting for work in the various classes and units form a random vector, the allocation model used was a stochastic programme with recourse. It was then transformed into a deterministic equivalent and solved.

Finally, we wish to mention Freund and Staats who developed a technique for describing 'elements' reflecting care task groups and patient conditions, obtained difficulty values for each element, and developed a heuristic procedure for allocating elements to nurses with difficulty as a measure of assignment 'load'.[44]

Most of the workload prediction techniques and allocation procedures are not used to monitor and adapt the procedures themselves or to bring about improved long-range staff balance. Quantitative benefit-cost analysis of alternative procedures and policies is generally not considered. However, Offensend used his workload predictor in experiments with various policies for admission control and assignment of patients to nursing teams.[45] He calculated the value of obtaining better information before making decisions, and he performed sensitivity analyses on several parameters.

Tani developed a model of a staffing reserve-resource system that supplies float and relief staff and scheduled voluntary absences and extra shifts.[46] Historical distributions of reserve demand and availability of relief, extra shifts and voluntary absences were estimated. A cost function was established and various sizes of the float pool were tried in order to find an optimal float pool size. The study exemplifies an approach to benefit-cost analysis that can be used to predict the effects of changes in the availability of various corrective allocation alternatives or changes in operating policies.

The simulation model developed by Hershey, Abernathy and Baloff focuses on:

1. the prediction of savings in manpower requirements of introducing a float pool under a variety of operating and policy parameters;
2. forecasting manpower requirements for a given allocation procedure and policy.[47]

Several criteria which an administrator might adopt for equating levels of patient care under alternative staffing schemes are suggested and studied. Although the examples indicate savings in manpower requirements of 9-12 per cent from introducing a float pool for the most realistic combinations of parameters, no general conclusions should be drawn because many costs and benefits were not included in the model and the data were hypothetical.

All of the allocation models discussed require large data bases for their operation. Furthermore, these data bases must be accurate for every shift when allocations are performed. To maintain such data bases in the absence of time sharing and/or distributed computer systems is virtually impossible. Consequently, none of these mathematical allocation models is operating at the present time. However, as more micro- and mini-computers are introduced into nursing administration departments, simple interactive allocation models will be used to aid corrective allocation decisions.

Some of this development is already under way. It involves the construction of individual nurse data bases which indicate their work schedules, their nursing specialty skills, their previous experience on different hospital units and their preferences for floating or pulling. In addition, data are needed on the manpower task substitutability and the trade-off of performance of a task by the different skill levels, since, for example, one practical nurse does not substitute for one registered nurse (although the reverse holds). As the shifts change, the nursing shortage or excess for each unit and skill level can be computed (based on previously entered patient classification workload calculations). By interactive heuristic allocation rules, nurses can be pulled or floated to appropriate units. Such data bases are under construction and others exist in partial form at a few leading medical centres, for example Fairview Hospital in Minneapolis, Rush Presbyterian St Luke in Chicago and Stanford Hospital in Palo Alto.

Given these data bases, simple or complex allocation models may then be tried. More importantly, linkages to other information and decision systems can be introduced. For example, the allocation information system can link to the payroll system to record who worked what shift and unit, to the admissions scheduling system to indicate not only bed availability and patient transfer but personnel availability for under- or over-staffed units, and to patient billing systems as hospitals begin to allocate manpower as well as supply costs to particular patients.

Shift Scheduling

The nurse scheduling process may be viewed as one of generating a configuration of nurse schedules that specify the number and identities of the nurses working each day of the scheduling period. By specifying nurse identities, a pattern of scheduled days off and on is created for individual nurses. These patterns, along with hospital staffing requirements, define the nurse scheduling problem: how to generate a configuration of nurse schedules that satisfy the hospital staffing requirements while simultaneously satisfying the individual nurse's preferences for various schedule pattern characteristics.

The most common formalised procedures for scheduling shifts on and shifts off for individual nurses are based on the development of a fixed schedule that repeats itself on a cyclic basis, normally every fourth week.[48] The major shortcomings of such 'cyclic schedules' are that they cannot normally take into account fluctuations in workloads and absences, except on a fixed weekday pattern, and they do not consider preferences or the capabilities of individual nurses. Such inflexible scheduling procedures require high flexibility within the corrective allocation and manpower planning system to avoid expensive overstaffing.

Two non-cyclical scheduling papers of note are those of Rothstein[49] and Warner.[50] Rothstein's application was to hospital housekeeping operations. He sought to maximise the number of day-off pairs (e.g. Monday-Tuesday) subject to constraints requiring two days off each week and integral assignments. Warner presented a two-phase algorithm to solve the nurse scheduling problem. Phase I is involved with finding a feasible solution to various staffing constraints, while Phase II seeks to improve the Phase I solution by maximising individual preferences for various schedule patterns while maintaining the Phase I solution.

Sanders let nurses distribute 1,000 disutility points among seven factors in their schedules, e.g. night duty and split weekend, to measure their attitudes concerning the relative unpleasantness of each factor.[51]

Substantial differences in attitudes from nurse to nurse and between wards were found. An evaluation of past schedules' disutility points for each individual showed great variances. He also found that nurses with relatively greater disutility points tended to be absent more often. The problem was then to find a scheduling procedure that minimises the sum of cumulative disutilities while considering all other constraints. He investigated alternative definitions of equitability, the existence of equitable solutions, the properties of some scheduling paradigms and the relationships between optimal and equitable solutions. A relatively equitable heuristic procedure seems to be to give the worst schedule to the nurse with the least accumulated disutility points and the best schedule to the one with the most, until all schedules have been distributed.

Despite the multitude of quantitative procedures that have been developed to assist in scheduling nursing staff, very few have been implemented and accepted; the vast majority of hospitals schedule nurses on an informal and subjective basis. One of the most successful implementations of quantitative nurse scheduling has been by Miller, Pierskalla and Rath,[52] Miller, Pierce and Pierskalla,[53] Miller, Pierce, Pierskalla and Rath[54] and Jelinek *et al.*[55] This computer-based nurse scheduling system has been successfully implemented in a number of hospitals in the United States and Canada. The theoretical basis is mathematical programming; the computer basis is the cyclic co-ordinate descent algorithm. This system is described in detail in a later case study section.

Although the above model has been implemented in several settings, it suffers from the extensive work needed to maintain a large data base, from the need for a large computer (although a mini would suffice) and from the lack of integration with other systems such as corrective allocations, payroll, admissions and other hospital activities. As with the corrective allocation level, little has been done continuously to evaluate and adapt scheduling systems themselves, and quantitative benefit-cost analysis of alternative design and operating procedures is even more exceptional.

Manpower Planning and Performance Monitoring

In contrast to the allocation and scheduling levels, for which many models and systems for decision support have been proposed and some adopted, few quantitative models have been developed to assist the planning of task substitution, hiring, training, transfer, discharge and other personnel allocation decisions. Instead, most studies concerned with this level of nurse staffing have stressed the importance of variable budgeting — that is, procedures for the evaluation of outcomes that correct for variations in uncontrollable factors, such as workload, wages and procedural changes.

For example the purpose of Kaplan's study was to perform monthly evaluations of efficiency and scheduling by comparing the actual number of nursing hours with a variable standard expressed as a linear function of the actual number of patient days.[56] The coefficients in the linear function were estimated from historical data.

Olson describes an operating system for the bi-weekly monitoring of budget performance.[57] The number of hours worked in each department is compared with standard hours, calculated from a linear function with or without a fixed component. The coefficients are obtained from CASH standards or from historical data.[58] The ratio of hours worked to standard hours is plotted, together with the occupancy rate for each department, in order to estimate the flexibility in staffing performance and changes in personnel efficiency or utilisation.

Davis and Cowie stress the measurement and evaluation of both cost and quality by means of variable budgeting and effectiveness indices, but no specific technique is described.[59] Even traditional hospital budgeting and accounting handbooks discuss the trade-off between cost and quality and recommend flexible budgets for nursing services.[60]

The American Hospital Association has a central computer processing service called Hospital Administration Services (HAS). Direct expenses, certain resources measures such as man-hours, and some output measures such as patient days, meals and pounds of laundry are reported monthly to HAS by each participating hospital. In return, each hospital receives statistics comparing its current performance with its historic performance and with the distribution of performance of other hospitals of the same size, geographical location or function. High relative ranges in some performance indicators have been reported, probably due to great variations in both variable definitions and actual performance.[61] Furthermore, very little information to support nurse staffing can be found in the HAS reports and, when fed back to each hospital, the data are about five weeks old, thus making it too late to take useful corrective actions. Hospitals must therefore rely on their own information systems for staffing monitoring.

A promising approach to budgeting and control is the Hospital Management Monitoring System Project.[62] Costs, man-hours and output measures (patient days for nursing, number of examinations for laboratories, etc.) are accumulated for each responsibility centre, a first-line supervisor post. The supervisors are then judged by their ability to meet man-hours to output standards that have been pre-established through negotiations between the administration and the supervisors. These standards, together with seasonally adjusted output volumes and expected wage rates, are also the basis for the annual budgeting of monthly expenditures. Furthermore, the volume forecast for each responsibility centre is updated monthly, using regression, indices and exponential smoothing. These forecasts, together with the man-hours to output standards, help the supervisors to foresee manpower requirements and then use part-time, overtime, transfer, vacation and attrition of personnel to adjust the workforce. Savings of $150,000 per year have been reported due to the introduction of this variable budgeting and control procedure in the demonstration hospital.

The MEDICUS system (Jelinek *et al.*[63]) also contains a management reporting system. Three categories of data are reported:

1. nursing performance (cost, manpower and activity levels);
2. nursing personnel status (utilisation, overtime, turnover, absenteeism and personnel satisfaction);
3. quality level measurements (questions of measurable 'process' attributes are randomly selected from a large 'question master file' and used to generate questionnaires that are filled out and then used to calculate quality indices).

Abernathy, Baloff, Hershey and Wandel divided the staffing process into three decision levels:

1. policy decisions, including the operating procedures for nursing units and for the staffing process itself;
2. permanent staff allocation, including hiring, discharge, training and reallocation;
3. short-term scheduling and allocation of available staff within the constraints determined by the two previous levels.[64]

These three levels are used as decomposition stages in the development of a probabilistic programming model of the staffing process. Solution procedures are developed and demonstrated with a hypothetical example application. The example also illustrates the type of information that can be generated by the model and the utility of this information:

1. for policy evaluation and decision;

2. as an informational basis for actual staff planning and control;
3. for co-ordination of staff allocation with patient admission, treatment scheduling, vacation planning and load forecasting;
4. to suggest standards for budgeting purposes;
5. to monitor nursing performance and staffing effectiveness.

However, the adaptability and acceptability of the model has yet to be demonstrated.

Shift Scheduling — A Case Study

This section discusses in detail a particular approach to quantitative nurse scheduling which has enjoyed some success.[65] The basis of the approach is a mathematical programming model which schedules days on and days off for all nurses on a given unit or ward for a given shift for a two, four, six or eight-week scheduling horizon, subject to certain hospital policy and employee constraints. Because of the large number of constraints, it is possible that no feasible solutions to the nurse scheduling problem would exist if all the constraints were binding. For this reason the constraints are divided into two classes: feasibility set constraints, which define the sets of feasible nurse schedules, and non-binding constraints, the violation of which incurs a penalty cost which appears in the objective function. Each hospital has the discretion to define which constraints go into each class.

Constraints: the Feasibility Set

Because of the possibility of special requests by nurses, no constraints are binding, in the sense that they hold under all circumstances except those constraints emanating from special requests. The model, however, distinguishes between constraints the hospital would like to hold in the absence of special requests and those which are allowed to be violated while incurring a penalty cost. These latter constraints (non-binding constraints) are discussed later.

The former constraints define the feasibility set π_i, i.e. π_i = the set of feasible schedule patterns for nurse i. In the absence of special requests, this set might include all schedules satisfying the following:

1. a nurse works ten days every pay period (i.e. 14-day scheduling period);
2. no work stretches (i.e. stretches of consecutive days on) are allowed in excess of σ days (e.g. $\sigma = 7$);

3. no work stretches for τ or fewer days are allowed (e.g. $\tau = 1$).

Hence one schedule in a π satisfying these values of σ and τ might be
1 1 1 1 1 1 0 0 1 1 1 0 0.

Now suppose a nurse has a special request. For example, suppose the nurse requests the schedule 1 1 1 1 1 1 1 0 1 0 0 0 B, where B indicates a birthday. In this case all of the above constraints would be violated and π_i would consist of only the schedule just given. Thus, in the general case π_i is the set of schedules which (a) satisfies a nurse's special requests, and (b) satisfies as many of the constraints the hospital would like to see binding as possible, given the nurse's special request.

The constraints the hospital would like to hold are a function of the hospital in which the model is applied. Thus, for example, the model could easily specify five out of seven days instead of ten out of fourteen or specify additional constraints such as one weekend off each pay period.

Constraints: Non-binding

Each schedule pattern $x^i \epsilon \pi_i$ may violate a number of non-binding schedule pattern constraints while incurring a penalty cost. Define $N_i =$ the index set of the non-binding schedule pattern constraints for nurse i. For example, if the hospital in which the model is being implemented deems them as non-binding, the following constraints might define N_i:

1. no work stretches longer than S_i days (where $S_i \leqslant \sigma$);
2. no work stretches shorter than T_i days (where $T_i \geqslant \tau$);
3. no day on, day off, day on patterns (1 0 1 pattern);
4. no more than κ consecutive 1 0 1 patterns;
5. Q_i weekends off every scheduling period (4 to 6 weeks);
6. no more than W_i consecutive weekends working each scheduling period;
7. no patterns containing four consecutive days off;
8. no patterns containing split weekends on (i.e. a Saturday on, Sunday off, pattern, or vice versa).

In addition to non-binding schedule pattern constraints, there are also non-binding staffing level constraints. Define $d_k =$ the desired staffing level for day k; and $m_k =$ the minimum staffing level for day k. Then (a) the number of nurses scheduled to work on day k is greater than or equal to m_k and (b) the number of nurses to work on day k is equal to d_k.

Objective Function

The objective function is composed of the sum of two classes of penalty costs: penalty costs due to violation of non-binding staffing level constraints and penalty costs due to violation of non-binding schedule pattern constraints.

Staffing Level Costs

The group to be scheduled is defined as the set of all the nurses in the unit who are to be scheduled by one application of the solution algorithm. A sub-group is defined as a sub-set of the group specified by the hospital. For example, the group to be scheduled may be all those nurses assigned to a nursing unit and the sub-groups may be registered nurses (RNs), licensed practical nurses (LPNs) and nursing aides. Alternatively, the group may be defined as all RNs and a sub-group might be those capable of performing as head nurses.

Then, for each day $k = 1, \ldots, 14$ (where there are I nurses), the group staffing level costs are given by:

$$f_k\left(\sum_{i=1}^{I} x_k^i\right), \text{ where } x^i = (x_1^i, \ldots, x_{14}^i).$$

For example, this function might appear as in Figure 8.2. Now let $B_j =$ the index set of nursing sub-groups j, and J = the index set of all sub-groups.

Figure 8.2: An Example of a Daily Staffing Level Cost Function for a Nursing Group

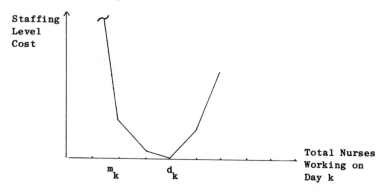

If m_k^j and d_k^j are the minimum and desired number of nurses required on day k for sub-group j, respectively, the staffing cost for violating those constraints on day k for sub-group j is:

$$h_{jk}\left(\sum_{i\epsilon Bj} x_k^i\right),$$

where h_{jk} (.) is defined similarly to f_k (.).

Then, the total staffing level costs for all 14 days of the pay period are:

$$\sum_{k=1}^{14} f_k\left(\sum_{i=1}^{I} x_k^i\right) + \sum_{k=1}^{14} \sum_{j\epsilon J} h_{jk}\left(\sum_{i\epsilon Bj} x_k^i\right).$$

Schedule Pattern Costs

For each nurse $i = 1, \ldots, I$, the schedule pattern costs for a particular pattern x^i measure:

1. the costs inherent in that pattern, in relation to which constraints in N_i are violated;
2. how nurse i perceives these costs in the light of her schedule preferences;
3. how this cost is weighed in the light of nurse i's schedule history.

For example, regarding (1), the pattern 1 1 1 1 1 0 0 1 1 1 0 0 1 1 may incur a cost for a nurse whose minimum desired work stretch is four days. This is a cost inherent in the pattern. Considering (2), we need to know how nurse i perceives violations of the minimum desired stretch constraint, i.e. how severely are violations of this non-binding constraint viewed *vis-à-vis* others in N_i. Finally (3) gives some indication of how to weight this revised schedule pattern cost on the light of the schedules nurse i has received in the past. Intuitively, if nurse i has been receiving pool schedules, the cost of a given schedule should be relatively higher than the costs for schedules of other nurses, in order to cause a good schedule to be accepted when the solution algorithm is applied and vice versa. Thus:

$g_{in}(x^i)$ = the cost of violating non-binding constraint $n\epsilon N_i$ of schedule x^i;

α_{in} = the 'weight' nurse i gives a violation of non-binding constraint

$n\epsilon N_i$, which is called the aversion coefficient;

A_i = the aversion index of nurse i, i.e. a measure of how good or bad nurse i's schedules have been historically *vis-à-vis* nurse i's preferences.

Then the total schedule pattern cost to nurse i for a schedule pattern x^i is:

$$A_i \sum_{n\epsilon N_i} \alpha_{in} g_{in}(x^i)$$

and the sum of these costs for all nurses $i = 1, \ldots, I$ is the total schedule pattern cost.

Problem Formulation

Let $\lambda \epsilon (0,1)$ be a parameter that weights staffing level and schedule pattern costs. It is chosen such that the weighted staffing and schedule pattern costs are of approximately equal magnitude. Experience has shown a trial-and-error procedure to be effective in arriving at satisfactory values of λ.

Given λ, the problem is to find $x^1, x^2, \ldots, x^I$ which minimise:

$$\lambda \left[\sum_{k=1}^{14} f_k \left(\sum_{i=1}^{I} x_k^i \right) + \sum_{k=1}^{14} \sum_{j\epsilon J} h_{jk} \left(\sum_{i\epsilon B_j} x_k^i \right) \right] + (1-\lambda) \sum_{i=1}^{I} A_i \sum_{n\epsilon N_i} \alpha_{in} g_{in}(x^i)$$

subject to $x^i \epsilon \pi_i, i = 1, \ldots, I$.

The solution procedure used is a near-optimal algorithm. It starts with an initial configuration of nurse schedules, one for each nurse. Fixing the schedules of all nurses but one, say nurse i, it searches π_i. The lowest present cost and best schedule configuration are updated if, when searching π_i, a schedule is found which results in a lower schedule configuration cost than the lowest cost to date. When all the schedules in π_i have been tested, either a lower cost configuration has been found, or no lower cost configuration has been found. The process cycles among the I nurses and terminates when no lower cost configuration has been found in I consecutive tests. For more detail on the solution procedures, see Miller, Pierskalla and Rath.[66]

The use of this algorithm has resulted in less variation between actual and desired staffing levels, more weekends off, fewer long stretches, more split days off, higher personnel satisfaction and lower costs than the previous manual or semi-automated systems. However, the data needs are great and require accurate maintenance. Consequently, in order to implement such a sophisticated system, the hospital must have access to systems programmers and a comprehensive mini- or full-sized computer.

As in any implementation which involves the preferences of hundreds (possibly thousands) of individuals, it is important that they are integrated with the implementation process. Once a hospital's top administrators have decided to install the computerised algorithm, the implementation process begins. It proceeds through a series of steps over several months. The initial step is to meet with the Director of Nursing to explain the system and gather data on hospital scheduling policies, such as the number of weekends off, maximum and minimum stretches, the start day and length of pay periods, schedule horizon (usually four or six weeks), rotation, use of part-time and/or float personnel, etc.

Next comes a group meeting with the head nurses to explain the operation of the system, what it can and cannot do for them, the types of reports and schedules they will receive, the time savings to them, the problems which it eliminates for them (and those it does not), and the need for timely data on special request. Emphasis is placed on the importance of co-operation on both sides and it is stressed that the computerised schedules do not take away any of the authority of the head nurse in approving special requests or changing the schedules to meet unanticipated needs. The computerised algorithm is a tool which removes some onerous tasks so that head nurses may have more time for more important tasks related to health care delivery.

Following the group meeting, individual meetings are scheduled with each head nurse. The purpose of these individual meetings is to answer any system questions and, more importantly, to gather data needed by the algorithm. The data comprise such items as who are the charge nurses, what groups and sub-groups must be scheduled together, what are minimum and desired group and sub-group staffing levels, and what specific scheduling problems are on the unit, such as parallel people, part-time restrictions, rotation restrictions, fixed patterns, team *v.* primary care groups, etc. Another important purpose of this meeting is to explain the limitations of the scheduler. For example, any group on a unit may specify which two days, Friday-Saturday or Saturday-Sunday, constitute a weekend; however, all of the nurses in that group must use the same definition for their weekend.

The next step is an orientation meeting with groups of nurses on the units. The main purpose here is to remove the fear of impersonalisation, to emphasise that the head nurse still controls the schedules and to point out that the computer gives nurses fairer and more individualised schedules that meet their particular requests and more nearly reflect their preferences.

After the general orientation meetings each individual is interviewed (including nurses' aides, orderlies and medical technicians) to obtain rankings of her (or his) preferences for weekends, stretches, split days off, etc. and to explain the way such preferences affect schedules. These individuals are also informed that all schedule changes or requests must be approved by the head nurse just as in the past.

Following each of the interviews, data are prepared and stored in the master file of the algorithm. After all the necessary data have been stored, trial schedules are run to adjust the various hospital and individual parameters. These trial schedules are reviewed by the respective head nurses in order to identify any items missed in prior interviews.

The nurse scheduling system is now in operating condition and periodic schedules are produced. Even in this production phase, however, the schedules are reviewed every time and adjustments are made for new hires, terminations, changes in workload requirements and/or nurse preferences, etc. On a continuing basis it usually requires the full-time involvement of one trained high school graduate, who works well with people and enjoys the challenge of producing the best schedule for each head nurse, to operate the algorithm for a 40-unit hospital with 900 full- and part-time nursing personnel. If the hospital is one-half this size, then only one-half the time is needed, since the effort in running and maintaining the algorithm is essentially linear with respect to the number of units and people being scheduled.

The savings in head nurse time alone constitute a minimum of one day per month per head nurse and more usually two to four days per month. Of course, head nurses' time is not the only advantage of the algorithm. Other advantages are fairer schedules which meet nurse preferences, the more even stafffing of units and the capability for the nursing administration to examine the effects of changes in policies prior to their implementation.

Among the locations where the algorithm has been implemented are: Mount Zion Medical Center, San Francisco, California; Pacific Medical Center, San Francisco, California; Stanford University Medical Center, Stanford, California; Kingston General Hospital, Kingston, Ontario; and Rush Presbyterian St Luke Medical Center, Chicago, Illinois.

Recommendations and Conclusions

In this chapter, we have conceptualised the nurse staffing process as a hierarchy of three tactical decision levels. The great bulk of research in nurse staffing has concentrated on the shift-scheduling and corrective allocation levels and on activity analysis and forecasting procedures to support staffing decisions. Exploration of the potential benefits of improved manpower-planning procedures has only begun. This is an important research area which we believe deserves greater attention in the future.

Another area which should be investigated further is the interdependence of the decision levels discussed in this chapter. Each decision level is constrained by the resources made available at higher levels and by the degree of flexibility for later correction at lower levels.

Consider the manpower-planning decision level. The week-to-week and day-to-day shift-scheduling decisions and shift-by-shift corrective allocations obviously depend upon the permanent staffing levels established through the manpower-planning process. On the other hand, the range and flexibility of shift-scheduling and corrective allocation options available to management should be known so that their performance can be anticipated and included in the staffing decisions made during the manpower-planning process. That is, the over-all staff requirements cannot be fully assessed until it has been decided how fluctuations in load are to be accommodated. If overtime, for example, provides the only flexibility in short-term scheduling, the full-time staff requirements might be substantially higher than if part-time help and a float pool were also available.

The interdependencies of the three levels should be recognised to bring about systematic nurse staffing improvements. One general conclusion from this review is that greater attention should be given to studying these interdependencies of the decision levels, rather than studying each level in isolation.

The need for co-ordination between nurse staffing and other hospital activities, such as task assignment, scheduling of admission and operating rooms, budgeting, payroll and facility planning, should also be stressed. Many studies have examined alternative approaches for balancing patient numbers and mix, allocating patients to nursing units and scheduling patient care activities, but the impact of these admission- and treatment-scheduling procedures upon nursing utilisation and upon the need for flexibility in staffing procedures has not yet been fully explored.

Very few studies have attempted to evaluate systematically alternative designs and methods of implementing nurse staffing systems and operating policies. We think it is crucial that the impact upon cost, quality and satisfaction of these strategic decisions be carefully investigated. There are many conflicting objectives, legal constraints and professional value systems in hospitals that place little emphasis on efficiency. More research and demonstration projects have to be undertaken before the adaptability, acceptability and significance of most of the reviewed procedures can be fully understood.

Notes

1. D.H. Stimson and R.H. Stimson, *Operations Research in Hospitals: Diagnosis and Prognosis* (Hospital Research and Educational Trust, Chicago, 1972).

2. M.D. Aydelotte, *Nurse Staffing Methodology: A Review and Critique of Selected Literature,* NIH Pub. 73-433 (US Department of HEW, Washington, DC, 1973).

3. W.J. Abernathy, N. Baloff and J.C. Hershey, 'The Nurse Staffing Problem — Issues and Prospects', *Sloan Management Review,* 13 (Fall 1971), pp. 87-99.

4. S.E. Wandel and J.C. Hershey, 'A Conceptual Framework for Nurse Staffing Management', *Omega, the International Journal of Management Science,* 3 (1975), pp. 541-50.

5. Aydelotte, *Nurse Staffing Methodology.*

6. Stimson and Stimson, *Operations Research in Hospitals.*

7. B. Pfefferkorn and C.A. Rovetta, *Administrative Cost Analysis for Nursing Service and Nursing Education* (American Hospital Association and National League of Nursing Education, Chicago, 1940).

8. American Hospital Association and National League of Nursing Education, *Hospital Nursing Service Manual* (National League of Nursing Education, New York, 1960).

9. F.L. George and R.P. Kuehn, *Patterns of Patient Care* (Macmillan, New York, 1955).

10. National League of Nursing Education, *A Study of Pediatric Nursing* (New York, 1947).

11. E. Bernstein *et al., A Study of Direct Nursing Care Consumed by Patients with Varying Degrees of Illness* (Office of Publications and Printing, New York University, New York, 1953).

12. H. Binhammer *et al., A Functional Analysis of Nursing Service* (University of California School of Nursing, San Francisco, 1951).

13. E. Claussen, 'Categorisation of Patients According to Nursing Care Needs', *Military Medicine,* 120 (1955), pp. 209-14.

14. F.G. Abedellah, 'Work Sampling Applied to the Study of Nursing Personnel', *Nursing Research,* 3 (June 1954), pp. 11-16; M.G. Arnstein, *How to Study Nursing Activities in a Patient Unit,* PHS Pub. 370 (US Department of HEW, Washington, DC, 1954); A.M. Feyerherm, 'Measures of Hospital Patient Care Loads', Final Research Report (GM 10344 and NU00064-02) (Kansas State University, 1964); W. Hudson, 'An Application of Management Engineering to Nonrepetitive Work — Hospital Nursing', unpublished PhD dissertation, University of Iowa, 1954; P.E. Torgerson, 'An Example of Work Sampling in the Hospital', *Journal of Industrial Engineering,* 10 (1959); M.J. Wright, *The Improvement of Patient Care* (G.P. Putnam's Sons, New York, 1954).

218   *Nurse Staffing Management*

15. R.J. Connor, 'A Hospital Inpatient Classification System', unpublished PhD dissertation, Johns Hopkins University, 1960; R.J. Connor, 'Hospital Work Sampling with Associated Measures of Production', *Journal of Industrial Engineering,* 12 (1961), pp. 105-7; R.J. Connor, 'A Work Sampling Study of Variations in Nursing Work Load', *Hospitals,* 35 (1 May, 1961), pp. 40-1 and 111; R.J. Connor *et al.,* 'Effective Use of Nursing Resources – A Research Report', *Hospitals,* 35 (1 May, 1961), pp. 30-9; C.D. Flagle *et al., Optimal Organisation and Facility for a Nursing Unit,* Progress Report, December 1957 to December 1959 (Operations Research Division, Johns Hopkins Hospital, 1960); C.D. Flagle *et al.,* 'The Problem of Organisation for Hospital Inpatient Care', in C.W. Churchman and M. Verhalst (eds.),, *Management Sciences: Models and Techniques,* Proceedings of the Sixth International Meeting of the Institute of Management Science, Paris, 1959, vol. 2 (Pergamon Press, New York, 1960), pp. 275-87.

16. Connor, 'A Hospital Inpatient Classification System'.

17. Ibid.; Connor, 'Hospital Work Sampling With Associated Measures of Production'.

18. Connor, 'A Hospital Inpatient Classification System'; Connor *et al.,* 'Effective Use of Nursing Resources'.

19. R.C. Jelinek, 'Nursing: The Development of an Activity Model', unpublished PhD dissertation, University of Michigan, 1964; R.C. Jelinek, 'A New Approach to the Analysis of Nursing Activities', *Hospitals,* 40 (1 October, 1966), pp. 89-91; R.C. Jelinek, 'A Structural Model for the Patient Care Operations', *Health Services Research,* 2 (1967), pp. 226-42.

20. R.P. White, D. Quade and K.L. White, *Patient Care Classification: Methods and Application,* Report on research supported by research grant NU-00080 from the Division of Nursing, Bureau of Health Services, United States Public Health Service, 1967.

21. E.L. Clark and W.W. Diggs, 'Quantifying Patient Care Needs', *Hospitals,* 45 (16 September, 1971), pp. 96-100.

22. CASH (Commission for Administrative Services in Hospitals), *Staff Utilisation and Control Program; Orientation Report, Medical/Surgical,* revised (Los Angeles, 1967).

23. SPRI (Sjukvardens och socialvardens planering-och rationaliserings-institut), 'Riktlinjer for beräkning och fördelning av sjukvards-personal vid vardavdelningar', Projekt 4016, Spri rapport 20, Stockholm.

24. W.H. Thomas, 'Model for Short Term Prediction of Demand for Nursing Resources', unpublished PhD dissertation, Purdue University, 1964; W.H. Thomas, 'Model for Prediction Recovery Progress of Coronary Patients', *Health Services Research,* 3 (1968), pp. 185-213.

25. J.L. Balintfy, 'A Hospital Census Predictor Model', in H.E. Smalley and J.R. Freeman (eds.), *Hospital Industrial Engineering* (Reinhold Publishing Corporation, New York, 1966), pp. 312-16.

26. P. Kolesar, 'A Markovian Model for Hospital Admission Scheduling', *Management Science,* 16 (1970), pp. 384-96.

27. J. Meredith, 'A Markovian Analysis of a Geriatric Ward', *Management Science,* 19 (1973), pp. 604-12.

28. S. Singer, 'A Stochastic Model of Variation of Categories of Patients within a Hospital', unpublished PhD dissertation, Johns Hopkins University, 1961.

29. D.M. Warner, 'A Two Phase Model for Scheduling Nursing Personnel in a Hospital', unpublished PhD dissertation, Tulane University, 1971.

30. R.E. Wendell and G.P. Wright, *A Simulation-Optimisation Model of Nursing Care in Intensive Care Units* (Design and Development Center, The

Nurse Staffing Management

219

Technological Institute, Northwestern University, 1968).
31. F.L. Offensend, 'Design, Control and Evaluation of Inpatient Nursing
Systems', unpublished PhD dissertation, Stanford University, 1971.
32. R.D. Smallwood, E.J. Sondik and F.L. Offensend, 'Toward an Integrated
Methodology for the Analysis of Health-Care Systems', *Operations Research,* 19
(1971), pp. 1300-22.
33. J.R. Griffith, *Quantitative Techniques for Hospital Planning and Control*
(Lexington Books, Lexington, 1972).
34. R.S. Kaplan, *A Statistical Model for Analysis and Control of Nurse
Staffing* (Graduate School of Business, University of Chicago, 1972).
35. Connor *et al.,* 'Effective Use of Nursing Resources'.
36. R.C. Jelinek, T.K. Zinn and J.R. Brya, 'Tell the Computer How Sick the
Patients Are and It will Tell How many Nurses They Need', *Modern Hospital,*
121 (December 1973), pp. 81-5; R.C. Jelinek, T.K. Zinn, G.L. Delon and R.A.
Aleman, *Nurse Scheduling and Allocation System in Operation,* Proceedings of
the 23rd Meeting of the American Institute of Industrial Engineers, Anaheim
(1972), pp. 273-81.
37. Medinet Corporation, *Nurse Staff Allocation* (100 Galen Street,
Watertown, Massachusetts, 1969).
38. H. Wolfe, 'A Multiple Assignment Model for Staffing Nursing Units',
unpublished PhD dissertation, Johns Hopkins University, 1964.
39. H. Wolfe and J.P. Young, 'Staffing the Nursing Unit, Part II: The Multiple
Assignment Technique', *Nursing Research,* 14 (1965), pp. 299-303.
40. Warner, 'A Two Phase Model for Scheduling Nursing Personnel in a
Hospital'.
41. D. Warner and J. Prawda, 'A Mathematical Model for Scheduling Nursing
Personnel in a Hospital', *Management Science,* 19 (1972), pp. 411-22.
42. J.S. Liebman, 'The Development and Application of a Mathematical
Programming Model of Personnel Allocation in an Extended Care Nursing Unit',
unpublished PhD dissertation, Johns Hopkins University, 1971; J.S. Liebman,
J.P. Young and M. Bellmore, 'Allocation of Nursing Personnel in an Extended
Care Facility', *Health Services Research,* 7 (1972), pp. 209-20.
43. H.E. Miller and W.P. Pierskalla, *Nurse Allocation with Stochastic Supply,*
Research Report no. 37-74-p7 (IE/MS Department, Northwestern University,
Evanston, Illinois, 1974).
44. L.E. Freund and G.E. Staats, *A Model for Allocating Nursing Resources
Based on Assignment Difficulties* (Department of Industrial Engineering, University
of Missouri-Columbia, 1972).
45. Offensend, 'Design, Control and Evaluation of Inpatient Nursing Systems'.
46. S. Tani, *An Analysis of the Staffing Reserve System* (Department of
Nursing Service, Stanford University Hospital, 1972).
47. J.C. Hershey, W.J. Abernathy and N. Baloff, 'Comparison of Nurse
Allocation Policies – A Monte Carlo Model', *Decision Sciences,* 5 (1974), pp.58-72.
48. M.A. Francis, 'Implementing a Program of Cyclical Scheduling of Nursing
Personnel', *Hospitals,* 40 (16 July, 1966), pp. 108ff; J.P. Howell, 'Cyclical
Scheduling of Nursing Personnel', *Hospitals,* 40 (16 January, 1966), pp. 77-85;
C. Maier-Rothe and H.B. Wolfe, *Cycle Scheduling and Allocation of Nursing
Staff* (Arthur D. Little, Inc., Cambridge, 1972); A.R. Morrish and A.R. O'Connor,
'Nursing Service-Cyclic Scheduling', *Hospitals,* 44 (16 February, 1970), pp.
66-71; E. Price, 'Techniques to Improve Staffing', *American Journal of Nursing,*
70 (October 1970), pp. 2112-15.
49. M. Rothstein, 'Hospital Manpower Shift Scheduling by Mathematical
Programming', *Health Services Research,* 8 (1973), pp. 60-6; M. Rothstein,
'Scheduling Manpower by Mathematical Programming', *Industrial Engineering,*
4 (1972), pp. 29-33.

50. D.M. Warner, 'Scheduling Nursing Personnel According to Nursing Preference: A Mathematical Programming Approach', *Operations Research,* 24 (1974), pp. 842-56.

51. J.L. Sanders, *Equitable Assignments in Small Nursing Units,* paper presented at the 41st Meeting of the Operations Research Society of America, New Orleans (1972).

52. H.E. Miller, W.P. Pierskalla and G.J. Rath, 'Nurse Scheduling Using Mathematical Programming', *Operations Research,* 24 (September-October 1976), pp. 856-70.

53. H.E. Miller, F.A. Pierce and W.P. Pierskalla, *The Implementation of Nurse Scheduling Using Mathematical Programming,* Proceedings of a Forum on Nurse Staffing, New York City, 8-9 September 1975 (National Cooperative Services Center of the Hospital Research and Educational Trust, 840 North Lake Shore Drive, Chicago, Ill. 60611).

54. H.E. Miller, F.A. Pierce, W.P. Pierskalla and G.J. Rath, 'Nurse Utilisation Algorithm', in George K. Chacko (ed.) *Health Handbook* (North-Holland Publishing Company, 1979).

55. See note 36.

56. Kaplan, *A Statistical Model for Analysis and Control of Nurse Staffing.*

57. C.H. Olson, *Projecting Manpower Requirements from Staffing Utilisation Charts,* Proceedings of the 23rd Meeting of the American Institute of Industrial Engineers, Anaheim (1972), pp. 283-93.

58. CASH, *Staff Utilisation and Control Program.*

59. R.N. Davis and J.M. Cowie, 'Variance Analysis for Patient-Centered Nursing Management', *Industrial Engineering,* 4 (July 1972), pp. 26-31.

60. E.g. L.E. Hay, *Budgeting and Cost Analysis for Hospital Management* (Pressler Publications, Bloomington, 1963), pp. 276-86.

61. Griffith, *Quantitative Techniques for Hospital Planning and Control,* p. 299.

62. Ibid., pp. 300-2.

63. See note 36.

64. W.J. Abernathy, N. Baloff, J.C. Hershey and S.E. Wandel, 'A Three Stage Manpower Planning and Scheduling Model – A Service Sector Example', *Operations Research,* 21 (May-June 1973), pp. 693-711; S.E. Wandel, 'A Three Stage Probabilistic Programming Model for Manpower Management: A Nurse Staffing Example', unpublished PhD dissertation, Stanford University, 1973; S.E. Wandel and J.C. Hershey, 'Evaluation of Nurse Staffing Policies Using a Manpower Planning and Scheduling Model', *Operational Research '75* (North Holland/American Elsevier, 1975).

65. See notes 36, 52, 53 and 54.

66. Miller *et al.,* 'Nurse Scheduling Using Mathematical Programming'.

9 PRIMARY HEALTH CARE

Tony Hindle

Introduction

In general, operational research (OR) in health has been looking either
for more efficient ways of providing service or, somewhat less frequently,
for innovation in providing health care. Although primary health care
has been subject to both approaches I believe it to be one of the most
fruitful areas of potential innovation. The reason is that many of the
fundamental decision problems are as much 'managerial' as they are
'professional' — medical or nursing, etc. Often the problem is not so
much the direct treatment of patients as deciding which patients should
be invited into the system for more specialist attention. The decision
problems are those of preliminary diagnosis, referral and the sign-
posting of services. It is certainly tempting to think that these decisions
are amenable to a more scientific approach. Unfortunately, however,
not all that much progress has as yet been made.

The primary health care service centres on the activities of the
generalist physician, variously called the family doctor, the family
practitioner or the general practitioner, who will often have helpers
or colleagues. For example, in the UK, his 'team' may include health
visitors, who are trained nurses with further experience in preventive
health care, and community nurses capable of providing a nursing
service in the patient's home. In the USA, the primary care physician
many employ physician's assistants, often with a scientific background
and further training in medicine, or family nurse practitioners with
some medical training to 'top up' their nursing background. In most
primary health care services the physician and his colleagues will have
access to technical help, particularly in the areas of pathology and
radiology.

Normally, the primary care physician and his team will have a 'list'
of people for whom they have a primary health care responsibility and
who regard the physician as 'their' doctor. In anything but severe
emergency conditions, the primary care 'practice' will be the first point
of call for the 'sick' patient. The organisation of such a service raises
a whole range of questions of considerable fascination to the
operational researcher:

1. Should the 'team' take the initiative and take preventive health
   care action or should it be passive and wait for the demands of
   'sick' patients?
2. What sort of decisions require what sort of training? Is a full medical
   school training needed for developing skills in preliminary diagnosis?
   Could a computer algorithm be more effective than a physician?
3. What size of population should a primary care team try to serve?
   How should teams be located?
4. How should teams be organised and tasks delegated?
5. How should the team 'optimise' its use of specialist service?

As already mentioned, not much progress has been made in helping to
answer these and other questions. Simpson puts most of the blame on
the fact that data problems are particularly severe, pointing out that
'most general practitioners make virtually no regular statistical returns,
apart from patient numbers in a few categories, and even these are
subject to significant error'.[1] Because of this, most studies to date have
concentrated on determining such basic facts as the frequency of visiting
by patients, consultation procedures, etc. These have been mainly
isolated 'one-off' studies, with the particular exception of those
undertaken by the author and also Professor Haley's group at Birmingham
University in the UK (in association with the Royal College of General
Practitioners).[2] Although not an OR book as such, Donald Hicks'
review of primary health care in the UK is written with a problem-
solving style and is a valuable source book for operational researchers
interested in this area of application.[3]

OR has a tremendous opportunity to make a contribution to many
crucial primary health care decision issues and the remainder of this
chapter discusses various illustrative applications in the UK and the USA.

The Geographical Distribution of Primary Care Physicians

In the USA one of the serious problems in the provision of primary
health care is that of geographical maldistribution. It is extremely
tempting, for professional, financial and cultural reasons, for primary
care physicians to set up practice in the major towns and cities and it is
difficult to persuade them to move to underprivileged areas. Since
primary care operates on a 'fee for service' basis, it is harder to make a
living in such areas and professional and social contacts are also more
difficult. In a study carried out by the author in Indiana, the State had

decided to implement a 'loan forgiveness' programme as a financial inducement to physicians to set up practice in currently underserved areas. The problem was how to define primary care service areas and how to judge the relative need for extra physicians.

Prior to the study the approach was simply to look at the number of primary care physicians per head of population in the administrative counties of the State. This was obviously inadequate; especially so because it ignored the interactions between counties, i.e. the cross-boundary flows. A somewhat arbitrary but more satisfactory approach, adopted in the study, was to define service areas as population centres and their environs with a population of at least 2,000 persons, which is the approximate number of people per primary care physician in the USA.

The environs were defined as the area within a five-mile radius of the population centre (five miles was thought to be a reasonable travel distance to a physician). If service areas defined in this way overlap, then a combined service area results. In addition, the State was divided into the twelve regions normally used by planning agencies. The result is the map shown in Figure 9.1, with 79 primary health care areas and the surrounding 'rural' area.

It was easy to find out the location and type of primary health care physician in practice in the State but there were no data on the patients actually being treated by each physician. A reasonably accurate picture of the demographic characteristics of each service area could, however, be obtained. The approach taken was to construct a plausible behavioural model which would assign patients to doctors and hence define those communities which were underserved, i.e. where the doctors would have insufficient capacity to meet potential demand.

The first step was to estimate the capacity of the primary care physicians in terms of patient visits per year. This was achieved by a study of *Reference Data on the Profile of Medical Practice*, a publication by the American Medical Association. The next step was to estimate 'potential demand', which is defined as the need for primary health care as perceived by the population, disregarding factors which would interfere with the satisfaction of that need. By definition, not all the potential demand will be expressed and this difference was estimated as a function of geographical accessibility (distance to the physician) and economic feasibility (income levels). Although this gap between need and expressed demand can be of relevance to decision makers, the principal interest lies in the extent to which expressed demand can be met by the primary health care physicians. An 'availability index' was derived where 'availability' was defined as the percentage of the

Figure 9.1: Primary Care Service Areas in Indiana

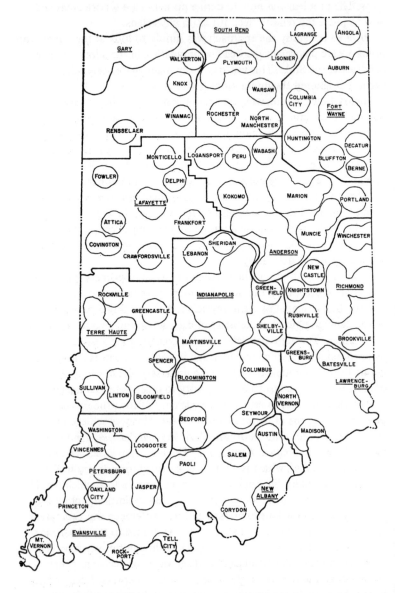

Source: reproduced, with permission, from *Health Services Research*, vol. 13, no. 3 (Fall 1978), p. 292. Copyright 1978 by the Hospital Research and Educational Trust, 840 North Lake Shore Drive, Chicago, Illinois 60611.

expressed demand which can be satisfied by the physicians. This index is based on a model of the services which flow across the service area boundaries. The basic assumptions made are:

1. if the physicians have spare capacity after all the expressed demand in their own service area has been met, this capacity is made available to the adjacent rural area;
2. If a person in a particular service area could obtain a better service (could satisfy more of his potential demand) in the adjacent rural area, his demand will be assigned to this latter area.

The availability index for a service area ($AVAIL_j$) is computed as:

$$AVAIL_j = (MD_j \times P) / V_j$$

where MD_j = the number of full-time equivalent primary care physicians in area j
P = the capacity of a full-time equivalent primary care physician (in visits per year)
V_j = the expressed demand on the physicians in area j in visits per year.

The results of this exercise for the service areas in Indiana clearly indicate those areas where availability is particularly low and hence where the need for extra physicians is high.

Other indices were also obtained from the analysis and in particular a 'primary care service index' ($PCSI_j$) which is defined as the ratio of satisfied demand to potential demand (need). Reducing this gap could be regarded as the overriding long-term objective.

From an OR viewpoint, a question of interest was the problem of determining the impact of distance to the nearest physician on demand and the expected distance to the nearest physician within service areas, given a particular allocation of physicians. A study in rural Kentucky (similar in many ways to Indiana) had shown clearly the fall-off in demand with distance to the physician giving rise to an accessibility index ($ACCESS_j$) where

$$ACCESS_j = 100 - 2.5D_j$$

where D_j is the expected road distance to physicians in service area j. In estimating D_j, use was made of the ideas developed by Eilon, Watson-Gandy

226 *Primary Health Care*

and Christofides.[4] Within a service area, the use of a nearest location algorithm will produce a set of polygons with the physician located centrally in each polygon. The area of the individual polygon can be estimated as the area of the service area divided by the number of physician locations (although account must be taken of the balance of solo and group practice in the area). Empirical study suggested that the expected distance to the physician in the areas obtained could be estimated quite well using the mathematical result obtained for circular areas and randomly located population giving

$$D_j = (1.3)(0.667)(A/(\pi L))^{\frac{1}{2}}$$

where A = the area of the service area
L = the number of physician locations.

Note that 1.3 is used as a conversion factor to give expected road distance.

Despite the assumptions made in developing these indices, the results seemed to fit in with medical school administrators' intuitive feelings and produce a fair and objective solution to their problems of allocation of the loan forgiveness programme's fund.

Beginning in April 1976, this research has been used to assist the members of the Board of Trustees of the Indiana Medical Distribution Loan Fund to determine the areas in Indiana in greatest need of additional primary care physicians. Around 30-40 students per year have so far participated in the programme which involves them in a selection of practice locations based on the need index, in return for which they receive financial help.

Primary Health Care Teams

In the UK, USA and elsewhere, an area of interest has been the development and organisation of primary health care teams. As already mentioned in the introduction, the main issues have involved the delegation of tasks and responsibilities to nurses and technicians with various levels of qualification and experience in primary health care.

In the UK, the approach has been a rather unusual one whereby health visitors and nurses have been 'attached' to primary care physicians. Prior to this innovation, community-based nurses were employed by local government agencies and not directly by the health service and hence were largely independent of the primary care physicians. In 1974, they became employees of the health service and were assigned to work with particular physicians to provide their specialist services to his patients. They are not the direct employees of the doctor. The change has been difficult and fairly traumatic. Perhaps the most difficult problems have centred around the role of the health visitor. Although she is a trained nurse, she does not carry out nursing duties as such but rather provides general health advice in the patients' homes, particularly in the mother and baby context. It has not been uncommon for doctor and health visitor to experience difficulties of mutual adjustment and acceptance of each other's relative status in the team.

A more straightforward problem faced in setting up a team arises from the geographical spread of the physician's patients. Whereas health visitors and community nurses had been accustomed to working in well-defined and non-overlapping geographical areas, a physician's patients can be much more widely scattered, leading to the possibility of significant increases in travel time and a corresponding reduction in effective patient contact time. A way of tackling this problem is to allow for 'partial' attachment whereby a community nurse (or health visitor) can hand over responsibility for the physician's more remote patients to a more conveniently located nurse. A study aimed at designing such arrangements was carried out by the author in a rural area of northern England.

In this study a wide range of possible 'team' arrangements and hand-over organisations could be considered and the main problem was to predict the consequences of any scheme in terms of travel time and effective patient contact time. What was needed was a model of the nurse's day.

The nurse's day can be divided into three phases:

1. administration;
2. travelling;
3. patient contact.

In the model, administrative time was regarded as a constant to be deducted from the time available for travelling to visit and provide a service to patients. The number of patients visited will depend on the demand but also on the constraints imposed by travel time and, of course, the time needed to deal with each patient. The travel time will, in turn, depend on the geographical characteristics of the area to which the nurse has been assigned. In the rural part of the study area, the population lived mainly in villages with the remainder in scattered farmhouses. Roads connected the villages. Thus a nurse's route could be seen as mainly a path between villages with detours to farmhouses. Since it is a simple matter to locate village centres in a model of the problem, this aspect was tackled first and an attempt made to estimate the average (or expected) travel distance between village centres, $\bar{D}_B$, for a given nurse trying to meet the demand placed upon her.

To estimate $\bar{D}_B$, use was made of the result obtained by Christofides and Eilon who simulated a similar problem and found a relationship between D_B and D_R: the sum of radial distances from the starting-point to the points of call, giving

$$D_B = \frac{1.8D_R}{C} + 1.1(a)^{\frac{1}{4}} . (D_R)^{\frac{1}{2}}$$

where a = the area of the region being served
and   C = the maximum number of calls that can be made before a
                  return to base.[5]

Several difficulties arise in adapting this result. Firstly, the demand on a nurse is stochastic in that, on any particular day, a village will only be visited if there is at least one patient needing a service. A second difficulty arises from the parameter C in that, although nurses do not have a capacity constraint as such, they usually do, in fact, return to base during the day for various administrative reasons. C was set as the average number of calls prior to return to base that were observed in practice.

The stochastic property was introduced by assuming that $\bar{D}_B$ could be regarded as a function of $\bar{D}_R$, i.e. the expected radial distance. For a set of random demands the probability that a village is included in a particular day's route is

$$1 - e^{-k_i p}$$

where k_i is the number of potential patients in the village
          p is the probability (average) that a patient will need a visit
              on a given day.

Thus:

$$\bar{D}_B = \sum_{i=1}^{m} d_i (1 - e^{-k_i p})$$

where m = number of villages
       d_i = radial distance to a particular village.

In order to estimate the extra distance travelled to the 'randomly' scattered patients ($\bar{D}_W$), use was made of the result obtained by Beardwood, Halton and Hammersley which suggests that:

$$D_W = k. \sqrt{a.N}$$

where a = the area of the region being served
       N = the number of randomly located calls.[6]

Again, in order to introduce the stochastic element, $\bar{D}_W$ was regarded as a function of $\bar{N}$, the expected number of calls. These extra calls were regarded as randomly scattered within each 'parish' which is the administrative area surrounding each village.

In order to examine the success or otherwise of any particular assignment of nurse to patients (and hence areas), one can either judge the number of hours per day needed to meet the expected demand or alternatively determine the proportion of the demand which can be satisfied if the nurse has a given number of hours available. In general, if $\bar{D}_T = \bar{D}_B + \bar{D}_W$, i.e. the total expected daily travelling distance, then for any particular area $\bar{D}_T$ is a function of p, the average probability of a patient needing a visit, and k is the population of potential patients. The number of hours required (H) is given by:

$$\frac{\bar{D}_T (p)}{S} + Vkp$$

where S = average road speed
       V = average contact time per patient.

To display this result in an easily usable form, the relationship can be written:

$$1 = \frac{D_T(p)}{Y} + \frac{k.p}{X}$$

and a set of contours plotted (as in Figure 9.2) relating X and Y for various values of p,

where X = H/V
       Y = H.S

Figure 9.2: The Effect of the Organisation of a Nurse's Day on the Level of Service she can Provide

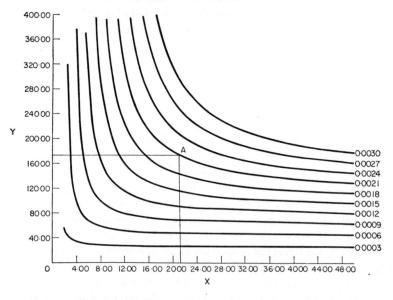

Source: reproduced, with permission, from *Operational Research Quarterly*, vol. 25, no. 2 (June 1974), p. 237.

Figure 9.2 also shows how the chart can be used to determine the calling rate achievable by a nurse having seven hours to spend on travelling and visiting in a particular area. If her average time per visit is 20 minutes and her average travelling speed is 25 mph, the resultant X and Y values are 175 and 21. The point A (175, 21) gives a p value of 0.0021, indicating that with this work pattern a service level of 2.1 calls per day per thousand people in her region could be achieved.

The analysis described was used to derive a particular 'partial' attachment plan in which the increase in mileage was assessed as 8 per cent compared with a 54 per cent increase for the best 'full' attachment plan, whereas only 3 per cent of calls needed to be handed over to non-attached nurses.

The level of implementation was almost unnervingly high in this project and the plan was put into effect almost exactly as recommended in the report. This is the only project in which the author has been involved where the report became a sort of 'bible' to be followed to the letter: an interesting experience but perhaps characteristic of a 'one-off' yet comprehensive reorganisation.

Around a year later the plan was monitored and seemed to be working well, although mileage had increased a little more than predicted by the model (by 12 per cent rather than 8 per cent). Some of this extra mileage was associated with independent changes in the 'cover' arrangements for nurses on holiday or sick, although some was no doubt due to inaccuracy in the model.

A current project is looking at the over-all health visiting service provided by partially attached health visitors; this is described below.

The Allocation of Health Visiting Effort

Given that a health visitor will only carry out part of her work for her doctor's patients as a member of a primary health care team, then she will also be available for other work — either work passed on from other teams *or* alternatively certain specialised work for the wider community. It is clearly important that this work should be in line with the priorities and needs of the community as a whole. The project described here examines how this might be done.

Because health visitors, like many other health professionals, are to some extent independent practitioners, it is important that the work allocated to them is in line with their own views and interests. Thus the approach suggested here has three elements:

1. a knowledge of the community's requirement for health visiting;
2. a knowledge of the extent to which the requirements are being met;
3. a knowledge of the interests and specialised skills of individual health visitors.

The objective is to fill the gaps identified in (2) above by allocating the 'extra' work in line with the findings of (3) above.

The study was carried out in a health district with 25 health visitors and a population of approximately 112,000. The need was defined by determining 'target' visiting and the numbers of persons in each of 25 care groups, such as 'mother and baby,' 'the elderly', 'metabolic disorders' and so on. Minimum acceptable visiting rates were also defined. These visiting levels were derived from discussion with the policy makers in the district.

The gaps in visiting were readily determined by a detailed activity survey and by comparing current activity with the targets. Some quite wide gaps emerged in terms of the quantity of visiting and also the balance of visiting. Figure 9.3 shows for seven aggregated care groups the current pattern of visiting compared with the target visiting pattern. It indicates the need for an increased emphasis on visiting to the 'elderly', to the 'handicapped' and to 'medico-social' problems (such as 'metabolic disorders'). Thus there was a need to identify health visitors who might increase their work in these directions.

A knowledge of interests and skills was obtained from a structured interview with each health visitor in which she expressed her interest in 'extra' visiting (and conversely 'reduced' visiting). There was a considerable agreement between 15 of the health visitors who essentially expressed an interest in the traditional 'mother-baby-children' role – in line with their current activity and suggesting that they would be willing to do more of the same. The other health visitors had more specialised interests not necessarily in line with these current activities. The majority of these had 'elderly' interests but other interests included social problems and also metabolic disorders. In general, there seemed to be scope for a reallocation in line with both the views of the health visitors and the needs of the community.

Reallocation of work is not an area of activity in which community nurse management has, as yet, much experience and this study is at the stage of selling the idea. Thus, precise methods have not yet been developed. However, the general approach will be to set visiting targets which move gradually towards the desired over-all pattern. Organisationally, the health visitors need to accept both a team and a community-wide responsibility.

Assisting the Primary Care Physician

Some OR has been carried out in the context of the primary care 'practice', ranging from early work on appointment systems through to studies of task delegation to various 'physician assistants'.

Appointment systems have, in general, been successfully implemented in the primary care setting following an excellent piece of work carried out by Jackson, Welch and Fry in 1964.[7] This study looked at the problem both from a doctor's and an OR point of view. Unfortunately, not many other aspects of practice organisation have been looked at in

Figure 9.3: The Current 'Pattern' of Health Visiting Compared with
the 'Target Pattern'

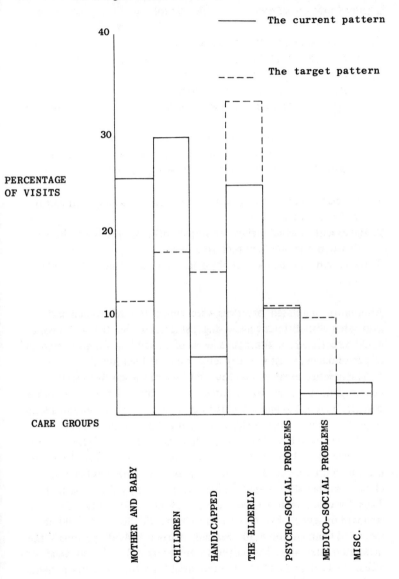

any great detail.

In making a start on this question, the author (and others) have built a general practice simulation capable of exploring such questions as:

1. the time-tabling of practice activities;
2. the balance of office sessions and home visiting;
3. the consequences of 'extra' practice activities;
4. the impact of the number of doctors;
5. the 'list size' (number of potential patients) capacity of the practice.

A particular experiment using this simulation helped a practice to evaluate alternative time-tables and examine the consequences of taking on an extra physician. The measures of performance used were:

1. the delay experienced by patients in obtaining an appointment to see the physician;
2. the extent to which delays led to patients having to see a physician other than the one they preferred to see;
3. the extent to which actual physician hours correspond to time-table hours.

Alternative 'simulated' practices were subject to levels of demand associated with different increasing 'list sizes' so that the performance could be assessed for alternative levels of demand or, for given standards of performance, a 'list size' capacity could be determined.

The practice involved had four full-time physicians who were contemplating changes in the surgery time-table and an extra full-time partner. Figures 9.4 and 9.5 illustrate the sort of results obtained with respect to 'appointment delays' and 'patient-doctor preference'.

T1 refers to the present practice time-table, T2 to a 'feasible' new time-table and T3 to the enlarged practice with an 'optimal' time-table together with a reduced level of 'extra' practice activities (such as clinical assistantship sessions in local hospitals) by existing partners. Thus, for example, if we decided on an average delay of two days as a standard of service, Figure 9.4 indicates that the 'list size' could be increased from around 8,500 persons to around 14,500 persons – the maximum attainable. The partners were interested in the financial effects of such a change and the potential for attracting extra patients to the practice 'list'. Figure 9.4 also shows that a time-table change alone could allow them to accept around 600 extra patients to their 'list', with a very direct effect on practice income.

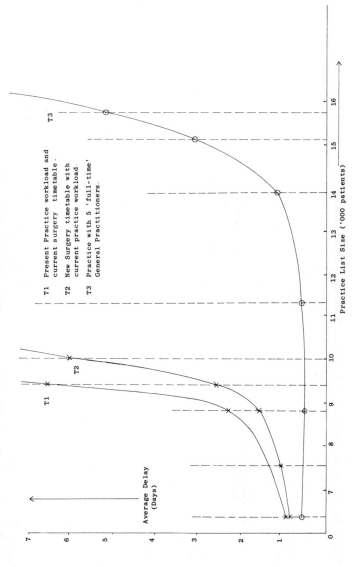

Figure 9.4: Average Delay (Days) for Non-urgent Appointments as List Size Increases

Figure 9.5: Percentage of Patients Failing to See their Preferred Doctor as List Size Increases

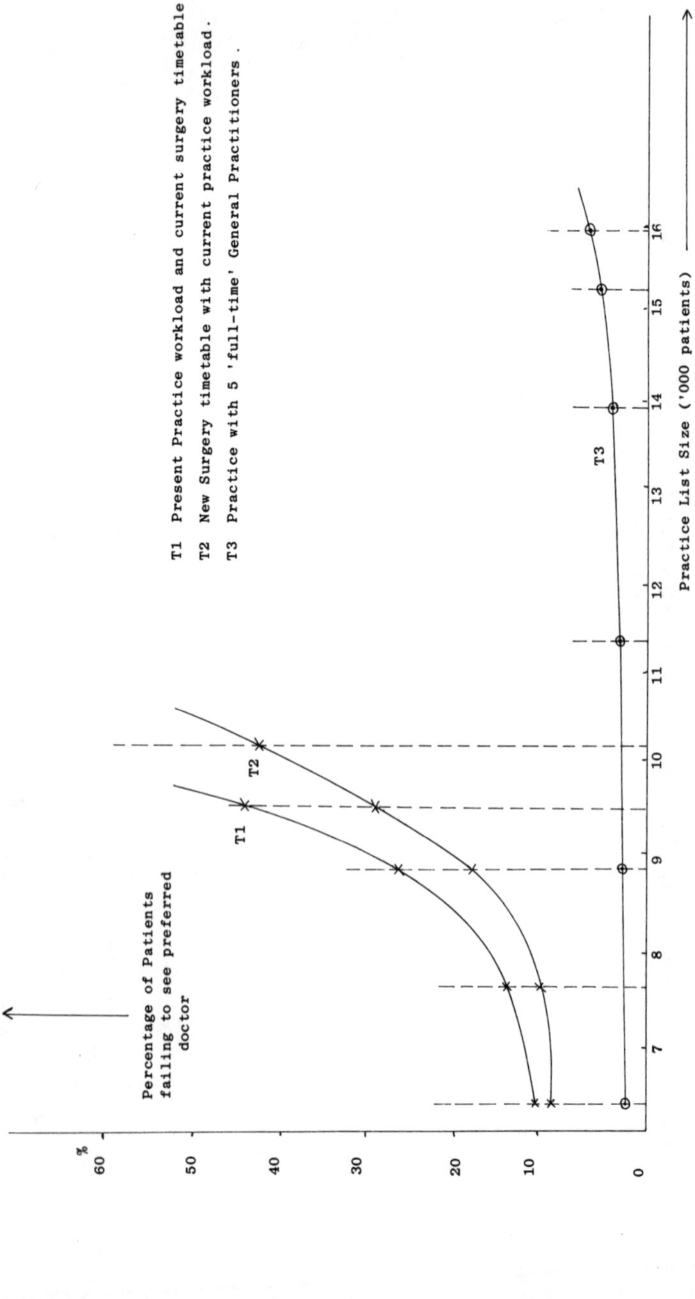
%
60
50
40
30
20
10
0
Percentage of Patients failing to see preferred doctor
T1
T2
T3
T1 Present Practice workload and current surgery timetable.
T2 New Surgery timetable with current practice workload.
T3 Practice with 5 'full-time' General Practitioners.
7
8
9
10
11
12
13
14
15
16
Practice List Size ('000 patients)

Perhaps the development which has been most challenging to the concept of primary care has been the emergence, particularly in the USA, of a new breed of 'physician assistants'. The basic idea is that graduates (preferably in the sciences) can be trained in the methodology of medical decision making and hence take the load off the physician. An alternative idea is to take nurses and give them a similar training, so producing 'family nurse practitioners'. Clearly, a key issue is the precise relationship between such intermediate-level health practitioners and the physicians and this could range from very close supervision through to almost independent status. These developments are challenging because they raise the questions of what knowledge and skills are really involved in primary care decision making. Similar questions are also raised by developments in computer diagnostics.

Much analysis has been carried out relevant to questions of optimal staffing in primary care but, as Smith *et al.* point out, very often the problems of data and measurement are glossed over when elegant models are presented.[8] The objective of most studies in the American context has been the minimisation of cost in meeting the demand for the various services. There are other considerations which may dominate this objective in other health care situations, particularly the low availability of trained doctors.

The methodology adopted in the analysis has involved either mathematical programming or simulation or some interactive use of both techniques. As Smith *et al.* point out, an important feature of the problem is that most health workers must be hired full-time and the primary care centre is not free to use a few minutes of a particular type of personnel's time per week. This leads to a mixed integer linear programming formulation.

The approach requires four types of information:

1. Encounters between the practice and the patients must be grouped such that encounters within a group can be argued to have received effectively the same service albeit from different personnel (referred to by Smith *et al.* as homogeneous encounter groups (HEGs)). The mix of patient problems presented to the practice must be specified in terms of HEGs.
2. For each HEG a collection of feasible techniques must be specified. This collection may be defined by observation or, possibly, in some applications from discussion of treatment policy with the doctors.
3. The maximum amount of time per week available per person of each provider type needs to be provided to the model.

4. The relative wages of the various practitioners must be specified.

The operation of the model provides not only an optimal staff selection but also an allocation of patient problems to each staff member. However, it must, of course, be remembered that there will be other aspects of organisation and that patient arrival is an inherently stochastic process.

Notes

1. M.G. Simpson, 'Health', *Operational Research Quarterly,* 27, no. 1(ii), (1976), p. 217.

2. R.J.F.H. Pinsent and J.B. Peacock, 'The Summary Card', *Journal of the Royal College of General Practitioners,* 23 (1973); R.J.F.H. Pinsent and J.B. Peacock, 'Package Programmes for Operational Research in General Practice', *Journal of the Royal College of General Practitioners,* 23 (1973).

3. Donald Hicks, 'Primary Health Care – A Review' (Department of Health and Social Security, HMSO, London 1976).

4. S. Eilon, C. Watson-Gandy and N. Christofides, *Distribution Management: Mathematical Modelling and Practical Analysis* (Hafner, New York, 1971).

5. N. Christofides and S. Eilon, 'Expected distances in distribution problems', *Operational Research Quarterly,* 20 (1969), p. 437.

6. J. Beardwood, H.J. Halton and J.M. Hammersley, 'The Shortest Route Through Many Points', *Proceedings of the Cambridge Philosophical Society,* 55 (1959), p.299.

7. R.R.P. Jackson, J.D. Welch and J. Fry, 'Appointment Systems', *Operational Research Quarterly* vol. 15, no. 3 (1964).

8. K.R. Smith, A. Mead-Over, M.F. Hansen, F.L. Golladay and E.J. Davenport, 'Analytic Framework and Measurement Strategy for Investigating Optimal Staffing in Medical Practice', *Journal of the Operations Research Society of America,* vol. 24, no. 5 (1976).

10 AMBULANCE SERVICE PLANNING

Robert Raitt

Ambulance service planning has attracted considerable attention from operational research practitioners, especially in the last ten years. At first sight the analysis of ambulance services appears to be a natural area for the application of traditional OR techniques, presenting a more readily quantifiable logistical problem than most other areas of health care planning. In many cases quantitative performance measures existed prior to the influence of management science, and one might assume that the cumulative experience of the OR profession in the facility location, vehicle scheduling, routeing and distribution fields would be applicable to ambulance services with only a modest investment of technical development. This, however, is not generally the case. Questions of ambulance deployment have exhibited many distinctive structural characteristics that have posed new modelling problems.

There are aspects of ambulance service management that are indeed common to the management of any fleet of vehicles. Vehicle replacement, maintenance policy and supplies of spares are examples of such aspects which have been subject to studies similar to those sponsored by operators of other large fleets of vehicles. In this chapter I intend to focus on the deployment problems which are unique to ambulance services.

The various approaches adopted in OR ambulance studies reflect the different operational features and contexts which shape particular service problems. A fundamental factor is whether an 'emergency only' service is provided, or whether out-patients and day-care patients are also provided with transport by the ambulance service. In the USA, most services are essentially emergency services, although a small number of admissions, discharges and out-patients may be carried. In the UK, emergency calls account for less than 10 per cent of ambulance journeys and day-time operations are dominated by the transport requirements of out-patients and day-care patients to and from hospitals and day-care centres. Another factor that has influenced the modelling approach is the scale of operation of a service. Analysis of the deployment of an extensive fleet of ambulances within a given geographical area is qualitatively different from determining the number of ambulances to provide services for a single hospital. A further factor is the geographical nature of the area to be covered, in particular the distinction between densely populated urban areas and rural areas. Data availability and computing resources have also influenced the nature of some of the OR work in this field.

The structural difference between planning emergency and non-emergency services is a fundamental one. The problems of emergency ambulance planning are similar to those of fire services, where a fast response to random events is required. The focus of attention in planning is usually on the locations of stations and the staffing levels required to provide efficient responses to the given pattern of calls. The main difference between emergency ambulance services and fire services is that the fire service has fewer calls, but each case is likely to be a serious one requiring a number of crews, while ambulance emergency calls are more frequent but usually require a single vehicle response.

In contrast, non-emergency ambulances provide a transport service to hospitals and health care centres. These services are structurally similar to a mail delivery service but they typically have loading and demand peaking problems resembling those of bus services. Improvements have been achieved by demand zoning and by applying analytical methods to improve routeing efficiency.

Most OR work has been applied to emergency service planning, since even where non-emergency services are provided, they are rarely considered relevant to location decisions. Thus, after a brief comment on non-emergency ambulance planning, the bulk of this chapter will review the OR contribution to emergency services.

Planning Non-emergency Journeys

Most of the developments in this area have taken place in the UK, where large fleets of 'sitting case' and dual-purpose vehicles are deployed for out-patient and day-care patient transport. This demand has pronounced peaks in the early morning and late afternoon, coinciding with clinic and day-care centre starting and finishing times. Typically, between 15 and 20 per cent of patients attending out-patient clinics at a hospital are carried by the ambulance service and these comprise over 90 per cent of ambulance patient journeys. Day-shift manning levels in the service are thus determined predominantly by the demand for out-patient transport, as already indicated.

Daily Scheduling of Out-patients

The recent development of incentive bonus schemes for ambulancemen has stimulated attempts to improve the efficiency of out-patient transport in the UK. A number of computer systems are under development within health authorities for patient routeing and scheduling. The various algorithms used in these systems employ unpublished heuristic methods — in some cases these merely serve as starting-points in an interactive process directed by a planning officer. Standard distribution planning techniques have proved of little value in this context. Most are based on the distribution of goods from a central warehouse to a number of delivery points. Such techniques applied in reverse, i.e. routeing vehicles through a number of pick-up points to a central hospital, could go some way in supporting route planning, but many practical limitations would remain. For example, there may be a considerable number of destinations, and at any given moment a vehicle may be carrying patients for different destinations. There are several distinct types of patient to be considered — especially walking, wheel-chair and stretcher cases. Whilst the technical problems raised by these difficulties are not insuperable, this formulation only covers the first journeys of the morning or afternoon into a hospital, and these journeys often present little difficulty to a manual scheduler. It is the subsequent allocation of crews to further inward and outward journeys throughout the day under conditions of uncertainty that presents a more intractable problem. A major source of uncertainty is the clinic throughput time for any patient or group of patients. Time at the clinic is known to vary between specialties, between individual consultants and between individual cases. Thus, it is rarely feasible for an ambulance crew to return the same group of patients that it delivered to the clinic, except on the longest journeys.

Most computerised schemes for non-emergency ambulance scheduling include a facility for interaction with a planning officer. The system may then provide an initial schedule for the day's workload, which can be modified in the light of events, as the day proceeds. The framework for these systems is established by dividing the geographical area into small demand zones and estimating within-zone travel and pick-up times, and between-zone travel times. Appropriate loads and routes may be compiled heuristically, for example, by starting at the periphery of an area and picking up patients in zones *en route* to a given destination, or by delivering patients from 'outer' zones first and accommodating patients from 'inner' zones on subsequent journeys.

The development of these scheduling systems by management services groups continues; to date, little has been implemented and few technical publications have been produced. Similar approaches have been employed for studies of specific planning issues by the National Health Service OR Group. Thus, by taking a sample of demand over a number of days or weeks and applying similar analytical principles to those employed in daily scheduling systems, it is possible to estimate the number of vehicles and men required to meet the demand for transport in a given authority.[1] It can also be shown that more flexible appointment times for patients carried by ambulance, or more stringent control of demand, often allow substantial savings in resources and/or improvement in service levels.[2]

Tiering

When ambulance services offer a non-emergency service, questions regarding the appropriate interaction between emergency and non-emergency work inevitably arise. At one extreme, a two-tier system operates these two aspects of the service with separate sets of vehicles. This system has the advantage that less expensive vehicles with single-man crews may be used for the non-emergency tier. At the other extreme a single-tier system offers complete flexibility, each vehicle being available for any type of journey, and higher vehicle utilisation is possible. In many services an intermediate arrangement is more effective than either extreme. Davidson has investigated the effect of different operating strategies on the waiting times of different priority patient groups with a given ambulance fleet size, formulating the problem as a priority queuing system.[3] He compares the expected waiting times for patient groups using nine ambulances under a combined fleet, and under a tiered system with two emergency and seven general-purpose vehicles. He estimates that a tiered system increases waiting times for low-priority patients without significantly improving waiting times for high-priority patients in an urban ambulance service. He concludes that a two-tier system is not cost effective, although he performs no cost analysis as such, e.g. comparison of manning requirements or vehicle costs. His results are also limited by the fact that he does not take the geographical distribution of demand or specific road conditions into account. The successful operation of a single tier service can be extremely demanding on the control officers, who have to decide continuously how best to ensure cover for each part of their areas. Indeed, an OR approach to this problem has been adopted by researchers at the Cranfield Institute of Technology; they have developed a simulation of control procedures, although their work is as yet unpublished. The experience of ambulance officers in various types of area and the results of other modelling work (see the final section of this chapter) confirm that the costs and benefits of tiering depend on the specific conditions and characteristics applying in an area.

Planning Emergency Cover

OR methods have made a substantial contribution to the planning of emergency ambulance services over the last ten years. As suggested at the beginning of this chapter, the variety of modelling approaches reflects the differing environmental and operational features of ambulance services. The location of depots (also referred to as stations and garages) or units (ambulances) has been the main focus of attention, as, in some cases, has been the number of ambulances required to cover a given area.

Performance Criteria

Various quantitative performance criteria were available as a basis for the study of alternative operational arrangements, prior to the application of OR methods. The concept of response time as a measure of service level was well established. This is the time elapsing from the receipt of a call by ambulance control to arrival of an ambulance at the scene of the incident. The mean expected response time for an area is a common measure, sometimes in combination with maximum response time. This focuses on the time a patient is awaiting the ambulance and its use implies that the crew on arrival can alleviate or at least stabilise the patient's condition. The time from the call to arrival at hospital — round-trip time — is occasionally used as a measure. Also, a more limited measure is ambulance availability or activation time, i.e. the time from receipt of a call to the despatch of an ambulance. The utilisation of ambulance vehicles has also been employed as a measure of operational efficiency, as opposed to service level or effectiveness measures. Gibson has reviewed evaluation criteria for emergency ambulance services.[4]

Modelling Approaches

The earlier OR applications in the USA tended to analyse the potential performance of services at single hospitals or in a particular hospital district. Savas, in a pioneering exercise, simulated the service in a district of New York.[5] Adopting response time and round-trip time as service level criteria, he simulated the despatch of ambulances over a long period in the district to compare various location policies. Subsequent cost-benefit analysis demonstrated that dispersion of ambulances improves service levels per unit cost.

Queuing theory was used by Bell and Allen to estimate the fleet size required to respond immediately to calls from a single location.[6] Their primary criterion is immediate response, or what has subsequently been termed availability or 'activation time', and their main analysis is concerned with the size of a small local ambulance service. No geographical or travel factors are included and, as the authors indicate, an analysis of the service for a larger community using similar principles would require simulation, unless such a service could realistically be divided into a number of small independent single-garage services. This paper gives one of the first clear descriptions of an emergency ambulance service as a queuing system, with emergency calls 'arriving' in the system for servicing by an ambulance. Their discussion also implies a formulation of larger-scale studies in terms of an assignment problem (assigning calls to depots) combined with a queuing problem (availability of an ambulance at depots). This formulation proved a productive one for further work. The assignment problem has attracted separate attention as an area of study. Carter, Chaiken and Ignall developed a model to investigate the effect of response area boundaries on average response times, using a co-ordinate system for a problem involving the location of two ambulances.[7]

Following Bell and Allen, Hall similarly emphasised the availability aspect of service, in a study of ambulance/police requirements in two precincts of Detroit.[8] The arrival process was modelled as a semi-Markov process for the occurrence of calls and a multi-function stochastic service process was developed, depending on the type of emergency and particular vehicle assigned. Again, the scale of the analysis was small as a multi-channel service system was employed, accommodating a maximum of four vehicles, and no detailed analysis of travel times to incidents was performed. Numbers and distributions of vehicles were suggested according to the availability criterion.

Volz extended this type of analysis by combining the availability consideration with 'drive time' to the incident.[9] The development of a drive time model between any two points in a county of Michigan enabled him to apply a mean response time criterion and to optimise local ambulance station locations on this basis. An iterative procedure was used to derive a solution. All calls within one square mile areas were considered to be located at a single point, and predetermined average speeds were applied to different types of road. This part of the method is clearly influenced by the rural nature of the service area. A constraint that the average response time to any point in the area be less than a specified minimum was also introduced. The analysis was extended up to six vehicles in the county.

Toregas, Swain, Revelle and Bergman formulate the problem of locating emergency service facilities as a set covering problem, emphasising travel times/distances rather than the stochastic aspect of the problem.[10] Availability is not explicitly taken into account and the method is possibly more appropriate for the location of fire stations than for ambulance stations. The sets are composed of combined potential facility and user points. The area is thus reduced to a finite number of points and a matrix of distances between points is obtained. The problem is then structured as an integer programming problem. The objective function to be minimised is the number of service facilities required, and upper limits on distance or travel times to given user points comprise the constraints.

An interesting and practical application, developed by Fitzsimmons, selects that sub-set of potential locations which minimises mean response time.[11] Availability is modelled on the basis of the probability of a given number of ambulances being busy, and solved by Monte Carlo methods. This eliminates the need to assume instantaneous relocation of ambulances when one is deployed, as for example does Volz.[12] Travel times are computed as a function of distance from point to point in the service area and a pattern search routine is used to find the most effective sub-set of locations. Thus, in the City of Los Angeles the system was used to select 14 emergency ambulance locations from 34 firehouses. Data were gathered on a grid of 308 census tract centroids. Again, this approach reflects the planning context in the USA, where ambulances are frequently based at fire stations when they are not hospital based. The selection of sites for purpose-built ambulance stations, as in the UK, tends to impose a different problem formulation.

Those studies concerning urban areas tend to place more emphasis on vehicle availability and the stochastic aspects of the problem, while those concerning rural areas pay relatively more attention to the distance and drive time. Thus Bell and Allen[13] and Hall,[14] working in urban areas, based their models on the stochastic problem, while Volz[15] and Toregas *et al.*[16] included detailed analyses of travel times from point to point in their rural service areas. Cantwell, Lenehan and O'Farrell provide another example of this, pointing out that in a rural area there is only a very slight possibility of a queue of calls forming and that travel times therefore tend to be more important than availability.[17] They simulate a service providing both emergency and non-emergency services on the basis of average speeds applied to distances between district centres. The response time distributions are predicted for various location strategies. In practical terms, the results of this study resemble several of those outlined above; i.e. it is recommended that ambulances be dispersed close to the sources of demand. This may seem an obvious conclusion but in fact the appropriate balance between a central depot and vehicle dispersion is often not apparent without some type of quantitative analysis.

A number of studies have built on the simulation work of Savas by developing a methodology that includes a combination of simulation and other analytical techniques.[18] Swoveland, Uyeno, Vertinsky and Vickson, for example, combine simulation with a branch and bound technique in an ambulance location study in Vancouver.[19] Zones are defined, central nodes identified and inter-nodal travel data gathered as in a number of other studies referred to above. Simulation runs determine the relationship between location strategies, despatch rules, demand and response times. An objective function is then developed and a branch and bound method used to derive a solution which provides minimum response times.

Berlin and Liebman combine simulation with a set covering model.[20] They formulate the emergency ambulance question as two related analytical issues — facility location and vehicle assignment. The location problem is addressed by the formulation of a set covering model similar to that of Toregas *et al.*[21] A network based on a system of nodes is developed and the minimum number of sites to reach all nodes within a maximum response time is determined by integer programming. This static model assumes continual availability at each site. The stochastic problem of availability is then examined by simulating the allocation of calls to ambulances at these sites. In combination, these models may then be used to evaluate alternative siting and manning levels.

The location problem has been formulated somewhat differently by Larson.[22] His hypercube queuing model has been applied to urban emergency services in general, including ambulance services. A geographical description of the region in terms of calls with associated travel time statistics is used as a basis for generating the state transition matrix for the Markov process. The vertices of the N-dimensional unit hypercube correspond to particular combinations of units occupied in attending calls. These vertices are 'toured' in a unit-step fashion and the optimal despatch units determined. Steady state probabilities are found by an iterative procedure and a range of performance measures are computed, including travel time-based measures and utilisation type measures by atom (cell), district and region.

Scott, Factor and Gorry also develop a distinctive approach, using probability theory to predict the entire probability distribution of response times from the demand distribution and the number and location of ambulances in an urban area.[23] Ambulance locations in this model are assumed to be a function of demand density at each point and travel speed is treated as a random variable, the distribution of average speed being estimated from a random sample of runs. Queuing theory is applied to model the availability factor.

This review is not intended to be exhaustive, but rather to indicate the main variations in approach in the literature. Revelle, Bigman, Schilling, Cohon and Church[24] provide a review of location models — both general and emergency service (EMS) — and emphasise the appropriate structure of a maximal covering model for EMS application, based on previous work by Church and Revelle.[25] This formulation has much in common with that of Toregas *et al.* and its attractiveness depends on the precise nature of the problem to be addressed and the characteristics of the area.[26]

Set covering models have a contribution to make where a large number of available locations exists, e.g. fire stations and hospitals in an urban area, and when few practical restrictions limit the use of these sites by an ambulance service, e.g. limited flexibility in the assignment of manpower between sites. The stochastic aspects of ambulance availability must be taken into account in these models, however, unless they are to be merely models of ambulance ranges expressed in terms of demand.

On the other hand, the simpler queuing models are limited to predicting availability only, unless they also incorporate geographical or road networks so that response times may be computed. They are also limited in the size of area and problem that can be addressed. The various simulation approaches overcome some of these limitations, although they often remain limited in size. Their event-by-event structure tends to make analyses of a wide range of options or operating conditions a time-consuming and expensive exercise.

Implementation

A general reservation which has frequently been expressed by ambulance officers and staff regarding OR models is the incorporation of apparently simplistic assumptions with respect to the travel times within a service area. The assumption of a uniform speed from point to point is certainly dubious in urban areas and, on dividing an area into districts, zones or cells, it is often intuitively felt that the results of the study will be sensitive to how the segmentation is performed, in determining both the number of zones and the principles used in zoning. Assumptions of straight-line distances and of neat circular service areas or rectangular cells with centroids have also been criticised. A few of the studies described above develop travel matrices based on detailed analyses of response time documentation but, even when this is done, ambulance staff frequently comment on the naivety of relying on a single data set. A characteristic view in the service, in the author's experience, is that travel times, and thus response times, vary considerably with traffic congestion and weather conditions. This variation is rarely felt to apply uniformly throughout an area. In London, for example, travel times along some roads can vary by a factor of three or more. Routes from a given point to another may vary with the time of day in order to avoid known delay points. Such factors, it is often suggested, determine the service level achieved. This intuitively held view is supported by much of the analytical work, for example that of Cantwell *et al.*[27] and the NHS OR Group in the UK (see below), which shows that the queuing of calls for ambulances rarely occurs and that response times are more sensitive to travel time estimates than to any other uncontrollable variable. Thus, it is surprising that more attention has not been directed towards the construction of detailed local data bases of travel times at various times of the day, week or year. It is especially surprising if the model is to be used to indicate manning levels in various shifts, as one would expect the travel times in different shifts to exhibit different patterns, especially in urban areas. As far as can be judged from published papers, the sophistication of mathematical modelling far exceeds that of the construction of key data bases.

The emphasis given to applications in the literature is in general slight, in many cases validation and application being described, if at all, in a small section at the end of the paper, or as an 'example'. The problems of implementing operational changes are rarely mentioned.

In some cases this may be due to the authors' need to select what they feel is the most appropriate material for publication, but in general implementation seems to be of secondary concern to the model designer. There is little evidence of awareness of the problems, for example, of compiling shift rotas to provide the cover in each shift as indicated by a model, or of ensuring that a planned staffing arrangement is feasible in terms of recruiting local staff at remote stations (especially at night), or of examining ways in which crews can support each other by relocating when a particular central location is left without cover.

The reader is left wondering how much practical impact this work has had on location selection, levels of staffing or operational planning. When applications are described, there is little reference to any participation or commitment on the part of the receiving organisations. Chaiken has reviewed the implementation record of six emergency service deployment models in the USA, although these are not designed particularly for ambulance services.[28] The record of these models is a mixed one; most of the implementation problems quoted by Chaiken — adequacy of documentation, need for subsequent programme modifications, and the availability of an appropriate computer system in the operating agency — clearly derive from the separation of the development and application functions in the case of these six models. The transfer of a model from one organisation to another inevitably poses problems.

In general, OR practitioners in recent years have tended to put greater emphasis on a participative approach in which model designers, operating management and planning staff from the receiving organisation collaborate in a project. The advantages of this approach in terms of influencing operations are more or less self-evident and it is to be expected that ambulance planning will be no exception. This was accepted as a premiss for the emergency ambulance planning work performed over the last five years in the UK by the National Health Service OR Group. Model design, the format of computer programmes and the development of relations with ambulance staff have been structured for such participation and for maximum ease of implementation. The success of this approach in introducing changes in ambulance services has been considerable. The following section briefly describes this work.

Ambulance Planning in the NHS OR Group

The Context of Emergency Ambulance Planning in the UK

The reorganisation of the National Health Service (NHS) in Britain, in April 1974, incorporated ambulance services into the NHS, organising them on an Area Health Authority basis, except for six metropolitan services. Most ambulance services were then faced with the problem of integrating services previously provided by local authorities. Questions of location, resource levels and organisation required a radical reassessment if the efficient provision of cover was to be achieved.

Performance criteria for emergency ambulances were developed by Orcon Services in 1974. The resulting standard performance levels and a method of measuring performance were accepted by the Department of Health and Social Security and issued to health authorities as recommended standards.[29] The method of measurement adopted was the distribution of response times achieved by each service, the recommended standard for an Area Health Authority being eight minutes or less for 50 per cent of calls and 20 minutes or less for 95 per cent of calls. For a metropolitan service these standards are seven and 14 minutes respectively.

In addition, it was recommended that activation time, defined as the interval between notification of an incident and the despatch of a vehicle, should not exceed three minutes for 95 per cent of calls. Subsequent to the acceptance of these standards, planning exercises have attempted to estimate the distribution of response times that would result from particular numbers and geographical distributions of emergency crews. The NHS Operational Research Group, which is not part of the NHS but a unit of the Royal Institute of Public Administration, has been particularly active in this field. In 1974 the Group developed an analytical approach to ambulance service planning, allowing the level of cover to be predicted in any health authority for any number and disposition of crews that the authority wished to consider. This computer model has demonstrated sufficient flexibility for application to extremely diverse areas in terms of geography, demography and urbanisation. In calibration exercises it has also been found to exhibit at least the level of accuracy required for the routine monitoring of operations. It is now an established tool for ambulance service planning within the UK, having been applied to approximately thirty different services.

The development of the model was sponsored by the Department of Health and Social Security on the grounds that the model should subsequently be instrumental in improving services in authorities throughout the UK.

Model Design

From the outset, a pragmatic design approach was adopted. In order to promote maximum ambulance staff participation, a model was developed which will predict the response time distribution for any set of locations and level of manning that officers of the service wish to specify, but which includes no normative features. Thus, no optimisation methods were used and the interactive capability was emphasised in conducting the studies. This design approach is far from unique — some of the models described above were based on similar principles, but the degree to which each project is controlled by ambulance officers themselves is perhaps unusual. Chief officers and control staff are invited to direct the study by posing questions for the model to address, the OR team acting as intermediaries in this process. No problems of programme modification or documentation arise, since the model design team are involved in the application work.

The construction of detailed data bases is approached in the same way. Ambulance personnel participate in developing a road network of the area. This is based on nodes which represent any point of significance for emergency work. Town centres, village centres, main intersections, industrial estates, shopping areas, hospitals, ambulance stations, danger points on roads — any point of potential significance is represented by a node. Travel time estimates from node to adjacent node along the network are prepared by the ambulance service, either by circulating the network to each station for local estimates or from available documentation. Several sets may be gathered for different times of the day, week or year. In particular, maximum times are estimated in addition to off-peak or average times. Similarly, a large sample of demand data is distributed geographically by node, and analysed by hour of the day, week, etc. For each run of the model, demand level may then be scaled to reflect a given 'rush hour' or shift.

The technical content of the model is described by Groom.[30] It is sufficient here to note that the ranges of crews at any location are computed by calculating the matrix of shortest route travel times between all specified points on a road network. The percentage of calls within $1, 2, 3, 4 \ldots$ etc. minutes of any combination of locations can then be computed. These 'potential' response time distributions must then be multiplied by availability distributions, i.e. the probability that for n locations, $n, n - 1, n - 2 \ldots 1$ of them will actually be manned at any given time, given the demand level and the service time to complete a call and return to provide cover. Availability distributions have been estimated from queuing theory. Sensitivity trials have shown the results to be insensitive to the assumptions inherent in the queuing model (e.g. Poisson arrivals).

Three basic variations of the availability model allow for different operating systems:

1. stations support each other when necessary, by relocating vehicles from less busy locations to busier ones when the latter are temporarily without cover (i.e. an assumption of instant relocation);
2. no such supporting activity is undertaken, and thus ambulances remain at their base station until mobilised for a call;
3. a single-tier system is in operation during day shifts (as described at the beginning of the chapter), under which a large fleet of vehicles on other duties may potentially respond to emergencies if required. This ensures very high availability.

Application of the Model

A study typically proceeds by a series of evaluations under the guidance of the Chief Ambulance Officer. The routine monitoring system requires that all response times are recorded and monthly comparisons against the recommended standards made. This facilitates validation exercises, in which performance with the present resources, locations and procedures can be predicted by the model for comparison with actual response times achieved. Officers are then encouraged to 'try' changes in locations, manning by shift, or operating procedures. The effect of the changes is then predicted and further evaluations specified in the light of the predictions. In fact, the location options to be considered are highly constrained, since new sites are in short supply and the costs of moving large, purpose-built stations would be considerable. There is no danger of a study producing results that are administratively or practically infeasible. Numbers of vehicles required can only be addressed by assessing cover levels for each shift and by taking the locally appropriate operating methods (tiering and support procedures) into account. A considerable number of evaluations are thus necessary, each based on the appropriate set of travel times and mean frequency of calls. A simulation model would be extremely expensive to rerun in this way.

Results indicate that apparently similar problems experienced by different authorities often require different measures to resolve them, given th variety of local circumstances and conditions. Rather than present a catalogue of results and measures implemented, I think it would be more appropriate to make some general observations. For example, analysis shows that, as Cantwell *et al.* found, the level of cover achieved is much more sensitive to changes in road conditions than to fluctuations in the frequency of calls.[31] Typically, a 100 per cent increase in the frequency of calls requires a 10-20 per cent increase in provision to maintain a given level of cover, while a 100 per cent increase in travel times due to traffic congestion or weather conditions requires a 50-80 per cent increase in provision for cover maintenance (depending predominantly on the degree of geographical clustering in the demand pattern). Moreover, the first of these conditions is not significantly improved by increasing the number of separate locations, while normally the second condition *requires* additional locations.

One output from the model is the potential contribution to cover from each location in the set being considered in terms of the percentage of calls it could respond to more quickly than any other. Also, the most appropriate site from which to respond to calls at each node in the network is given for control guidance. Location policies may then be examined by determining the marginal contribution of a crew at each location. A strategy, under which cover is built up by manning locations in order of their potential contribution, is clearly more effective than alternative location strategies, especially in rural areas (see Figures 10.1 and 10.2).[32] The hatched areas in these figures indicate the scope that exists for improving cover by location policy alone.

The distribution of crews between stations requires separate runs of the model by shift, with demand patterns and travel times appropriate to each shift. Many types of options may be considered, including the use of crews on call at home and the dispersion of crews at a large number of locations. A trade-off often exists between the number of locations and the number of crews required to meet the recommended standards (see Figure 10.3).

Generalisations about tiering are fraught with difficulties, since there are many factors to consider apart from operational efficiency, e.g. the training requirements for emergency work and the present mix of vehicle types in the fleet. Operational efficiency itself presents problems of measurement. A single-tier system inevitably allows higher utilisation of ambulances — this has been confirmed both by the application of the model and in practice. But the double-manning requirement can make it an expensive system. There is a stronger case for a two-tier system in urban areas than in rural areas, as the higher frequency of calls ensures

Figure 10.1: Emergency Cover in East Sussex

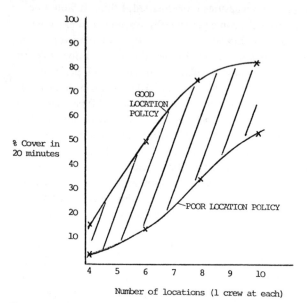

Figure 10.2: Emergency Cover in Greater Manchester — Division I

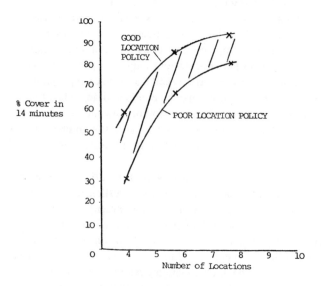

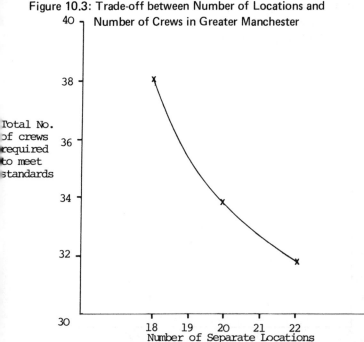

Figure 10.3: Trade-off between Number of Locations and Number of Crews in Greater Manchester

that the extremely low utilisations that can occur in rural areas are not experienced here. This is shown by the availability distributions calculated by the model. In a city the size of Manchester, for example, the mean of this distribution, i.e. the mean number of vehicles out attending calls at any given moment, can be greater than twelve, while in a rural area it is often less than two, and can be less than one.

The analysis of intermediate tiering arrangements has frequently been conducted. One common approach in the service is to employ a type of tiering where the emergency tier also performs some general work and is thus larger than would be necessary under a strict mutually exclusive two-tier system. Another system is the designation of a small number of exclusively emergency crews, other emergency calls being met from the general fleet. In these cases the availability distribution can be used to predict the probability distribution for the number of disruptions that face the out-patient service per hour or shift with any specified number of designated emergency crews. Figure 10.4 shows this predicted relationship for West Sussex in the evening rush-hour.

Figure 10.4: Disruption to Out-patient Services between 3 p.m. and 7 p.m. Necessary to Meet the Recommended Standards For Emergency Calls

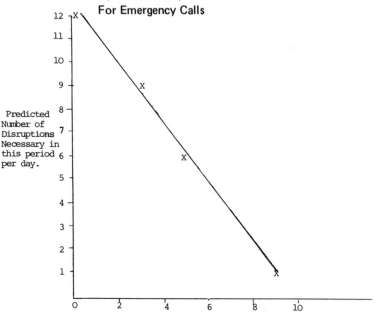

Number of Designated Emergency Crews

The model has also been used for the following purposes:

1. to search a given area for the most effective site for a new station, given the locations of other stations;
2. to examine disparities in service levels between different parts of an area;
3. to predict the effect of plannned road and motorway developments or population movements on the pattern of cover;
4. to assess whether changes in the times of shift changes would improve the efficiency of manning rotas.

The record of implementing the recommendations of these studies is a successful one in terms of closing some stations, resiting others, changing manning rotas and introducing new control methods. The Group attributes this success to the participation and commitment of ambulance officers, which, in turn, are facilitated by the flexible form of the model and the careful construction of realistic data bases.

Notes

1. K.E. Holloway, 'Clwyd Ambulance – Non-Emergency Service', NHS ORG Report 77/6 (1977); R.A. Raitt, 'Mid-Glamorgan Ambulances – Non-Emergency Services', NHS ORG Report 76/8 (1976).

2. R.A. Raitt, 'Outpatient Services at Neath General Hospital', NHS ORG Report 76/3 (1976); R.A. Raitt, 'Non Emergency Transport to the Royal East Sussex Hospital', NHS ORG Report 77/8 (1977).

3. D. Davidson, 'The Stretcher Ambulance Problem' (The Institute of Mathematics and its Applications, 1974), p. 16.

4. G. Gibson, 'Evaluative Criteria for Emergency Ambulance Systems', *Social Science and Medicine*, vol. 7 (1973), p. 425.

5. E.S. Savas, 'Simulation and Cost-Effectiveness Analysis of New York's Emergency Ambulance Service', *Management Science*, vol. 15, no. 12 (1969), pp. B608-B627.

6. C.E. Bell and D. Allen, 'Optimal Planning of an Emergency Ambulance Service', *Socio-Economic Planning Sciences*, vol. 3 (1969), pp. 95-101.

7. G.M. Carter, J.M. Chaiken and E. Ignall, 'Response Areas for Two Emergency Units', *Operations Research*, vol. 20, no. 3 (1972), pp. 571-94.

8. W.K. Hall, 'The Application of Multifunction Stochastic Service Systems in Allocating Ambulances to an Urban Area', *Operations Research*, vol. 20, no. 3 (1972), pp. 558-70; W.K. Hall, 'Management Science Approaches to the Determination of Urban Ambulance Requirements', *Socio-Economic Planning Sciences*, vol. 5 (1971), pp. 491-9.

9. R.A. Volz, 'Optimum Ambulance Location in Semi-Rural Areas', *Transportation Science*, vol. 5, no. 2 (1971), pp. 193-203.

10. C. Toregas, R. Swain, C. Revelle and L. Bergman, 'The Location of Emergency Service Facilities', *Operations Research*, vol. 19, no. 6 (1971), pp. 1363-73; C. Toregas and C. Revelle, 'Optimal Locations Under Time or Distance Constraints', *Papers of the Regional Science Association* (1972), p. 133.

11. J.A. Fitzsimmons, 'A Methodology for Emergency Ambulance Deployment', *Management Science*, vol. 19, no. 6 (1973), pp. 627-36.

12. Volz, 'Optimum Ambulance Location in Semi-Rural Areas'.

13. Bell and Allen, 'Optimal Planning of an Emergency Ambulance Service'.

14. Hall, 'Management Science Approaches to the Determination of Urban Ambulance Requirements'.

15. Volz, 'Optimum Ambulance Location in Semi-Rural Areas'.

16. Toregas *et al.*, 'The Location of Emergency Service Facilities'.

17. J. Cantwell, B. Lenehan and J. O'Farrell, 'Improving the Performance of a Local Authority Ambulance Service', in M. Ross (ed.), *OR '72* (North-Holland Publishing Company, London, 1973), pp. 443-53.

18. Savas, 'Simulation and Cost-Effectiveness Analysis of New York's Emergency Ambulance Service'.

19. C. Swoveland, D. Uyeno, I. Vertinksy and R. Vickson, 'Ambulance Location: A Probabilistic Enumeration Approach', *Management Science*, vol. 20, no. 4, pt. 2 (1973), pp. 686-98.

20. G.N. Berlin and J.C. Liebman, 'Mathematical Analysis of Emergency Ambulance Location'. *Socio-Economic Planning Sciences*, vol. 8, no. 6 (1974), p. 323.

21. Toregas *et al.*, 'The Location of Emergency Service Facilities'.

22. R.C. Larson, 'A Hypercube Queuing Model for Facility Location and Redistricting in Urban Emergency Services', *Computers and Operations Research*, vol. 1 (1974), pp. 67-95; R.C. Larson, 'Approximating the Performance of Urban Emergency Service Systems', *Operations Research*, vol. 23, no. 5 (1975), pp. 845-68.

23. D.W. Scott, L.E. Factor and G.A. Gorry, 'Predicting the Response Time of an Urban Ambulance System', *Health Services Research*, vol. 13, no. 4 (1978), pp. 404-17.

24. C. Revelle, D. Bigman, D. Schilling, J. Cohon and R. Church, 'Facility Location: A Review of Context-free and EMS Models', *Health Services Research*, vol. 12, no. 2 (1977), p. 129.

25. R. Church and C. Revelle, 'The Maximal Covering Location Problem', *Papers of the Regional Science Association*, vol. 32 (1974), p. 101.

26. Toregas *et al.*, 'The Location of Emergency Service Facilities'.

27. Cantwell *et al.*, 'Improving the Performance of a Local Authority Ambulance Service'.

28. J.H. Chaiken, 'Transfer of Emergency Service Deployment Models to Operating Agencies', *Management Science*, vol. 24, no. 7 (1978), pp. 719-31.

29. Orcon Services, 'Ambulance Service Performance Standards and Measurements', Report to DHSS (Cranfield Institute of Technology, Cranfield, 1974).

30. K.N. Groom, 'Planning Emergency Ambulance Services', *Operational Research Quarterly*, vol. 28, no. 3, pt. 2 (1977), pp. 641-51; K.N. Groom, 'The Estimation of Emergency Ambulance Cover', NHS ORG Report 75/16 (1975).

31. Cantwell *et al.*, 'Improving the Performance of a Local Authority Ambulance Service'.

32. R.A. Raitt, V.A. Kempner and K. MacMahon, 'Emergency Ambulance Cover in East Sussex', NHS ORG Report 76/2 (1976); R.A. Raitt and L. Adams, 'Study of Emergency Cover in Division I of the Greater Manchester Metropolitan Ambulance Service', NHS ORG Report 75/14 (1975).

NOTES ON CONTRIBUTORS

Duncan Boldy: Senior Operational Research Scientist, Institute of Biometry and Community Medicine, University of Exeter; Chairman of the European Working Group 'Operational Research Applied to Health Services'.

Mårten Lagergren: Director of Government Study on Care in Society, Stockholm.

Richard Gibbs: Senior Principal Scientific Officer, Department of Health and Social Security, London.

Reginald Canvin: Director, Institute of Biometry and Community Medicine, University of Exeter.

John Russell: Operational Research Scientist, British Gas, London.

Geoffrey Royston: Senior Scientific Officer, Department of Health and Social Security, London.

Dietrich Fischer: Director of Central Studies, IABG, Munich.

Richard Burton and David Dellinger: Associate Professors, Graduate School of Business Administration, Duke University, North Carolina.

Ciaran O'Kane: Director, Health and Social Services Management Research Unit, Department of Business Studies, The Queen's University, Belfast.

Jack Hershey and William Pierskalla: National Health Care Management Centre, University of Pennsylvania.

Sten Wandel: Professor of Transportation Systems, Linkoping University, Sweden.

Tony Hindle: Lecturer, Department of Operational Research, University of Lancaster.

Robert Raitt: Head, Health Operational Research Unit, Royal Institute of Public Administration, Reading.

INDEX